THE ASSOCIATION FOR SCOTT

NUMBER TWEN

# THE COMPLETE POEMS
# OF EDWIN MUIR

# THE ASSOCIATION FOR SCOTTISH LITERARY STUDIES

THE ASSOCIATION FOR SCOTTISH LITERARY STUDIES

GENERAL EDITOR – C. J. M. MACLACHLAN

# THE COMPLETE POEMS
# OF EDWIN MUIR

An Annotated Edition
edited by
Peter Butter

THE ASSOCIATION FOR
SCOTTISH LITERARY STUDIES
ABERDEEN
1991

First published in Great Britain, 1991
by The Association for Scottish Literary Studies
c/o Department of English
University of Aberdeen
Aberdeen AB9 2UB

ISBN 0 9488 7713 8

British Library Cataloguing in Publication Data

Muir, Edwin, *1887–1959*
   The complete poems of Edwin Muir.
   I. Butter, P. H. (Peter Herbert), *1921–*
821.912

ISBN 0-9488-7713-8

The Association for Scottish Literary Studies
acknowledges subsidy from the Scottish Arts Council
towards the publication of this volume.

Typeset in Garamond by Speedspools, Edinburgh
Printed by Bell and Bain, Glasgow

# CONTENTS

* Not in *Collected Poems* (1984)

v

## THE LABYRINTH (1949)

LAST POEMS

I

II

# Contents

## APPENDICES

### I. UNCOLLECTED POEMS

### II. EARLY VERSIONS

# THE ASSOCIATION
## FOR
## SCOTTISH LITERARY STUDIES

The Association for Scottish Literary Studies aims to promote the study, teaching and writing of Scottish literature, and to further the study of the languages of Scotland.

To these ends, the ASLS publishes works of Scottish literature (of which this volume is an example), literary criticism in *Scottish Literary Journal*, scholarly studies of language in *Scottish Language*, and in-depth reviews of Scottish books in *SLJ Supplements*. And it publishes *New Writing Scotland*, an annual anthology of new poetry, drama and short fiction, in Scots, English and Gaelic, by Scottish writers.

All these publications are available as a single 'package', in return for an annual subscription. Enquiries should be sent to:

**ASLS**
**c/o Department of English**
**University of Aberdeen**
**ABERDEEN**
**AB9 2UB**

# FOREWORD

This edition aims to combine inclusiveness with respect for the author's choices. Muir published eight volumes of poetry, not including the small limited edition, *Six Poems*; and *Collected Poems 1921–1951* (1952), the selection for which was made by Mr John Hall. When this last came up for reprinting in summer 1958 it was agreed between Muir and his publisher T. S. Eliot that what was really a large selection should be extended into a true collected poems. It was not, however, to include poems written since *One Foot in Eden* (1956) because it was hoped there would soon be enough for a new small volume. During the late summer Muir went through the published volumes, choosing and in some cases amending poems for the new collection. One poem, 'Ballad of Eternal Life' renamed 'Ballad of the Soul', was considerably rewritten, so that it is in its final form one of his last as well as one of his very first poems. The work was completed by October – fortunately, for his health was failing. He died in January 1959 before the collection could be published, leaving the new poems mostly unrevised and some unfinished. Mrs Muir and Mr Hall edited the late poems for inclusion, with those chosen by Muir from the earlier volumes, in *Collected Poems 1921–1958* (1960). The late poems were added to and amended in subsequent editions down to 1984.

This edition includes the eight volumes published by Muir complete, the poems not chosen by him for the final collection being distinguished by an asterisk. Texts are, with few amendments, as in *Collected Poems* (1984) or, for poems not included in it, as in the original volumes. New readers are advised to start with the non-asterisked poems in these volumes – these alone make up the body of poetry finally revised and endorsed by Muir. Then they might go on to *Last Poems*. The notebook in which some of these were drafted and which contains plans for unwritten ones, shows Muir, like the aged Blake, 'feeble and tottering' in body, 'but not in Spirit and Life, not in the Real Man The Imagination which Liveth for Ever'. These poems include some of his strongest and most moving ones, but it should be remembered that a few would probably have been rejected, some are unfinished and some would probably have been amended. Then the reader might go back to the asterisked poems. Though probably agreeing with Muir's decisions, he may find that not all the builder's rejected stones are without value and that less good work sometimes helps towards understanding and appreciation of the best.

Everything else has been relegated to Appendices. In Appendix I are poems written before *One Foot in Eden* was sent to the publisher and not chosen by Muir for any volume. These are presumably rejects, but since 'Scotland's Winter' was brought in from the cold after twenty years in the wilderness one cannot be quite sure that some others may not have been overlooked. Two poems hitherto in the collected editions, 'You will not leave us' and 'Do not mourn still' have been transferred to this Appendix because they could have been, and were not, included in *One Foot in Eden*. No judgement on their value is implied. In Appendix II are rejected versions of some early poems, 'Ballad of Eternal Life' being of special interest because closer than the revised 'Ballad of the Soul' to 'the most strange and the most beautiful experience', according to Muir, that he ever had. In Appendix III are revisions of three poems, one at least of which, 'The Song', would probably, with further revision, have become the final version of a good poem. Only heroic devotees will wish to go further; for them are listed in Appendix IV juvenilia and some occasional verses and translations. The late poems show that Muir was still a poet at seventy; the juvenilia that he was right to say he became one at thirty-five.

Willa loved Edwin's last poem 'I have been taught'; she and John Hall made a readable whole out of a difficult MS which, if merely transcribed, would be a messy draft. Her version, as amended with her consent for *Collected Poems* (1963), has been left almost unchanged, followed by a photocopy of the MS. This broken sentence expressing gratitude and faith fittingly ends his work as a poet; and in the published version embodies the creative collaboration between the two of them.

# ACKNOWLEDGEMENTS

Thanks for permission to quote and for other help are due to the copyright-holder, the Executors of the late Mr Gavin Muir; to the Librarians and staffs of the British Library, Harvard University Library, the Library of Congress, St Andrews University Library and, especially, to the Trustees of the National Library of Scotland; to Muir's publishers, Faber and Faber and the Hogarth Press; and to the authors, especially Professor Robert Hollander, of the bibliographies and other work cited in the Bibliography.

# *First Poems*

## TO P.W.

# *1925*

# POEMS

## CHILDHOOD

Long time he lay upon the sunny hill,
　To his father's house below securely bound.
Far off the silent, changing sound was still,
　With the black islands lying thick around.

He saw each separate height, each vaguer hue, 　　5
　Where the massed islands rolled in mist away,
And though all ran together in his view
　He knew that unseen straits between them lay.

Often he wondered what new shores were there.
　In thought he saw the still light on the sand, 　10
The shallow water clear in tranquil air,
　And walked through it in joy from strand to strand.

Over the sound a ship so slow would pass
　That in the black hill's gloom it seemed to lie.
The evening sound was smooth like sunken glass, 　15
　And time seemed finished ere the ship passed by.

Grey tiny rocks slept round him where he lay,
　Moveless as they, more still as evening came,
The grasses threw straight shadows far away,
　And from the house his mother called his name. 　20

## * THE LOST LAND

And like a mist ere morning I am gone;
My whispering prow through silence furrows on,
I fare far in through circles vast and dim,
Till a grey steeple lifts above the rim,

3

From which a chime falls far across the waves.          5
I see wind-lichened walls the slow tide laves;
The houses waver towards me, melt and run,
And open out, in ranks, and one by one.

I see the prickly weeds, the flowers small,
The moss like magic on the creviced wall,          10
The doors wide open where the wind comes in,
And is a whispering presence, salt and thin;

The still church standing lonely on the mound,
The leaning tombs which slumber with no sound.
Here would I stay, thus dreaming, evermore,          15
And watch the white ships flocking to the shore.

I look again. Alas! I do not know
This place, and alien people come and go.
Ah, this is not my haven; oft before
I have stood here and wept for the other shore.          20

And now it lies ten leagues across the sea,
And smiles, and calls on me perpetually;
But mountains and abysses lie between,
And I must fare by uplands coarse and lean,

Where towering cliffs hem in the thin-tongued strait, 25
And far below like battling dragons wait
The serpent-fangéd caves which gnash the sea,
And make a hollow barking constantly;

And where in pale moon-charméd valleys stay
Dreadful and lovely mists at full noon-day.          30
I gather giant orchids, light and dead,
And make a pallid garland for my head,

And sleep upon a green and watching mound
Which some child's wizardry has girdled round;
And I have been here many times before,          35
And shall return hereafter many more,

While past huge mountains and across great seas
That haven lies, and my long-sought release.
There tranquil spirits stand forevermore,
And watch the white ships flocking to the shore.          40

4

## * REMEMBRANCE

O places I have seen upon the earth,
  Your silence is not virginal any more,
For one still wanders there whose mortal birth
  Was mine. And now, gaze bent on buried lore,

A child, a youth, a man – O is it I? –                    5
  In silence stands by every lake and tree,
Or leans lost poring face where flickering by
  The bright stream moves on to another sea.

And all is changed, the shining fields, the host
  Of shapes who were myself years long ago.         10
'Tis these who live! And I am but a ghost
  Exiled from their sole light and jealous glow.

Ah no, it was not I who, laughing there,
  Walked with the crowd, and there, in solitude,
Wandered a summer's day through windless air,        15
  In a once-visited far-northern wood.

It was not I from morn till noon who went
  The white road's length to the white noisy town
So many years ago. That light is spent,
  And he who saw it, long since fallen down.          20

And he no less, the child who, walking grave,
  Saw beauty of tiny weed, of moss and stone;
And all his comrades, diffident and brave –
  They each have perished, silent and alone.

I can no more have speech with them, nor know     25
  The light which lights them. Vaster than the sea,
The yawning distances o'er which we go
  On our frail paths of sundering destiny.


## HORSES

Those lumbering horses in the steady plough,
On the bare field – I wonder why, just now,
They seemed terrible, so wild and strange,
Like magic power on the stony grange.

Perhaps some childish hour has come again,       5
When I watched fearful, through the blackening rain,
Their hooves like pistons in an ancient mill
Move up and down, yet seem as standing still.

Their conquering hooves which trod the stubble down
Were ritual that turned the field to brown,       10
And their great hulks were seraphim of gold,
Or mute ecstatic monsters on the mould.

And oh the rapture, when, one furrow done,
They marched broad-breasted to the sinking sun!
The light flowed off their bossy sides in flakes;       15
The furrows rolled behind like struggling snakes.

But when at dusk with steaming nostrils home
They came, they seemed gigantic in the gloam,
And warm and glowing with mysterious fire
That lit their smouldering bodies in the mire.       20

Their eyes as brilliant and as wide as night
Gleamed with a cruel apocalyptic sight.
Their manes the leaping ire of the wind
Lifted with rage invisible and blind.

Ah, now it fades! it fades! and I must pine       25
Again for that dread country crystalline,
Where the blank field and the still-standing tree
Were bright and fearful presences to me.


## * HOUSES

The far house shines so clear, it seems to come
    Towards me across the green estranging land.
The chimneys clustering watch; a tiny hum
    Fills the closed rooms; the mute walls listening stand.

When as a child I walked upon the earth,       5
    In burning inquisition, half afraid,
Too empty seemed the wide horizon's girth,
    But there were nooks with magic thick inlaid;

But most where in a house in one green place
   Doors opened wide to low voice of a stream,    10
Where through still-standing days I seemed to pace,
   As if the years were tarrying in a dream.

There was a line around on every side,
   And all within spoke to me and was home.
Beyond, the empty fields spread waste and wide,    15
   To the dark sea where ships cut white the foam.

How long, how long I pored on stone and tree,
   In happy inward dream day after day!
Slow lifting up my heavy head to see
   Tall men walk on the white roads far away,    20

And houses standing still in sun and rain,
   With dreamt-of rustlings filled from roof to floor, –
Then I would watch for hours to see again
   The folk go out and in about the door.

Now I can see once more, once more can feel    25
   That human magic on the stony earth.
See, through their struggling web of stone and steel,
   Those distant houses shine with grief and mirth!

## * MAYA

Ah, could I put this viewless strife aside,
   And lie forever on a sunny hill,
And see the unregarded river glide
   Through the small plain, and it be morning still! . . .

I watch the clear blank houses standing low,    5
   Their windows gleaming black in the pale sun.
The walls grow brighter; unseen ripples flow
   Up to the eaves, where smoky shadows run.

Around, the fields are greener, and the trees
   Their slowly wakening branches bend more down; 10
Unquiet memories stir beneath the leas,
   Whose knolls rise like a green deserted town.

Along the roads the tiny people move,
    Between the shining meadows, far and clear.
They go towards the mountains; and above      15
    The ridge the fresh young firmament looks near.

Now from the hills a slow unwinding sound
    Comes of bells swinging in a distant dale.
Through unseen valleys nearer it is wound,
    Loudens, and falls upon the sunlit vale. . . .    20

And all at once those fields and mountains seem
    A little gleaming strip of grass and light,
Bordering the million-fold and shapeless dream
    Which keeps our souls apart in strangest night.

We seek in inner cloud our formless way,      25
    In mystery without ground, beginning, end.
And when we lift our eyes we see the day
    Astonished, and stand motionless, and attend.

## * THE ENCHANTED PRINCE

Here lying on the ancient mount,
    Through days grown stagnant and too rich,
My half-raised eyes keep sleepy count
    Of wild weeds springing in the ditch,

Of turf so quiet and so clean,      5
    The sun's light seems more ancient there,
As if the chill and slumbering green
    Had grown indifferent to the air.

And all worn smooth 'neath deadened years
    Which have forgotten that they roll,    10
Though at its secret term appears
    The lawful grass upon the knoll.

Here is the peace of ended toil
    Heavy and rich, too rich, as though
A race were mingled with the soil,    15
    And could no more rise up and go.

A willow hangs above the vale,
  Here at my foot, and I have sight,
Through twisted branches dusty pale,
  Of distant hills in different light.          20

So inaccessible and so clear;
  The houses gleam on every hill!
The silent valley tumbles sheer,
  Like an abyss where time is still.

Yet here upon the enchanted mount          25
  I look out towards the farther heights,
And, lost far onward, strive to count
  Ambiguous shapes in shifting lights,

Till, where peaks battle in the haze
  In mortal strife without a cry,          30
Upon unnameable things I gaze,
  And dragons rearing at the sky.

If now, turned back, I think again
  That all those lines which heaved and strove
Just now, were quiet earth, I fain          35
  Would perish of a boundless love.

Here lying on the ancient mount,
  Through days grown stagnant and too rich,
My heart is dust, the while I count
  The wild weeds springing in the ditch.          40

## OCTOBER AT HELLBRUNN

The near-drawn stone-smooth sky, closed in and grey,
  Broods on the garden, and the turf is still.
The dim lake shines, oppressed the fountains play,
  And shadowless weight lies on the wooded hill.

The patient trees rise separate, as if deep          5
  They listened dreaming through the hollow ground,
Each in a single and divided sleep,
  While few sad leaves fall heedless with no sound.

9

The marble cherubs in the wavering lake
    Stand up more still, as if they kept all there,    10
The trees, the plots, in thrall. Their shadows make
    The water clear and hollow as the air.

The silent afternoon draws in, and dark
    The trees rise now, grown heavier is the ground,
And breaking through the silence of the park    15
    Farther a hidden fountain flings its sound.


## * REVERIE

The dark road journeys to the darkening sky,
    The twilight settles like a circling pool,
The railway bridge is lifted up on high,
    And the unerring lines are beautiful.

A soldier and his girl in casual walk    5
    Pass heavily, their garments creased with woe,
Like stiff, slow-labouring statues; yet they talk
    In peace, and gather comfort as they go.

In the small cabin by the railway-side
    A lonely concertina by some priest    10
Of guileless joy is played; its sound goes wide,
    Like the blunt brumming of a vague-voiced beast.

I stand, and thin-toned anguish frets my heart
    Over the cabin boy who all the night
Sits in his thoughtless paradise apart,    15
    And in his lonely monologue finds delight;

And over those two, who, in half-dumb talk,
    With broken gestures, and half-shapen speech,
In unintelligible rapture walk,
    Too far for vain and longing thought to reach.    20

O why should fading form and falling sound
    Such sculptured shapes of deep division take?
Why do we walk with muted footsteps round
    In this strong trance called life from which none wake?

Whither do these blind-journeying lovers go?    25
  What does he wait, the boy with idle hands?
And I who stand in idle questioning so?
  We walk all four in strange and different lands.

Those lovers never will return again.
  That sound has died long since within the gloam.  30
Why do I wait still with my foolish pain?
  All, all at last must take their sorrow home.


## * ON THE MEDITERRANEAN

Now it comes back again, the thought of peoples
  In populous lands, who live and doubt and die,
Comes here in this small town with trivial steeples,
  On the stiff gulf, beneath the foreign sky.

Dark-featured children gambol in the ocean,    5
  The blistering light burns on the stony hills,
And tranquil women pass with cloud-like motion
  O'er the wet sands; and pain my spirit fills

For stubborn silence of those rocky highlands,
  Those simple fields I cannot understand,    10
And those half-glimpsed and enigmatic islands,
  Which hang, a torment teasing the vexed land.

I think of thousand-citied, distant races,
  Who in one baffling image ever change;
The hieroglyphic silence of old places    15
  Our listening makes more taciturn and strange;

Of oceans, deserts, rivers, forests, mountains,
  Seen but by vacant night, incurious day;
Deserted temples, palaces, gardens, fountains,
  Left lying like wrecks of interrupted play.    20

Why in our lonely, swiftly-ended passion
  Should we o'er such gigantic pathways move?
Stretch featureless space around us as a fashion,
  And feel the fathomless tides of hate and love?

Why are all these in wild mutation shaken?    25
  See, the sun, sinking, stains the ocean red.
In flames the vineyards sleep, the mountains waken,
  And common crimson gilds each casual head!

We know not Him Who stretched in rapture o'er us
  Mystery and Beauty; and with fear is fanned    30
Our trembling memory of the Hour which bore us,
  And shut us 'twixt the bastions of the land.


## * AN ANCIENT SONG

I thought of all the passions men have known:
Despair which hardens to a moveless stone;
Rage running round and round until it falls,
And fallen, deaf and blind, in narrow stalls
Is fastened, self-consenting, unappeased;    5
Bereavement which, by deathless Memory teased,
Pores o'er the same, forever-altered track,
Turns, ever on the old lost way turns back;
Lost Love which flies aghast it knows not where,
And finds no foothold but the dreadful air;    10
Deep Misery which knows not its own cries;
And sightless Hope with ever straining eyes:

      Yet this, this, for ages long
      Will turn to story and sweet song.


## BETRAYAL

Sometimes I see, caught in a snare,
  One with a foolish lovely face,
Who stands with scattered moon-struck air
  Alone, in a wild woody place.

She was entrapped there long ago.    5
  Yet fowler none has come to see
His prize; though all the tree-trunks show
  A front of silent treachery.

And there she waits, while in her flesh
   Small joyless teeth fret without rest.      10
But she stands smiling in the mesh,
   While she is duped and dispossest.

I know her name; for it is told
   That beauty is a prisoner,
And that her gaoler, bleak and bold,      15
   Scores her fine flesh, and murders her.

He slays her with invisible hands,
   And inly wastes her flesh away,
And strangles her with stealthy bands;
   Melts her as snow day after day.      20

Within his thicket life decays
   And slow is changed by hidden guile;
And nothing now of Beauty stays,
   Save her divine and witless smile.

For still she smiles, and does not know      25
   Her feet are in the snaring lime.
He who entrapped her long ago,
   And kills her, is unpitying Time.


## \* ANATOMY

My feet walk to a hidden place
   Whence no path issues, my eyes range
Through immobility of space.
   Towards changelessness my members change.

My flesh a ripening fruit, my blood      5
   A crimson brook which tends towards death;
My reins a black and secret bud
   Which breaks in everlasting breath.

My lusts, a beauty-bearing tide,
   Move stealthily as if bent on crime.      10
My heart, self-moved, against my side
   Beats, like Eternity in Time.

13

## * LOGOS

Over the slumbering ocean
With wavering feet I travel.

Far back, the land, a leaden
Blue shadow slowly melting,
Sinks in the gnawing circle.                          5
The hills are eaten
Away in silence.

The smooth-backed serpent-hided ocean
Under my footfall whispers.
Pale gossamer lies upon the billows,                 10
And far it sounds a crystal tinkling.
The strengthless sun is smouldering
In the soft sky, drained and wounded.

Thou heaven, bent twice around me,
Keep still! Mounts fast my terror,                   15
On the bright silence rocking,
The chalk-pale heavens reel; in silence
The ocean streams to the white horizon.
I fall through blackness.

End and Beginning!                                   20
Thy tides are warm and stagnant.
In caverns, snow-white giants
Sprawl on great rocks, and the currents
Lift and let fall their foam-soft crumbling
Limbs, and their eyes more clear than water          25
Laugh when the waves comb out their tresses.
Their hands are vague and careless
As lazy tree-tops swaying.
On their huge breasts hang generations
Asleep, like sunless forests.                        30
Light shall bear these, whom darkness ripened.
They shall know naught save that in slumber
Mysterious fingers
Touched them, and their blood yearned upward,
Chafing against sealed ears and eyelids.             35

Amazed they rise. The ocean
Is strewn with silent forms which, standing,
Blaze on the gulf. Before them
They see the outspread and soundless morning,
And their immense eternal pathway.                    40


## WHEN THE TREES GROW BARE
## ON THE HIGH HILLS

When the trees grow bare on the high hills,
And through still glistening days
The wrinkled sun-memoried leaves fall down
From black tall branches
Through the gleaming air,                                5
And wonder is lost,
Dissolving in space,
My heart grows light like the bare branches,
And thoughts which through long months
Have lain like lead upon my breast,                     10
Heavy, slow-ripening thoughts,
Grow light and sere,
And fall at last, so empty and so beautiful.

And I become
Mere memory, mere fume                                   15
Of my own strife, my loud wave-crested clamour,
An echo caught
From the mid-sea
On a still mountain-side.
The leaves fall faster,                                  20
Like a slow unreturning fountain of red gold.
The billow of summer breaks at last
In far-heard whispering.
And in mere memory, mere dream,
Attainment breathes itself out,                         25
Perfect and cold.

## AUTUMN IN PRAGUE

The ripe fruit rests here,
On the chill ground,
In the sterile air,
All meanings have fallen into your lap,
Uncomprehending earth.                                    5

The stubble shines in the dry field,
Gilded by the pale sun.
The trees, unburdened, with light limbs,
Shiver in the cold light.
In the meadow the goat-herd,                              10
A young girl,
Sits with bent head,
Blind, covered head,
Bowed to the earth,
Like a tree                                               15
Dreaming a long-held dream.

The gossamers forge their cables
Between the grasses,
Secure,
So still the blue air hangs its sea,                      20
That great sea, so still!
The earth like a god,
Far withdrawn,
Lies asleep.


## * SALZBURG – NOVEMBER

The bells are chiming in the town.
   It's four; and on the darkening streets
The mountains scatter chilling down
   The wintry dusk. The shrill bell beats

And stops. Startling our footsteps ring;                  5
   Our voices sound more sharp and clear;
The bright shop windows burn and sting;
   Around, the snow-streaked hills come near.

We had been walking all the day
    Through miry lanes, 'twixt fields new-ploughed. 10
White peaks drew near and dropped away
    On either hand, and one pale cloud

Covered the sky and closed it up.
    The world seemed small: we could but see
The black wet fields in their wet cup:         15
    The roadside brook flowed drearily.

But when at dusk the town drew nigh
    We saw it glittering dark and bright,
And one near spire stood up so high
    It showed above the distant height.       20

The church, the mountain, side by side,
    Stood there as childish pictures stand;
The great spanned roof rose, curved and wide
    And clear and tiny lay the land.

We gazed; as on we trudged again       25
    The small green landscape drank us in.
A great brown horse stood in a wain,
    His nostrils smoking silvery thin.

Gleaming he seemed to warm the air:
    His warm bright bridle jingled high:     30
He stood so solitary there,
    There seemed naught else beneath the sky.

Then through chill narrow streets to see
    From bright doors clattering men burst out
One breath the door swung brilliantly,     35
    Then the dark street rang with the shout.

Now night has fallen, and far up
    The hills climb back into the sky.
The valley is a misted cup;
    The sparkling city walks on high.     40

17

## \* GRASS

The vague immutable contour of the earth –
This insubstantial phantom of green hills
Which ever falling away forever stand,
Perpetual mirage hung beyond Time's reach –
Is grass, which sets the round world in our sight.    5
Grass standing thick and still in soundless vales
No eye has seen, or straggling into wastes,
Beat down but spared by winds which tear up oaks;
Green in the sun and beneath smothering mists
Where each moist blade sweats one clear glistening drop;  10
Grass growing below huge rocks and round lone graves;
Climbing, a tiny host, up mountain-sides;
Hanging on mist-locked keeps above dun lakes;
Tossing on low small islets on the tide,
Soft meadows 'mid the currents of the sea,    15
Where the green glossy blades drink the blue wave;
Grass waiting in the dark 'neath table-lands of snow,
O'er new-riven chasms weaving its light veil,
And quiet fields o'er fallen and jagged peaks:
The invulnerable vesture of the world.    20

# BALLADS

## BALLAD OF HECTOR IN HADES

Yes, this is where I stood that day,
  Beside this sunny mound.
The walls of Troy are far away,
  And outward comes no sound.

I wait. On all the empty plain           5
  A burnished stillness lies,
Save for the chariot's tinkling hum,
  And a few distant cries.

His helmet glitters near. The world
  Slowly turns around,           10
With some new sleight compels my feet
  From the fighting ground.

I run. If I turned back again
  The earth must turn with me,
The mountains planted on the plain,      15
  The sky clamped to the sea.

The grasses puff a little dust
  Where my footsteps fall.
I cast a shadow as I pass
  The little wayside wall.          20

The strip of grass on either hand
  Sparkles in the light;
I only see that little space
  To the left and to the right,

And in that space our shadows run,     25
  His shadow there and mine,
The little flowers, the tiny mounds,
  The grasses frail and fine.

But narrower still and narrower!
  My course is shrunk and small,     30
Yet vast as in a deadly dream,
  And faint the Trojan wall.
The sun up in the towering sky
  Turns like a spinning ball.

The sky with all its clustered eyes     35
  Grows still with watching me,
The flowers, the mounds, the flaunting weeds
  Wheel slowly round to see.

Two shadows racing on the grass,
  Silent and so near,     40
Until his shadow falls on mine.
  And I am rid of fear.

The race is ended. Far away
  I hang and do not care,
While round bright Troy Achilles whirls     45
  A corpse with streaming hair.


\* BALLAD OF REBIRTH

I flew aloft on frozen wings,
  I clove a waveless sea,
And sat upon a glittering star
  In glory and penury.

And, lapped round like the Cherubim     5
  With waves of my own fire,
I felt the secret moving lust
  For the unmoving mire.

I cast myself in wild disdain
  From that vast precipice.     10
I fell, a splintered lance of light,
  On a blank ball of ice.

Snowy and red, with wings outspread,
  In palsied trance I lay,
And waited with the unwilling dead       15
  The certain Judgment Day.

The terror drove my spirit forth
  Into the quivering air.
The ice heaved, and the sleeping beast
  Rose reeling from his lair.       20

That vast, remorseless, ageless beast,
  Heaven-high and ocean-wide,
Came from the ice and looked at me,
  Pondered, and pitying cried:

'As light is lost in deeper light,       25
  Gloom swallowed up in gloom,
You must in your own infinite
  Your infinite entomb.

'A sprite, you must in mire be dipt,
  A worm, take wings and fly;       30
You must in great indifferent seas
  Your purity purify.'

Then in the cavern of his maw
  He took my limbs and ate,
And turned again, and went behind       35
  The eternal icy gate.

But my soul hovered, trembling still,
  On the bleak empty air,
Waited, and feared, and knew full well
  What still must happen there.       40

A lovely youth, jocund and free,
  Out of the ribbed ice came,
Across his breast a serpent lay
  Like a brown band of flame.

'My limbs are strong as the deep hills,       45
  Set on the enduring slime,
But my eyes were forged in Paradise,
  And have forgotten Time!'

## BALLAD OF THE SOUL

### I

I did not know whence came my breath
  Nor where had hid my clay,
Until my soul stood by my side
  As on my bed I lay.

I looked across a dark blue shore                    5
  Under a dark blue sky,
The light came from no wandering star,
  The sun had not passed by.

Faintly uprose like graven mist
  A wraith upon the sea –                            10
Woman or wraith or mist – I thought
  It made a sign to me. ,

The waters rose, down sank the land,
  The sea closed in like lead,
The waves like leopards tumbled on                   15
  Far above my head.

There closed the mesh and waxed the flesh
  That brought my soul to birth.
I rose, the sky was white as snow,
  As ashes black the earth.                          20

The ashes of memorial fires
  Extinguished utterly;
In towering blocks the twisted rocks
  Stuck up above the sea.

And now I swam, a moving thing                       25
  On the vast and moveless mere,
And headless things swam all around;
  I saw and did not fear

Till when I reached the saving shore
  A soft sea-creature caught                         30
My bonéd hand with boneless hand;
  For all a day I fought.

And it was gone. I walked alone
  Over sands and barren dunes;
The low-browed voiceless animals          35
  Were my companions.


## II

What next I saw I cannot tell
  And ill can understand,
Though well I know that once I went
  Through that hollow land.          40

It was a waste of jagged rock
  (No beast nor bird was by),
And there what seemed a palace lay
  Like ruins of the sky.

I stood without, I stood within;          45
  Far down the toppling ledge,
Scaffolds of wood, scaffolds of wood
  From edge to yawning edge.

And spiders wove and silence lay
  On each deserted wall;          50
I poured myself from beam to beam,
  Dived deep and knew my fall,

And that one beam would hold me there
  And then like spouted light
That I should climb from beam to beam          55
  Until I scaled the height.

But now the roof with final seal
  Lay full upon my head;
My body like a battering ram
  Beat on it, beat and bled,          60
The blood dyed me head to foot
  Like a fierce fury red.

And the dumb stone shuddered and cried,
  Turned back and made a way.
The sky leapt up, the stars showered out,          65
  In peace the planets lay.

## III

Now day came on me and I saw
  A tarn, a little mound,
And rushes like an army's spears
  Stood as at watch around.                    70

Then on the white field of the sky
  Two clouds like phantoms fell.
They grew, they moved together like
  Two armies terrible.

They met, they broke in fiery smoke,          75
  A red ball in the sky,
A ball of fire, it raged and turned
  To ashes suddenly.

In the white sky a round black sun
  In furious circles whirled,                  80
From which two serpents broke and shook
  Their flames over the world.

Their pennon fires shot out and in
  And split the cracking mail;
You'd say all hell with plumes of fire        85
  Upon the air did sail.

That sun drank up its fires, it stood
  In heaven immovably;
As if some fear had clamped it there
  It stood immovably.                          90

But now its rage in furious spawn
  A hundred legs gave birth;
Like a great spider down the air
  It clambered to the earth.

Its head was like a wooden prow                95
  That had voyaged silently
Over the seas of perished worlds:
  It smiled disdainfully.

24

I stood; a sword was in my hand
  Fallen from the empty sky.      100
I struck the beast full on the brow,
  It did not move nor cry,

But like an image melting slow
  It softly, softly smiled.
My body was a storm wherethrough    105
  The sword in lightnings wild
Rove and rent: *it* sidewards bent
  Obedient as a child.

The sword streamed out in running fire,
  The hard mail burst in two,    110
The white-robed white-winged spirit up
  In wavering circles flew.

Hastily sank the empty mail
  Deep in the secret ground.
Nothing was there but trampled grass,    115
  The tarn, the watching mound.

## IV

Then as I looked above I saw
  The sweet sky rain with wings.
I was so happy I longed to be
  With one of these fair things.    120

And now they flew over seas so clear
  That their bright wraiths below
Like mute and pilgrimaging thoughts
  Obediently did go.

Two linked their hands till one they seemed, 125
  Rose up in wavering rings;
Two plumes fell down the glittering air,
  They mounted on two wings.

I thought: Must these in mire be dipt,
  Reborn, take wings and fly,    130
And in such strange indifferent seas
  Their purity purify?

I asked, but then the fading dream
Had nothing more to say
That night my soul stood by my side                    135
As on my bed I lay.


## * BALLAD OF THE NIGHTINGALE

In his book on *German Philosophy and Religion* Heine relates that in the
May of 1433, at the time of the Ecumenical Council, a party of ecclesiastics
took a walk in a grove near Basle. In the midst of their discourse 'they
paused transfixed before a blooming linden tree, on which sat a nightingale,
trilling and trolling the sweetest and tenderest strains.' For a time they were
ravished by the sweetness of the song; but finally one of them had the
sagacious thought that the nightingale might be the devil, who was trying to
interrupt their pious conversation. He proceeded to exorcise it, and the bird
did in fact reply, 'Yes, I am the devil!' and flew away laughing. This ballad
is an imaginary continuation of the incident.


The priest sleeps, he sleeps soundly;
  The bell strikes the midnight.
See, on the blank wall brightening,
  A flame, a wavering sprite?
    In the bare cell,                                     5
    Weaving a spell,
  A gentle, gambolling light?

It mounts, a moveless column,
  And One is standing there.
Straight as a flame is lifted                            10
  From his bright head His hair;
    Like strings of fire
    On a burning lyre.
  A cresset of quivering hair.

He does not touch the sleeper;                           15
  He draws him with His eyes.
With one slow sliding motion
  The priest begins to rise:
    Nor sound, nor word,
    Like a tight cord,                                    20
  To his full height doth rise.

26

They pass the moon-ribbed cloister,
  And walk the throngéd street;
They move like souls in slumber
  Which know not those they meet:       25
    Their eyes as far
    Voyagers' are,
  And soundless are their feet.

Lo, the sun stands straight in heaven,
  For it is full noon-day.       30
The folk march with loud shouting,
  But yet as tranced are they:
    With garlanded hair,
    They smile as 'twere
  Some strange redemption day.       35

And murderers in red raiment
  Move as the blessed move:
Their eyes like frozen daggers
  Are fixed, still-held, above,
    As quivering       40
    Unwavering
  Pulses of naked love.

And harlots robed for bridal
  Bring peace on all who see:
Their brows have naught left on them       45
  Save first virginity.
    As risen from deep
    Clear gulfs of sleep
  Their eyes are pure and free.

And ribbed wood-scented creatures       50
  Stalk noiseless here and there:
The mountain-headed lion,
  The doe, star-browed and fair:
    By their blunt heads
    A maiden leads       55
  Two tigers stark and bare.

The beasts lift up their faces
  Like statues, and adore;
They seem as they would never
  Look earthwards any more.       60

27

So still they are,
They look like far
Cliffs on some quiet shore.

But they rise like ranked waves rising;
  The birds' song bursts like a gale;                    65
The priest stands still and listens
  To hear the nightingale;
    His ear-drums burst
    For dreadful thirst
  Of the songless nightingale.                           70

Songless! and all slow-turning,
  Gaze at him silently.
Their eyes burn in so deeply,
  They are as one great eye
    Of some mystical                                     75
    Huge animal.
  He shrieks: ''Tis I! 'Tis I!   '

And 'neath the farthest circle
  They sweep wild-voiced away.
The day is void, is perished,                            80
  And it is but our day.
    The priest awakes,
    With numb hand takes
  Back, back his torpid clay.


## * BALLAD OF THE MONK

I wandered in the woods my lane;
I heard a wind did sab and mane.

A dowie wind passed me by,
Yet there was nae wind in earth or sky.

I sat me doon beside a tree;                              5
The eerie ghaist shak waefully.

It soomed the swounding air upon;
It was a snaw-white skeleton.

It picked its banes oot ane by ane,
And cast them doon wi' sab and mane.          10

It cast and cast them dreamfully,
Like light leaves frae a late hairst tree.

It cast them doon fell and fast,
As it wad lose its banes at last.

But the sma' banes were fu' o' grace;          15
They moved each to his rightfu' place.

They gathered like a rank o' men;
They knit themselves in ane again.

They claithed themsels in dowie flesh,
Weel-woven like a wabster's mesh.          20

They covered the heid wi' close-weaved hair;
They set twa eyes to blink and stare.

And the puir clay to move began:
It was a coal-black naked man.

It cam' and stood before the tree,          25
And spak, the tear fell frae its e'e:

'I was a monk o' the order white,
But noo I'm black as the midmost night.

'I gave my lands, I gave my board,
And a' that blythe sinners sweetly hoard,          30

'And my eternal part I gave,
For I was minded my saul to save.

'But my fause flesh I couldna gi'e,
And I maun live anither day,

'And I maun live forevermair!'          35
It lap awa' through the mirky air.

29

## BALLAD OF THE FLOOD

'Last night I dreamed a ghastly dream,
    Before the dirl o' day.
A twining worm cam out the wast,
    Its back was like the slae.

'It ganted wide as deid men gant,                5
    Turned three times on its tail,
And wapped itsel the warld around
    Till ilka rock did wail.

'Its belly was blacker than the coal,
    It wapped sae close about,                   10
That it brak the hills in pieces sma'
    And shut the heavens out.

'Repent, repent, my folk, repent,
    Repent and turn around.
The hills are sinking in the sea,               15
    The warld has got a stound.'

The braw lads woke beside their makes
    And drowsy were their een:
'O I wat this is anither day
    As every day has been.                       20

'And we sall joy to-day, my luve,
    Sall dance to harp and horn,
And I'll devise anither play
    When we walk out the morn.

'But on the neist high day we twa               25
    Through the kirk door maun gae,
For sair I fear lest we sall brenn
    In living fire alway.'

They looked around on every wa'
    And drowsy were their een.                   30
The day rase up aboon the east
    As every day had been.

But Noah took a plank o' aik,
  Anither o' the pine,
And bigged a house for a' his folk     35
  To sail upon the brine.

'Gang out, gang out and ca' the beasts,
  Ca' twa o' every kind
To sail upon this crackling shell
  When a' the hills are blind.     40

'Ca' but, ca' but, and they'll rin fast
  As sune's they hear your voice,
For they hae heard amang the hills,
  I wat, a boding noise.

'They cry a' night about the house,     45
  And I hae ruth to see
Sae mony innocent creatures die
  For man's iniquity.'

Noah's sons went out into the fields,
  Ca'd twa o' every kind.     50
They cam frae the east, they cam frae the wast,
  And followed close behind.

And some were brighter than the sun
  Some blacker than the coal.
The lark was wiléd frae the sky,     55
  The serpent frae the hole.

And they were as meek as blessed sauls
  Assoilzied o' their sin,
They bowed their heids in thankfulness
  Whenas they entered in.     60

'Come in, come in, my people a',
  The sea has drunk the plain,
The hills are falling in the flood,
  The sun has downward gane.'

The rain it rained baith day and night     65
  And the wind cam together.
The water rase in a lang straight line
  Frae ae hill to the tither.

The Ark span like a cockle shell,
  Ran east and then ran wast. 70
'Now God us save,' auld Noah cried,
  'The warld is sinking fast.'

The beasts they hid amang the shaws
  And loud and sair cried they.
They sabbed and maned the leelang night 75
  And fought the leelang day,

That the creatures in the Ark were sair
  Astonied at the sound.
They trembled sae they shak the house
  As it were in a swound. 80

But syne there was nae crying mair
  Across the dowie sea.
'I wat,' said Noah, 'the warld is sunk
  Frae plain to hill-top heigh.'

The first day that auld Noah sailed 85
  The green trees floated by.
The second day that auld Noah sailed
  He heard a woman's cry.

And tables set wi' meats were there,
  Gowd beakers set wi' wine, 90
And twa lovers in a silken barge
  A-sailing on the brine.

They soomed upon the lanely sea
  And sad, sad were their een.
'O tak me in thy ship, auld man, 95
  And I'll please thee, I ween.'

'Haud off, haud off,' auld Noah cried,
  'Ye comena in to me!
Drown deep, drown deep, ye harlot fause,
  Ye wadna list to me.' 100

She wrang her hands, she kissed her make,
  She lap into the sea.
But Noah turned and laughed fu' loud:
  'To hell, I wat, gang ye!

'To hell the haill warld gangs this day,   105
   But and my folk sae gude.
Sail on, sail on till Ararat
   Lifts up aboon the flood.'

The third day that auld Noah sailed
   There was nae sign ava'.   110
The water rase on every side
   Like a weel biggéd wa'.

The astonied ships upon the sea
   Tacked round and round about
Till the dragons rising frae the deep   115
   Sucked a' their timbers out.

Ane after ane, ane after ane,
   They sank into the sea,
And there was nane left on the earth
   But the Ark's companie.   120

But every day the dragons came
   And played the Ark around.
They lay upon the faem and sang;
   It was a luvely sound.

'Why stand ye at the window, my sons?   125
   What hope ye there to see?'
'We wad see a gudely ha', faither,
   Set in the green countrie.

'But we see naught but water, water,
   We've seen this mony a day,   130
And the silly fishes in the faem
   That soom around in play.'

'Sail on, sail on,' auld Noah cried,
   'Sail on, sail on alway!
I wat we'll sail about the warld   135
   Until the Judgment Day.'

Noah sent a doo far owre the sea,
   It flew into the south.
It stayed four days and cam again
   Wi' a leaf within its mouth.   140

Noah sent a doo far owre the sea,
    It to the wast is ta'en.
It tarried late, it tarried lang,
    And cam'na back again.

'O what's yon green hill in the wast      145
    Set round wi' mony a tree?'
'I wat it is Mount Ararat
    New risen frae the sea.'

He's set the Ark for Ararat,
    He's plied her owre the faem,      150
He's lighted down at Ararat,
    And there he's made his hame.

# Chorus of the Newly Dead

## TO JOHN HOLMS

## *1926*

# ⁕ CHORUS OF THE NEWLY DEAD

CHORUS:

The sundering doom has fallen. We have lived.
   No more, no more these empty eyes turn back
To catch light's arrowy harvests, spent and sheaved.
   Beat thin as air is Life's wide-trodden track.
The mountains and great isles like giants falling     5
Plunge in oblivion beyond recalling.

But wavering towers we see in transient light,
   And fleeting temples on the opening sea
That shift like breath, and plains where armies fight,
   While the sun lies on red limbs changelessly;     10
And smoking cities by far rivers dreaming,
And half-glimpsed sails which perish in their gleaming.

And sometimes like full-armoured foes arise
   Our strange forgotten faces in the light,
Our blind brows and disaster-facing eyes,     15
   And the short stony path; and in the night,
From that vast inarticulate memory turning,
Sudden we mourn and know not we are mourning.

THE IDIOT:

They flung me out;
   They broke my brain.     20
Down beat the sun,
   Down beat the rain.
They broke upon me:
   All was vain.
The truth is hard,     25
   The false is plain.

A judgment light,
  A prison ray,
Fell around me:
  That was day.
Then sleep sank down
  And far away
I saw three angels
  Run and play.

The angels played
  In silence there;
Their brows were calm,
  Their limbs were bare.
Slow dawned the day
  Of bright despair:
The sun leapt up
  To stare and stare.

I laughed and hopped,
  My head was so light;
I walked in a field,
  The sun shone bright.
Quick passed a maiden
  Full of spite;
Her bosom was round,
  Her arms were white.

The dizzy day
  Went round and round.
Each minute was like
  A senseless sound.
And I was freed,
  And I was bound;
But I found again
  What I always found.

I laughed, I wept,
  Felt stinging pain,
Over and over
  But all was vain,
For bright and vacant
  Was my brain;
The truth is hard,
  The false is plain.

38

CHORUS:

What did he see? What rancour in the rim
  Of the harsh moon? Disaster on the sea?
What did the tiger's striped head spell to him?
  And clouds like signs? What made him still when he  70
  In his mother's eyes sat gazing peacefully?

He could but learn to fear what others loved,
  And none could know the phantoms of his fear:
Mountain and plain confounded and removed;
  And all pressed on his steps, too near, too near!  75
  While a close pattering whisper filled his ear.

Once he had suffered more than human wrong,
  Before man's unapproachable face he saw.
He did not know the place, the alien throng;
  The light was strange to him, bound by the awe  80
  Of a once-broken long-forgotten law.

THE BEGGAR:

  They cast me crippled in the sun,
    The mighty nameless powers.
  The fight was fought, and they had won,
    Ere I could count the hours.  85

  A child, I fawned on each fair thing
    Betwixt desire and doubt.
  They laughed and fought within the ring;
    Yearning I watched without.

  I sat by doors forever close;  90
    I knew each blackened stone,
  Heard on hot walls the sunlight doze,
    And heard dry pavements groan;

  Till Time, fallen inward, was so still
    That stone and shadow were  95
  Naught but myself; and soul and will
    Rose in mute matter there.

39

I slept in hovels. Morn again
  Sent up its demon towers.
From painted steeples fell in rain      100
  The false and clattering hours.

Like glittering steeds the swift years' pride
  Went crashing o'er my head.
I wandered senseless where the wide
  Cities lay bright and dead.      105

Ye Who, inscrutable, sent me forth,
  Was it that You might lay
The splendour of the cruel earth
  Around me like a play?

That lust and glory, myriad-eyed,      110
  Might be an alien show?
And Beauty that I am denied
  Be mirrored in my woe?

CHORUS:

Did They, all-knowing, Who bade the dust
Spawn him, did They give him in trust      115
Aught of Their light to realise
In gutted temples of his eyes?
From him was all but longing taken
  That in the gulf of appetite
The world's dark glory might awaken      120
  And gleam like gardens in the night?

He saw lust, myriad limbed and eyed,
Grey dust in dust, like lightning glide,
And deep within, a prisoned prize,
Burned the fury of proud men's eyes.      125
The proud who knew not rage nor glory
  Which o'er their burning faces fell –
These were to him a fearful story
  Which, heard, his awed tongue could not tell.

The look of doors which never ope      130
He knew, knew well the dwindling hope
Of those whom dogs and children spurn
If once too often they return.

The mountains spurned him; a derision
  Fenced him outside field, wood and plain,   135
That he might see an earthly vision,
  And suffer an unearthly pain.

THE COWARD:

The cities hounded me; I fled;
An angry cloud hung o'er my head;
It flew above me through the day   140
To where great stones in deserts lay.

I climbed the sultry mountain track;
The hill reared up and struck me back.
My feet sank in the soundless fen;
The forest was a dragon's den.   145

And, spawn of earth, in waning light
Arose far off from gulfs of fright,
Encircling all the plain, the crests
Of small round hills like angry breasts.

And on that waste where slept the dust   150
Lo! a little tree upthrust;
But stiff and dry, a dead man's arm;
Evil, but impotent to harm.

The tame town mongrels seemed to know
My secret fear. They watched me go   155
With shameless and considering eyes,
Turned to each other in surmise.

And still the cloud hung o'er my head!
Now it has burst, and I am dead.
And to mysterious nooks of clay   160
That mighty dream has rolled away.

CHORUS:

To him the world, a valley-cloven shadow,
  Spread dragon paths, but there was none to lead
Through encircling terror to a sunlit meadow.

He saw Life only in its wounds that bleed.     165
Nature he knew but in the grappling greed
Of waxing roots, the gluttony of the weed.

But still he could not stay, borne onward by
    A vision and a pain greater than ours.
He flew into the net when he would fly,     170
    Found ever, and could not face, the hidden powers.
    Anger he saw among the tossing flowers,
    And turning madness in branch-woven bowers.

Did They decree that still he should recall
    The haughty fear concealed in human fears?     175
Should see at noon tall men like pillars fall,
    And in the streets the mutinous mourning biers?
    They sent him out to range the inhuman years
    That one might pass the bound of mortal tears.

THE HARLOT:

The mean great street in evening heat     180
    Shot pistons to the sunset sky.
Up to my room the traffic's beat
    Arose and fell: 'A whore am I!'

Stale powder's dust on everything;
    Faint scents of flesh upon the walls:     185
I sat within a shambles' ring,
    Where a perpetual victim falls.

As down the darkening street I fared
    The pavement rose and struck at me.
Each doorway was a cannon bared,     190
    Each block a naked battery.

I walked between. Naught could I hear
    Save the loud echoing of my feet
On pavements neither far nor near.
    Past time stretched on the brazen street.     195

The blocks went blind, weak lamps were lit,
    The dark bridge held me like a claw –
A pinioned captive to be hit
    By all the naked eyes I saw;

42

Until, delivered, I turned back                                  200
  With someone with a form and face;
Our trivial heels, click-clack, click-clack,
  Went with us to the offering place,

Where 'mid the powder and the scent,
  As down a dark and dusty well,                            205
Through all the toppling tenement,
  Laughing I fell, and fell, and fell!

CHORUS:

What power decreed that one mean street
  Should be her fate-beleaguered way?
Why on those roofs did Time repeat                               210
  For her the self-same night and day?
A dusty room, a street to pace,
Week after week, were Time and Space
To her. She knew no longer track
Than the waste circle turning back.                              215

And where she walked the forms she saw
  Were animals of thicker dust,
With eyes considering without awe
  The open labyrinths of lust.
She fell away. There was no tear                                 220
Shed for her sake. Deathly and sere
The air. But on that arid ground
Pain rolled a surly ball around.

It was decreed. We cannot tell
  Why harlot, idiot or clown                                 225
Lived, wept and died. We cannot spell
  The hidden word which drove them down.
But looking towards the earth we see
The chart, deep-scored, stretched rigidly.
And all they did beneath the sun                                 230
Writ clear until the world is done.

THE POET:

The plains and cities, the great roads which run
　　Across ribbed continents to meet strange seas –
Where are you, neighbouring peoples in the sun,
　　Dawn-rustling glades, vast sunset-glancing leas?　　235

Perchance by now last autumn is on the earth;
　　A million leaves, a million mortals fall;
The savage land is mute, shorn clean by dearth,
　　Above the sea, a brown and naked wall.

How, through what wastes of time, can I return,　　240
　　Who wait, and in a distant picture see
The small red ranks of fading forests burn,
　　And blacken on the black hills gradually?

Have we this stubborn love for passing things
　　That we might seek behind Death's towering hill　245
Forests and rivers of eternal Kings,
　　Where beast and tree like blocks of light are still?

O surely all that beauty found far off
　　By falling mountains and long-sunken seas
Shall go with us as when, in burning love,　　250
　　We walked through shining stillness of bright trees,

And through our souls the vast tormented world
　　Passed slow in splendid pictures without pain.
Where, in what distant night, have these been hurled?
　　When shall dawn rise on those lost mounts again?255

CHORUS:

　　Once more a transient beauty burns,
　　　　And we forget earth's misery,
　　And like a traveller who turns
　　　　From a high ledge, we look and see,
Distant and clear, the silent land of doom,　　260
Porched by the sunlit backward-calling tomb.

　　Once before we stood as now
　　　　And longed for life, a wavering band;
　　We saw the trembling of a bough,

44

And heard bells ring from hidden land.    265
We could not turn away; a little sound
And light waylaid us; we were snared and bound.

Life closed around us. Dark shapes stood
    Near by us, and we found our way
Within Life's vast and glittering wood.    270
    On either side existence lay
Unending. When we sought to leave the track,
The earth, awake or slumbering, turned us back.

But sometimes there the bonds were torn
    Asunder, and the forests seemed    275
To wake in everlasting morn,
    And changed the brightening branches gleamed.
Immortal seemed those blossoming trunks which bare
The still leaves woven into crystal air.

THE HERO:

He lay on mounds of treasure,    280
The sun poured blinding measure,
    The smooth-grained sand was hot.
The dragon crouched there blinking;
Rich sound of metal clinking
    Filled all the sultry spot.    285

The sand shot up in mountains
Soared up in stony fountains;
    Far sank the horizon.
O'er great beast-imaged boulders
Where hate, fast-fettered, smoulders,    290
    Fainting I stumbled on.

From ledges dry and choking
I saw the valleys smoking,
    The plains were dim with light.
Far down smooth lakes uncovered,    295
Great hills climbed up where hovered
    Sharp birds which dived in fright.

But with close ranks, unyielding,
The mountains stood round shielding
    That serpent old and wise;    300

45

And, like old walls inshrifted,
Their angry sides were rifted
    With great and burning eyes.

Day, month and year went o'er me;
I felt my foe before me;                                   305
    Close, mind to mind, I fought.
Intense in toil and slumber
I pierced in legioned number
    The lying mists of thought.

They melted, sullen sinking.                               310
Thin sound of metal clinking
    Poured near. The dragon old
Shuddered, the combat ending,
And, back his black throat bending,
    I slew him on his gold.                                315

CHORUS:

What sent him out against the vengeful air?
What spurred him, vulnerable in Time, and bare?
The archer stars stood round him, morning's light
Ambushed him; yet he held the prey in sight.

The phantom quarry sped through Time and Space    320
Is here; the hunt is ended in this place.
We scent the trail of blood. Time's deer is slain.
The hunter and the hunted rise again.

What did he seek in mocking flesh and bone?
The dream is dreamed and he is overthrown.                 325

THE MYSTIC:

The tiny demon shapes that warn
    In field and city wake again:
The hillock, lightning clawed and torn,
    The nettles in the stifling lane,

The mangled thicket where, half-shown,                     330
    Three tracks like twisting vipers meet,
The squat façade of tortured stone
    Close ambushed in the sultry street.

46

None read their lineaments but I,
  Who knew what grinding levers move          335
To change the orbit of an eye
  Towards death, towards hate or full towards love.

All shape was matter, working blind.
  Appearance was stern flesh and blood.
If evil was there, then behind                340
  Evil the universes stood;

As, ever unremovable,
  Behind all beauty Beauty lay.
The braided paths of Heaven and Hell
  Writhed 'neath my feet, turned every way.   345

But oh, that clear angelic host
  Of mountains standing in the sky!
That dragon-wrought long silent coast
  Where wheeling sun and stars went by!

Those proud heraldic animals                  350
  Like pictures in a primal dream,
Holding unconscious festivals
  Which past our primal darkness gleam!

That stationary country where
  Achilles drives and Hector runs,            355
Making a movement in the air
  Forever, under all the suns!

And that ghostly eternity
  Cut by the bridge where journeys Christ,
On endless arcs pacing the sea,              360
  Time turning with his solar tryst!

They sink behind me. Fate is here,
  Approaching, stumbling through the deep.
And once again the primal fear
  Falls, and I wake from sleep to sleep.      365

CHORUS:

They cease, and at the telling of their woe
   We turn away, our alien sorrows end.
And now the earth is but a phantom show
   Whose lighted shapes through deepening darkness wend.
   The mountain tops through evening light descend.    370
Into perpetual evening they are led,
The earth, her multitudes, and all her dead.

And lovely now the standing plains of corn
   Which countless dying eyes in parting see,
And million trees bowed with red fruit forlorn,    375
   And dusk on every no more wakening lea,
   And golden navies on the level sea,
And silent rivers hurrying to their home,
And for all sound the loudening of the foam.

But change will fall on change ere time is o'er.    380
   Last youth into blank sunset light will go,
And last sons weep to leave their fathers' shore,
   Flying from woe through silent lands of woe,
   Where, level-lit, the dead horizons grow
Unending. Then all hearts will turn aside    385
From life, and dreams will walk where flesh has died.

Then saviours will arise, and fainter clay,
   And evening realms casting long-shadowed towers,
And ransomed peoples turning all one way,
   In ranks beside red westward-facing bowers;    390
   No fruit, but only hills of empty flowers:
Men, blazoned beasts, and rocks, and flowers, and peace.
Last light will fall from them and Time will cease.

Lament! ye exiled dead, the mighty play,
   The infinite play begun, and still begun,    395
And all the universes deep in day.
   The obedient worlds roll vacant round the sun,
   Their great limbs spent, their solar service done,
Buried in endless light, immaculate tomb
Sealed on their unimaginable doom.    400

48

# *Variations*
# *on a Time Theme*

## TO THE MEMORY OF
## JOHN FERRAR HOLMS
## 1897–1934

# *1934*

And another king shall rise after them . . . and think that he may change times and laws, and they shall be given into his hands, until a time, and times, and dividing of times.

I

After the fever this long convalescence,
Chapped blood and growing pains, waiting for life,
Turning away from hope, too dull for speculation.

How did we come here to this broken wood?
Splintered stumps, flapping bark, ringwormed boles,                5
Soft milk-white water prisoned in jagged holes
Like gaps where tusks have been.
                                Where did the road branch?
Where did the path turn like an enemy turning
Stealthily, suddenly, showing his other face                       10
After the knife-stroke?
                        Or did we choose, and if we chose
Did we choose idly, following the fawning way,
Or after years of obstinate dubitation,
Night sweats, rehearsed refusals, choose at last                   15
For only the choice was left?
                              Did we come here
Through darkness or inexplicable light,
The road all clear behind us and before us,
An answer and a riddle?                                            20
                        Was it truth
That lured us here, or falsehood? Virtue itself,
Or weakness on weakness, an open stanchless wound?
Did we fight step by step, hacking our way
Through rank green flourishing hopes to come to this?              25

We did not know life held a place like this,
Or not for us, for others.
                          Yet we saw
Good halting stations on our road here, open doors,
Lights in windows, lighted shrines, and human faces               30
Not such as these.
                  We have seen Heaven opening,
And fields and souls in radiance. We have walked
In radiance and in darkness. Now this twilight.

Can we build a house here, make friends with the mangled stumps    35
And splintered stones, not looking too closely
At one another?

        Can we sing our songs here,
Pray, lift a shrine to some god? Can we till these nameless fields,
Nameless ourselves, between the impotent dead      40
And the unborn, cut off from both, fateless,
Yet ruled by fate? Many will follow us.


## II

At the dead centre of the boundless plain
Does our way end? Our horses pace and pace
Like steeds for ever labouring on a shield,
Keeping their solitary heraldic courses.

Our horses move on such a ground, for them      5
Perhaps the progress is all ease and pleasure,
But it is heavy work for us, the riders,
Whose hearts have flown so far ahead they are lost
    Long past all finding
While we sit staring at the same horizon.      10

Time has such curious stretches, we are told,
And generation after generation
May travel them, sad stationary journey,
Of what device, what meaning?

                  Yet these coursers   15
Have seen all and will see all. Suppliantly
The rocks will melt, the sealed horizons fall
Before their onset—and the places
Our hearts have hid in will be viewed by strangers
Sitting where we are, breathing the foreign air      20
Of the new realm they have inherited.
But we shall fall here on the plain.

                      It may be
These steeds would stumble and the long road end
(So legend says) if they should lack their riders.   25
    But then a rider
Is always easy to find. Yet we fill a saddle
At least. We sit where others have sat before us
And others will sit after us.

It cannot be                                           30
These animals know their riders, mark the change
When one makes way for another. It cannot be
They know this wintry wilderness from spring.
For they have come from regions dreadful past
All knowledge. They have borne upon their saddles      35
Forms fiercer than the tiger, borne them calmly
As they bear us now.

               And so we do not hope
That their great coal-black glossy hides
Should keep a glimmer of the autumn light             40
We still remember, when our limbs were weightless
As red leaves on a tree, and our silvery breaths
Went on before us like new-risen souls
Leading our empty bodies through the air.
A princely dream. Now all that golden country         45
Is razed as bare as Troy. We cannot return,
And shall not see the kingdom of our heirs.

These beasts are mortal, and we who fall so lightly,
Fall so heavily, are, it is said, immortal.
Such knowledge should armour us against all change,   50
And this monotony. Yet these worn saddles
Have powers to charm us to obliviousness.
They were appointed for us, and the scent of the ancient leather
Is strong as a spell. So we must mourn or rejoice
For this our station, our inheritance                 55
As if it were all. This plain all. This journey all.


### III

A child in Adam's field I dreamed away
My one eternity and hourless day,
Ere from my wrist Time's bird had learned to fly,
Or I had robbed the Tree of which I die,
Whose boughs rain still, whose fruit wave-green shall fall   5
Until the last great autumn reddens all.
Thence lured by demons or by angels driven,
A lonely shaft loosed from the bow's calm heaven,
Blind as an arrow I sped upon my race
And swiftly reached the sole remaining place,         10
My first and last since then. There soon I found

My restless home, my heaven, my hell, my ground,
And that to these allegiance I might vow,
Took quick the bloody sign upon my brow,
Fell Edenwards in innocent Abel slain                    15
And rose twice-armoured in the flesh of Cain.
Thus harnessed, thus baptized, I now could go
Unscathed through my confederate crowd and show
The badge the world likes best. Till came the river
That scoured the world blind, and sunk for ever,         20
Drowned in ten thousand shapes I lay, though still
My only flesh no shame nor loss could kill
Rode on the flood to Ararat's safe hill.

Thenceforth oblivious of Heaven's foundered ship,
A youthful Abraham with bearded lip,                     25
I walked the shrunken hills and clouded plains
Among my flocks, pleased with a shepherd's gains,
A shepherd's joys, not yet too wild or proud
For a small Eden in a wandering cloud.
Alas! no heavenly voice the passing told                 30
Of that last Eden; my own bliss I sold.
Weary of being one, myself conspired
Against myself and into bondage hired
My mortal birthright. On dark Egypt's brow
As at the world's great helm behold me now,              35
Highest among the fallen, a man's length more
From what I sought than I had been before.

As he who snatches all at last will crave
To be of all there is the quivering slave,
So I from base to base slipped headlong down             40
Till all that glory was my mountainous crown.
Set free, or outlawed, now I walk the sand
And search this rubble for the promised land.


IV

                    Now at the road's quick turn
The enemy stands like a tower. The serpent rears
Its crest in blindness and light. Time dies
Its minute death, stiffens, moves on again.
The heroes march out to the unknown field.               5
The veterans return, bearing in feeble hands

54

The peace that is won and lost. The peasants
Climb the path in the rain to the mountain church.
The priest prays. The panting messenger
Falls by the way, his eyes and thoughts set onward,   10
And arm rigid. The prophet dreams on the peak.
The ark is borne unseen through the wilderness.


V

Yet I thought they moved.

Or can it be this ground that heaves about them
Its giant mole-hills, lengthening league by league
The ghastly thin anatomy of Space Time
Stripped to the nerve?                                5

                There's nothing human here
To entertain these wraiths but night and day
Saluting them, and spring opening their hearts
To emptiness, and autumn shutting their hearts
On emptiness, stirring their hearts, not them.        10
The scenery summer shifts around them is
Dusty and frayed, and winter is a floor,
Swept and polished, where the devils weave
Their dance more cleanly and more honestly.

Once there were ancient cities here, and shrines      15
That branched from Adam's world.
                    Now these dead stones
Among dead stones, where the late nomads pitch
Their nightly tents, leaving a little refuse,
The comfortless smell of casual habitation,           20
Human or bestial—indistinguishable.
These; and light and water casting back
Our shallow masks to shame us. Or at most
The shades of our ancestors, lingering yet,
Play in the ruins of their former house,              25
Remembering the eyes once bent upon them
That one day left them.

That is long ago;
A memory of our fathers. We have known
Only this debris not yet overgrown, 30
Never to be removed.
            Dead and our own.


## VI

Forty years this burning
Circuitous path, feet spurning
The sliding sand and turning
The wheel, turning again
Sharp rock, soft dust, a land 5
Choked in sand.

Once in the wilderness
A stream leapt from the smitten rock, flowed on,
flowed on, and then
The rock was sealed again,
Our hearts were dry again. 10
Since then we have marched through emptiness
Over the sea-ground of the sealess plain.

To Sinai's hill one day
Jehovah came. His way
Was silent; silence rested 15
On the bright cloud, the bright and shadowy hill.
The rocks where the wild-birds nested
With glittering eyes were still.

The stream light-winding from His secret throne
Spoke to itself and was its own. 20
Till silence, come too near,
Grew loud and turned to fear.
We made a golden toy, with idle sound
Shattered the peace, and danced, and spurned the sacred ground.
At evening Moses came 25
Down from the Mount bearing the Law and saw our shame,
The brazen calf, the naked youths and men,
And broke the tables of the law again.
The wilderness has been our home since then.

All that is now a memory,                                              30
Burning, burning,
With Pharaoh's body floating on the sea
Among his wide-robed seers, his men and cavalry,
And the dim desert slowly turning,
And the evening shadows                                                35
On temple-mirroring Nile, the wells and shining meadows.

We have passed great kingdoms by
In a separate dream.
We have seen tame birds wheel homing through the sky,
And towers caught in a distant gleam,                                  40
And smelt the searching scent of roots, the moist and dry,
And stopped remembering,
In this hard torrid winter without spring,
Something once tender and green,
But wakening we have seen,                                             45
At the waste's ruined bounds,
Pale whirlwinds racing round like spectral hounds
And falling through the air with whispering sounds.

And we have loved these lonely shapes
At their disconsolate play,                                            50
Have looked up to the stony capes
Battered with scalding surf of sand
Like sailors watching after many a day
Their home hills rising from the spray.
Where is our land?                                                     55

There is a stream
We have been told of. Where it is
We do not know. But it is not a dream,
Though like a dream. We cannot miss
The road that leads us to it. Fate                                     60
Will take us there that keeps us here.
Neither hope nor fear
Can hasten or retard the date
Of our deliverance; when we shall leave this sand
And enter the unknown and feared and longed-for land. 65

## VII

Ransomed from darkness and released in Time,
Caught, pinioned, blinded, sealed and cased in Time;
Summoned, elected, armed and crowned by Time,
Tried and condemned, stripped and disowned by Time;
Suckled and weaned, plumped and full-fed by Time,    5
Defrauded, starved, physicked and bled by Time;
Buried alive and buried dead by Time:

If there's no crack or chink, no escape from Time,
No spasm, no murderous knife to rape from Time
The pure and trackless day of liberty;             10
If there's no power can burst the rock of Time,
No Rescuer from the dungeon stock of Time,
Nothing in earth or heaven to set us free:
Imprisonment's for ever; we're the mock of Time,
While lost and empty lies Eternity.                15

## VIII

Time's armies are the seconds soft as rain,
Whose wound's so fine it leaves no scar nor stain,
Whose feathery arrows rankle in my heart,
Yet are so light, though each a mortal dart,
That like Sebastian in the picture I              5
Can watch vicarious battles in the sky,
While this cruel plumage, stagy and absurd,
Of a plucked angel or half-naked bird,
Betrays my state to all eyes but my own.
Or I'm like Socrates at Marathon,                 10
An absent hero with a pensive sword,
Ears cocked for his wise daimon's lightest word
Touching the scene, the cast, the spurious play,
The Gods and Time, while Time brings down the day
Like a great wrestler, fells it like a tree       15
With all its fruit, defeat or victory.

What though? All strategy here is plain retreat,
And the sure issue of this war defeat.
See, at the thought these arrow pricks grow sharper!
Oh, Plato himself was only Time's poor harper      20
Playing to bid him pause, Shakespeare a wile

To make him turn his head and once beguile
His wolfish heart. I know where ends the course,
And there my body like a headstrong horse
Will bear me without stop or hindrance. There          25
These archers will surround me quite, the air
Turn to a sea of feathers, and all art
End in a new yet long-foresuffered smart.

Time is a sea. There, if I could but sail
For ever and outface Death's bullying gale          30
I'd ask no more. From that great pond I'd fish
At pleasure every poet's and conqueror's wish.
The treasure of that deep's unbattened hold
I'd rifle clean till it and I were old,
And of that salvage worlds on worlds would make          35
Newer than tarried for Columbus' sake.
Until I dream, in that vast more and more,
I'd find Eternity's unhidden shore,
And the Gods, so old, so young, I'd not know which,
And Time between shrink to a shallow ditch.          40
Each wish is traitorous and a dupe the wisher.
It is not I but Time that is the fisher.
Me he will catch and stuff into his net
With mortal sweepings, harp and banneret.
He'll dredge the very heavens; dull stars will rust          45
Among my own and miscellaneous dust,
Light dust of fame that floats, heavy that sinks
Into this drunken sea that drinks and drinks.

Time's a fire-wheel whose spokes the seasons turn,
And fastened there we, Time's slow martyrs, burn.          50
To some that rage is but a pleasant heat,
And the red fiery bower as summer sweet.
Others there are who lord it in the flame,
And, while they're burning, dice for power and fame.
A choicer company ignore the pyre,          55
And dream and prophesy amid the fire.
And a few with eyes uplifted through the blaze
Let their flesh crumble till they're all a gaze
Glassing that fireless kingdom in the sky
Which is our dream as through Time's wood we fly          60
Burning in silence or crying the ancient rhyme:
'Who shall outsoar the mountainous flame of Time?'

## IX

Packed in my skin from head to toe
Is one I know and do not know.
He never speaks to me yet is at home
More snug than embryo in the womb.
His lodgings are but poor; they neither please     5
Nor irk him greatly, though he sees
Their cracks, rents, flaws, impossibilities
As in a glass. He is safe, he has no doubt,
He sits secure and will not out.

His name's Indifference.     10
Nothing offending he is all offence;
Can stare at beauty's bosom coldly
And at Christ's crucifixion boldly;
Can note with a lack-lustre eye
Victim and murderer go by;     15
Can pore upon the maze of lust
And watch the lecher fall to dust
With the same glance; content can wait
By a green bank near Eden's gate
To see the first blood flow and see naught then     20
Except a bright and glittering rain.
If I could drive this demon out
I'd put all Time's display to rout.
It's wounds would turn to flowers and nothing be
But the first Garden. The one Tree     25
Would stand for ever safe and fair
And Adam's hand stop in the air.
Or so I dream when at my door
I hear my Soul, my Visitor.

He comes but seldom and I cannot tell     30
If he's myself or one that loves me well
And comes in pity, for he pities all:
Weeps for the hero's and the beggar's fall;
The conqueror before his fallen foe
(Fingering his useless sword he cannot go,     35
But stands in doltish silence, unappeased);
Bereavement that, by deathless memory teased,
Pores on the same for-ever-altered track,
Turns, always on the old blind way turns back;
Lost Love that flies aghast it knows not where     40

And finds no foothold but the dreadful air;
The unending open wound in Jesus' side;
And all that has to die and that has died.

Pity would cancel what it feeds upon,
And gladly cease, its office done.                    45
Yet could it end all passion, flaw, offence,
Would come my homespun fiend Indifference
And have me wholly. On these double horns
I take my comfort, they're my truckle bed;
Could Pity change the crown of thorns                 50
To roses peace would soon be fled,
And I would have no place to rest my head.

Then must dead Pity, quickened by my plight,
Start up again and make for my delight
A mimic stage where all the day                       55
A phantom hound pursues a phantom prey,
Where the slain rise and smile upon the slayer,
And the crowned victor is a harmless player,
And cunning is a fond deceit,
Treachery feigned and loss imaginary,                 60
And friends consent to meet
To stage a slaughter and make up a story.

Oh, then, at such deceitful art,
Tears, real and burning, from my lids would start,
And peace would burst into my heart.                  65

## X

Who curbed the lion long ago
And penned him in this towering field
And reared him wingless in the sky?
And quenched the dragon's burning eye,
Chaining him here to make a show,                      5
The faithful guardian of the shield?

A fabulous wave far back in Time
Flung these calm trophies to this shore
That looks out on a different sea.

These relics of a buried war,    10
Empty as shape and cold as rhyme,
Gaze now on fabulous wars to be.

So well the storm must have fulfilled
Its task of perfect overthrow
That this new world to them must seem    15
Irrecognizably the same,
And looking from the flag and shield
They see the self-same road they know.

Here now heraldic watch them ride
This path far up the mountain-side    20
And backward never cast a look;
Ignorant that the dragon died
Long since and that the mountain shook
When the great lion was crucified.

# *Journeys and Places*

## TO FLORA GRIERSON
## AND JOAN SHELMERDINE

## *1937*

# JOURNEYS

## THE STATIONARY JOURNEY

Here at my earthly station set,
  The revolutions of the year
Bear me bound and only let
  This astronomic world appear.

Yet if I could reverse my course                    5
  Through ever-deepening yesterday,
Retrace the path that led me here,
  Could I find a different way?

I would see eld's frosted hair
  Burn black again and passion rage              10
On to its source and die away
  At last in childhood's tranquil age.

Charlemagne's death-palsied hand
  Would move once more and never rest
Until by deadlier weakness bound              15
  It lay against his mother's breast.

Saint Augustine gives back his soul
  To stumble in the endless maze.
After Jesus Venus stands
  In the centre of his gaze,                            20

While still from death to life to naught
  Gods, dynasties, and nations flit;
Though for a while among the sand
  Unchanged the changing Pharaohs sit.

Fast the horizons empty. Now                      25
  Nothing's to see but wastes and rocks,
And on the thinning Asian plains
  A few wild shepherds with their flocks . . .

65

So, back or forward, still we strike
  Through time and touch its dreaded goal.          30
Eternity's the fatal flaw
  Through which run out world, life and soul.

And there in transmutation's blank
  No mortal mind has ever read,
Or told what soul and shape are, there,          35
  Blue wave, red rose, and Plato's head.

For their Immortal Being in
  Solidity more pure than stone
Sleeps through the circle, pillar, arch,
  Spiral, cone, and pentagon.          40

To the mind's eternity I turn,
  With leaf, fruit, blossom on the spray,
See the dead world grow green within
  Imagination's one long day.

There while outstretched upon the Tree          45
  Christ looks across Jerusalem's towers,
Adam and Eve unfallen yet
  Sleep side by side within their bowers.

There while fast in the Roman snare
  The Carthaginian thinks of home,          50
A boy carefree in Carthage streets,
  Hannibal fights a little Rome,

David and Homer tune their harps,
  Gaza is up, sprung from its wreck,
Samson goes free, Delilah's shears          55
  Join his strong ringlets to his neck.

A dream! the astronomic years
  Patrolled by stars and planets bring
Time led in chains from post to post
  Of the all-conquering Zodiac ring.          60

## THE MOUNTAINS

The days have closed behind my back
  Since I came into these hills.
Now memory is a single field
  One peasant tills and tills.

So far away, if I should turn           5
  I know I could not find
That place again. These mountains make
  The backward gaze half-blind,

Yet sharp my sight till it can catch
  The ranges rising clear           10
Far in futurity's high-walled land;
  But I am rooted here.

And do not know where lies my way,
  Backward or forward. If I could
I'd leap time's bound or turn and hide      15
  From time in my ancestral wood.

Double delusion! Here I'm held
  By the mystery of the rock,
Must watch in a perpetual dream
  The horizon's gates unlock and lock,     20

See on the harvest fields of time
  The mountains heaped like sheaves,
And the valleys opening out
  Like a volume's turning leaves,

Dreaming of a peak whose height        25
  Will show me every hill,
A single mountain on whose side
  Life blooms for ever and is still.

## THE HILL

And turning north around the hill,
The flat sea like an adder curled,
And a flat rock amid the sea
That gazes towards the ugly town,

And on the sands, flat and brown,                                    5
A thousand naked bodies hurled
Like an army overthrown.

And turning south around the hill,
Fields flowering in the curling waves,
And shooting from the white sea-walls                               10
Like a thousand waterfalls,
Rapturous divers never still.
Motion and gladness. O this hill
Was made to show these cliffs and caves.

So he thought. But he has never                                     15
Stood again upon that hill.
He lives far inland by a river
That somewhere else divides these lands,
But where or how he does not know,
Or where the countless pathways go                                  20
That turn and turn to reach the sea
On this or that side of the hill,
Or if, arriving, he will be
With the bright divers never still,
Or on the sad dishonoured sands.                                    25

## THE ROAD

There is a road that turning always
  Cuts off the country of Again.
Archers stand there on every side
  And as it runs time's deer is slain,
  And lies where it has lain.                                 5

That busy clock shows never an hour.
  All flies and all in flight must tarry.
The hunter shoots the empty air
  Far on before the quarry,
  Which falls though nothing's there to parry.    10

The lion crouching in the centre
  With mountain head and sunset brow
Rolls down the everlasting slope
  Bones picked an age ago,
  And the bones rise up and go.                    15

There the beginning finds the end
  Before beginning ever can be,
And the great runner never leaves
  The starting and the finishing tree,
  The budding and the fading tree.          20

There the ship sailing safe in harbour
  Long since in many a sea was drowned.
The treasure burning in her hold
  So near will never be found,
  Sunk past all sound.                      25

There a man on a summer evening
  Reclines at ease upon his tomb
And is his mortal effigy.
  And there within the womb,
  The cell of doom,                         30

The ancestral deed is thought and done,
  And in a million Edens fall
A million Adams drowned in darkness,
  For small is great and great is small,
  And a blind seed all.                     35


## THE MYTHICAL JOURNEY

First in the North. The black sea-tangle beaches,
Brine-bitter stillness, tablet-strewn morass,
Tall women against the sky with heads covered,
The witch's house below the black-toothed mountain,
Wave-echo in the roofless chapel,                      5
The twice-dead castle on the swamp-greeen mound,
Darkness at noon-day, wheel of fire at midnight,
The level sun and the wild shooting shadows.

How long ago? Then sailing up to summer
Over the edge of the world. Black hill of water,      10
Rivers of running gold. The sun! The sun!
Then the free summer isles.
But the ship hastened on and brought him to
The towering walls of life and the great kingdom.

Where long he wandered seeking that which sought him 15
Through all the little hills and shallow valleys.
One whose form and features,
Race and speech he did not know, shapeless, tongueless,
Known to him only by the impotent heart,
And whether at all on earth the place of meeting,          20
Beyond all knowledge. Only the little hills,
Head-high, and the winding valleys,
Turning, returning, till there grew a pattern,
And it was held. And there stood both in their stations
With the hills between them. And that was the meaning.  25

Though sometimes through the wavering light and shadow
He thought he saw it a moment as he watched
The red deer walking by the riverside
At evening, when the bells were ringing,
And the bright stream leapt silent from the mountain  30
Far in the sunset. But as he looked, nothing
Was there but lights and shadows.

                                        And then the vision
Of the conclusion without fulfilment.
The plain of glass and in the crystal grave                  35
That which he had sought, that which had sought him,
Glittering in death. And all the dead scattered
Like fallen stars, clustered like leaves hanging
From the sad boughs of the mountainous tree of Adam
Planted far down in Eden. And on the hills               40
The gods reclined and conversed with each other
From summit to summit.

                                        Conclusion
Without fulfilment. Thence the dream rose upward,
The living dream sprung from the dying vision,          45
Overarching all. Beneath its branches
He builds in faith and doubt his shaking house.


### TRISTRAM'S JOURNEY

He strode across the room and flung
    The letter down: 'You need not tell
Your treachery, harlot!' He was gone
    Ere Iseult fainting fell.

He rode out from Tintagel gate,     5
  He heard his charger slowly pace,
And ever hung a cloud of gnats
  Three feet before his face.

At a wood's border he turned round
  And saw the distant castle side,     10
Iseult looking towards the wood,
  Mark's window gaping wide.

He turned again and slowly rode
  Into the forest's flickering shade,
And now as sunk in waters green     15
  Were armour, helm, and blade.

First he awoke with night around
  And heard the wind, and woke again
At noon within a ring of hills,
  At sunset on a plain.     20

And hill and plain and wood and tower
  Passed on and on and turning came
Back to him, tower and wood and hill,
  Now different, now the same.

There was a castle on a lake.     25
  The castle doubled in the mere
Confused him, his uncertain eye
  Wavered from there to here.

A window in the wall had held
  Iscult upon a summer day,     30
While he and Palomide below
  Circled in furious fray.

But now he searched the towers, the sward,
  And struggled something to recall,
A stone, a shadow. Blank the lake,     35
  And empty every wall.

He left his horse, left sword and mail,
  And went into the woods and tore
The branches from the clashing trees
  Until his rage was o'er.     40

And now he wandered on the hills
    In peace. Among the shepherd's flocks
Often he lay so long, he seemed
    One of the rocks.

The shepherds called and made him run        45
    Like a tame cur to round the sheep.
At night he lay among the dogs
    Beside a well to sleep.

And he forgot Iseult and all.
    Dagonet once and two came by        50
Like tall escutcheoned animals
    With antlers towering high.

He snapped their spears, rove off their helms,
    And beat them with his hands and sent
Them onward with a bitter heart,        55
    But knew not where they went.

They came to Mark and told him how
    A madman ruled the hinds and kept
The wandering sheep. Mark haled him to
    Tintagel while he slept.        60

He woke and saw King Mark at chess
    And Iseult with her maids at play,
The arras where the scarlet knights
    And ladies stood all day.

None knew him. In the garden once        65
    Iseult walked in the afternoon,
Her hound leapt up and licked his face,
    Iseult fell in a swoon.

There as he leaned the misted grass
    Cleared blade by blade below his face,        70
The round walls hardened as he looked,
    And he was in his place.

## HÖLDERLIN'S JOURNEY

When Hölderlin started from Bordeaux
  He was not mad but lost in mind,
For time and space had fled away
    With her he had to find.

'The morning bells rang over France        5
  From tower to tower. At noon I came
Into a maze of little hills,
    Head-high and every hill the same.

'A little world of emerald hills,
  And at their heart a faint bell tolled;    10
Wedding or burial, who could say?
    For death, unseen, is bold.

'Too small to climb, too tall to show
  More than themselves, the hills lay round.
Nearer to her, or farther? They      15
    Might have stretched to the world's bound.

'A shallow candour was their all,
  And the mean riddle, How to tally
Reality with such appearance,
    When in the nearest valley    20

'Perhaps already she I sought,
  She, sought and seeker, had gone by,
And each of us in turn was trapped
    By simple treachery.

'The evening brought a field, a wood.    25
  I left behind the hills of lies,
And watched beside a mouldering gate
    A deer with its rock-crystal eyes.

'On either pillar of the gate
  A deer's head watched within the stone.    30
The living deer with quiet look
    Seemed to be gazing on

'Its pictured death—and suddenly
   I knew, Diotima was dead,
As if a single thought had sprung        35
   From the cold and the living head.

'That image held me and I saw
   All moving things so still and sad,
But till I came into the mountains
   I know I was not mad.        40

'What made the change? The hills and towers
   Stood otherwise than they should stand,
And without fear the lawless roads
   Ran wrong through all the land.

'Upon the swarming towns of iron        45
   The bells hailed down their iron peals,
Above the iron bells the swallows
   Glided on iron wheels.

'And there I watched in one confounded
   The living and the unliving head.        50
Why should it be? For now I know
   Diotima was dead

'Before I left the starting place;
   Empty the course, the garland gone,
And all that race as motionless        55
   As these two heads of stone.'

So Hölderlin mused for thirty years
   On a green hill by Tübingen,
Dragging in pain a broken mind
   And giving thanks to God and men.        60

# PLACES

## THE FALL

What shape had I before the Fall?
  What hills and rivers did I seek?
What were my thoughts then? And of what
  Forgotten histories did I speak

To my companions? Did our eyes                    5
  From their foredestined watching-place
See Heaven and Earth one land, and range
  Therein through all of Time and Space?

Did I see Chaos and the Word,
  The suppliant Dust, the moving Hand,           10
Myself, the Many and the One,
  The dead, the living Land?

That height cannot be scaled again.
  My fall was like the fall that burst
Old Lear's heart on the summer sward.            15
  Where I lie now I stood at first.

The ancient pain returns anew.
  Where was I ere I came to man?
What shape among the shapes that once
  Agelong through endless Eden ran?              20

Did I see there the dragon brood
  By streams their emerald scales unfold,
While from their amber eyeballs fell
  Soft-rayed the rustling gold?

It must be that one time I walked                25
  By rivers where the dragon drinks;
But this side Eden's wall I meet
  On every twisting road the Sphinx

Whose head is like a wooden prow
    That forward leaning dizzily          30
Over the seas of whitened worlds
    Has passed and nothing found to see,

Whose breast, a flashing ploughshare, once
    Cut the rich furrows wrinkled in
Venusberg's sultry underworld          35
    And busy trampled fields of sin,

Whose salt-white brow like crusted fire
    Smiles ever, whose cheeks are red as blood,
Whose dolphin back is flowered yet
    With wrack that swam upon the Flood.    40

Since then in antique attitudes
    I swing the bright two-handed sword
And strike and strike the marble brow,
    Wide-eyed and watchful as a bird,

Smite hard between the basilisk eyes,    45
    And carve the snaky dolphin side,
Until the coils are cloven in two
    And free the glittering pinions glide.

Like quicksilver the scales slip down,
    Upon the air the spirit flies,    50
And so I build me Heaven and Hell
    To buy my bartered Paradise.

While from a legendary height
    I see a shadowy figure fall,
And not far off another beats    55
    With his bare hands on Eden's wall.


# TROY

He all that time among the sewers of Troy
Scouring for scraps. A man so venerable
He might have been Priam's self, but Priam was dead,
Troy taken. His arms grew meagre as a boy's,
And all that flourished in that hollow famine    5
Was his long, white, round beard. Oh, sturdily

76

He swung his staff and sent the bold rats skipping
Across the scurfy hills and worm-wet valleys,
Crying: 'Achilles, Ajax, turn and fight!
Stop cowards!' Till his cries, dazed and confounded,    10
Flew back at him with: 'Coward, turn and fight!'
And the wild Greeks yelled round him.
Yet he withstood them, a brave, mad old man,
And fought the rats for Troy. The light was rat-grey,
The hills and dells, the common drain, his Simois,    15
Rat-grey. Mysterious shadows fell
Affrighting him whenever a cloud offended
The sun up in the other world. The rat-hordes,
Moving, were grey dust shifting in grey dust.
Proud history has such sackends. He was taken    20
At last by some chance robber seeking treasure
Under Troy's riven roots. Dragged to the surface.
And there he saw Troy like a burial ground
With tumbled walls for tombs, the smooth sward wrinkled
As Time's last wave had long since passed that way,    25
The sky, the sea, Mount Ida and the islands,
No sail from edge to edge, the Greeks clean gone.
They stretched him on a rock and wrenched his limbs,
Asking: 'Where is the treasure?' till he died.


## A TROJAN SLAVE

I've often wandered in the fields of Troy
Beneath the walls, seen Paris as a boy
Before youth made him vicious. Hector's smile
And untried lion-look can still beguile
My heart of peace. That was before the fall,    5
When high still stood Troy's many-tunnelled wall.
Now I am shackled to a Grecian dolt,
Pragmatic, race-proud as a pampered colt.
All here is strange to me, the country kings,
This cold aspiring race, the mountain-rings    10
On every side. They are like toppling snow-wreaths
Heaped on Troy's hearth. Yet still an ember breathes
Below to breed its crop of yearly ills,
The flowering trees on the unreal hills.
These bring Troy back. And when along the stone    15
The lizard flickers, thirty years I'm thrown
At odds and stand again where once I stood,

77

And see Troy's towers burn like a winter wood.
For then into their country all in flame,
From their uncounted caves the lizards came              20
And looked and melted in a glaze of fire,
While all the wall quivered and sang like wire
As heat ate all. I saw calamity
In action there, and it will always be
Before me in the lizard on the stone.                   25
   But in my heart a deeper spite has grown,
This, that they would not arm us, and preferred
Troy's ruin lest a slave should snatch a sword
And fight even at their side. Yet in that fall
They lost no more than we who lost our all.             30
Troy was our breath, our soul, and all our wit,
Who did not own it but were owned by it.
We must have fought for Troy. We were its hands,
And not like those mere houses, flocks, and lands.
We were the Trojans; they at best could swell           35
A pompous or a bloody spectacle.
And so we watched with dogs outside the ring
Heroes fall cheap as meat, king slaughtering king
Like fatted cattle. Yet they did not guess
How our thoughts wantoned with their wantonness.        40
They were too high for that; they guessed too late,
When full had grown our knowledge and our hate.
And then they thought, with arms as strong as theirs,
We too might make a din with swords and spears,
And while they feared the Greeks they feared us most,   45
And ancient Troy was lost and we were lost.

Now an old man—why should that one regret,
When all else has grown tranquil, shake me yet?
Of all my life I know one thing, I know,
Before I was a slave, long, long ago,                   50
I lost a sword in a forgotten fight,
And ever since my arm has been too light
For this dense world, and shall grow lighter still.
Yet through that rage shines Troy's untroubled hill,
And many a tumbled wall and vanished tree               55
Remains, as if in spite, a happy memory.

## * JUDAS

Judas Iscariot drearily
Wheeling round the deadly tree:
Adders sleep
Awake and keep
Their watch, encircling scale to scale          5
The tree of bale.
From whose cleft fastnesses glare out
Basilisks furnace-eyed;
Within whose shade like matted hair,
About, about,                                   10
Pronged hornets cruise and glide,
Sting, sting the glassy air.

And all around the labouring ground is torn;
Hoof and horn
Thrice-deep their hieroglyphs have lined,        15
Lead in and in his mind,
And wind him in a maze forlorn.
Judas, awake and pass
Dryfoot the charmed morass,
Break the bright fence of glass,                 20
Lift up your eyes!
Asleep in light great-limbed Judaea lies;
Dark wood and sunny hill
Will let you where you will,
And by some road perhaps young Judas waits,      25
Not found yet by his twelve doom-bearing mates.

*O that all time had stopped then, had rolled back*
*A little way, let Judas out again!*
*I saw Him stand in the Garden, by the snare*
*The dove-eyed Decoy. Had I taken my life*        30
*Just then it would have been in time. O that*
*I had stumbled and fallen then, died suddenly!*
*I stumbled and did not fall; the vast earth turned,*
*Then stopped awry, half-way, all mad and strange,*
*The ponderous heavens heeled over, stars, rocks, soldiers,*   35
*The very roots run wrong, locked wrong forever!*
*Now Time beats on, all changed, and yet the same.*

79

Judas Iscariot wearily,
Wheeling round the darkening tree:
Now winds the sting                        40
Deeper,
Now the faint fairy death-bells ring,
Now the mind's surly keeper
Makes the thirty death-coins spin,
Winding Judas in:                          45
*With such thin-edged unearthly sound*
*As ours the stones cry from the ground:*
*The little stones that cut the feet*
*Of travellers going up the hill,*
*Of sad and merry, lame and fleet,*        50
*And cannot show*
*Compassion though*
*Their little arrows striking make*
*With such mean war some heart to break*
*That thought to die undaunted on the hill.*   55

Now all the air is still.

*He chose, and I was chosen. No one knew Him.*

Judas Iscariot by the tree.


MERLIN

O Merlin in your crystal cave
Deep in the diamond of the day,
Will there ever be a singer
Whose music will smooth away
The furrow drawn by Adam's finger          5
Across the meadow and the wave?
Or a runner who'll outrun
Man's long shadow driving on,
Break through the gate of memory
And hang the apple on the tree?
Will your magic ever show                   10
The sleeping bride shut in her bower,
The day wreathed in its mound of snow
And Time locked in his tower?

80

## THE ENCHANTED KNIGHT

Lulled by La Belle Dame Sans Merci he lies
  In the bare wood below the blackening hill.
The plough drives nearer now, the shadow flies
  Past him across the plain, but he lies still.

Long since the rust its gardens here has planned,     5
  Flowering his armour like an autumn field.
From his sharp breast-plate to his iron hand
  A spider's web is stretched, a phantom shield.

When footsteps pound the turf beside his ear
  Armies pass through his dream in endless line,     10
And one by one his ancient friends appear;
  They pass all day, but he can make no sign.

When a bird cries within the silent grove
  The long-lost voice goes by, he makes to rise
And follow, but his cold limbs never move,     15
  And on the turf unstirred his shadow lies.

But if a withered leaf should drift
  Across his face and rest, the dread drops start
Chill on his forehead. Now he tries to lift
  The insulting weight that stays and breaks his heart.  20

## MARY STUART

My brother Jamie lost me all,
Fell cleverly to make me fall,
And with a sure reluctant hand
Stole my life and took my land.

It was jealousy of the womb     5
That let me in and shut him out,
Honesty, kingship, all shut out,
While I enjoyed the royal room.

My father was his, but not my mother,
We were, yet were not, sister, brother,     10
To reach my mother he had to strike
Me down and leap that deadly dyke.

Over the wall I watched him move
At ease through all the guarded grove,
Then hack, and hack, and hack it down,                    15
Until that ruin was his own.


## IBSEN

Solness climbs the dwindling tower
    And all the hills fall flat.
Hilda Wangel down below
    Now is no bigger than her hat.

Solness steps into the air,                               5
    All Norway lies below him, Brand
Frowning on the rusty heath,
    Peer's half-witted fairyland,

Nora stumbling from a door,
    Hedda burning a book,                                10
Doctor Stockman fishing up
    Bacilli from the brook,

Rebecca circling in the weir,
    The Rat Wife whipping round a wall;
The Pillars of Society                                   15
    Fall thundering with his fall.

And flashing by his house he sees it
    Split from earth to sky,
And his wife and children sitting
    Naked to every passer-by.                            20


## THE TOWN BETRAYED

Our homes are eaten out by time,
    Our lawns strewn with our listless sons,
Our harlot daughters lean and watch
    The ships crammed down with shells and guns.

82

Like painted prows far out they lean:      5
  A world behind, a world before.
The leaves are covering up our hills,
  Neptune has locked the shore.

Our yellow harvests lie forlorn
  And there we wander like the blind,     10
Returning from the golden field
  With famine in our mind.

Far inland now the glittering swords
  In order rise, in order fall,
In order on the dubious field      15
  The dubious trumpets call.

Yet here there is no word, no sign
  But quiet murder in the street.
Our leaf-light lives are spared or taken
  By men obsessed and neat.     20

We stand beside our windows, see
  In order dark disorder come,
And prentice killers duped by death
  Bring and not know our doom.

Our cattle wander at their will.     25
  To-day a horse pranced proudly by.
The dogs run wild. Vultures and kites
  Wait in the towers for us to die.

At evening on the parapet
  We sit and watch the sun go down,     30
Reading the landscape of the dead,
  The sea, the hills, the town.

There our ancestral ghosts are gathered.
  Fierce Agamemnon's form I see,
Watching as if his tents were time     35
  And Troy eternity.

We must take order, bar our gates,
  Fight off these phantoms. Inland now
Achilles, Siegfried, Lancelot
  Have sworn to bring us low.     40

## THE UNFAMILIAR PLACE

I do not know this place,
Though here for long I have run
My changing race
In the moon and the sun,
Within this wooded glade                          5
Far up the mountainside
Where Christ and Caesar died
And the first man was made.

I have seen this turning light
For many a day.                                   10
I have not been away
Even in dreams of the night.
In the unnumbered names
My fathers gave these things
I seek a kingdom lost,                            15
Sleeping with folded wings.
I have questioned many a ghost
Far inland in my dreams,
Enquired of fears and shames
The dark and winding way                          20
To the day within my day.

And aloft I have stood
And given my eyes their fill,
Have watched the bad and the good
Go up and down the hill,                          25
The peasants on the plain
Ploughing the fields red,
The roads running alone,
The ambush in the wood,
The victim walking on,                            30
The misery-blackened door
That never will open again,
The tumblers at the fair,
The watchers on the stair,
Cradle and bridal-bed,                            35
The living and the dead
Scattered on every shore.

All this I have seen
Twice over, there and here,
Knocking at dead men's gates            40
To ask the living way,
And viewing this upper scene.
But I am balked by fear
And what my lips say
To drown the voice of fear.             45
The earthly day waits.


# THE PLACE OF LIGHT AND DARKNESS

Walking on the harvest hills of Night
Time's elder brother, the great husbandman,
Goes on his ancient round. His massive lantern,
Simpler than the first fashion, lights the rows
Of stooks that lean like little golden graves       5
Or tasselled barges foundering low
In the black stream.
                        He sees that all is ready,
The trees all stripped, the orchards bare, the nests
Empty. All things grown                              10
Homeless and whole. He sees the hills of grain,
A day all yellow and red, flowers, fruit, and corn.
The soft hair harvest-golden in darkness.
Children playing
In the late night-black day of time. He sees         15
The lover standing by the trysting-tree
Who'll never find his love till all are gathered
In light or darkness. The unnumbered living
Numbered and bound and sheaved.
                        O could that day             20
Break on this side of time!
                        A wind shakes
The loaded sheaves, the feathery tomb bursts open,
And yellow hair is poured along the ground
From the bent neck of time. The woods cry:           25
*This is the resurrection.*

O little judgment days lost in the dark,
Seen by the bat and screech-owl!
                        He goes on,
Bearing within his ocean-heart the jewel,            30

85

The day all yellow and red wherein a sun
Shines on the endless harvest lands of time.


## THE SOLITARY PLACE

O I shall miss
With one small breath these centuries
Of harvest-home uncounted!
I have known
The mead, the bread,                                              5
And the mounds of grain
As half my riches. But the fields will change,
And their harvest would be strange
If I could return. I should know again
Only the lint-white stubble plain                               10
From which the summer-painted birds have flown
A year's life on.

But I can never
See with these eyes the double-threaded river
That runs through life and death and death and life,    15
Weaving one scene. Which I and not I
Blindfold have crossed, I and not I
Will cross again, my face, my feet, my hands
Gleaned from lost lands
To be sown again.                                               20

O certain prophecy,
And faithful tragedy,
Furnished with scenery of sorrow and strife,
The Cross and the Flood
And Babel's towers                                              25
And Abel's blood
And Eden's bowers,
Where I and not I
Lived and questioned and made reply:
None else to ask or make reply . . .                            30

If there is none else to ask or reply
But I and not I,
And when I stretch out my hand my hand comes towards me
To pull me across to me and back to me,
If my own mind, questioning, answers me                         35

86

And there is no other answer to me,
If all that I see,
Woman and man and beast and rock and sky,
Is a flat image shut behind an eye,
And only my thoughts can meet me or pass me or follow me,    40
O then I am alone,
I, many and many in one,
A lost player upon a hill
On a sad evening when the world is still,
The house empty, brother and sister gone,                    45
Beyond the reach of sight, or sound of any cry,
Into the bastion of the mind, behind the shutter of the eye.


## THE PRIVATE PLACE

This stranger holding me from head to toe,
This deaf usurper I shall never know,
Who lives in household quiet in my unrest,
And of my troubles weaves his tranquil nest,
Who never smiles or frowns or bows his head,          5
And while I rage is insolent as the dead,
Composed, indifferent, thankless, faithful, he
Is my ally and only enemy.

Come then, take up the cleansing blade once more
That drives all difference out. The fabled shore      10
Sees us again. Now the predestined fight,
The ancestral stroke, the opening gash of light:
Side by side myself by myself slain,
The wakening stir, the eyes loaded with gain
Of ocean darkness, the rising hand in hand,           15
I with myself at one, the changed land,
My home, my country. But this precious seal
Will slowly crumble, the thief time will steal
Soft-footed bit by bit this boundless treasure
Held in four hands. I shall regain my measure,        20
My old measure again, shrink to a room, a shelf
Where decently I lay away myself,
Become the anxious warder, groan and fret
My thankless service to this martinet
Who sleeps and sleeps and rules. I hold this life     25

Only in strife and the aftertaste of strife
With this dull champion and thick-witted king.
But at one word he'll leap into the ring.


## THE UNATTAINED PLACE

We have seen the world of good deeds spread
With its own sky above it
A length away
Our whole day,
Yet have not crossed from our false kindred.          5
We could have leapt straight from the womb to bliss
And never lost it after,
Been cradled, baptized, bred in that which is
And never known this frontier laughter,
But that we hate this place so much                   10
And hating love it,
And that our weakness is such
That it must clutch
All weakness to it and can never release
The bound and battling hands,                         15
The one hand bound, the other fighting
The fellow-foe it's tied to, righting
Weakness with weakness, rending, reuniting
The torn and incorruptible bands
That bind all these united and disunited lands,—      20
While there lies our predestined power and ease,
There, in those natural fields, life-fostering seas.

If we could be more weak
Than weakness' self, if we could break
This static hold with a mere blank, with nothing,     25
If we could take
Memory and thought and longing
Up by the roots and cast them behind our back,
If we could stop this ceaseless ringing and singing
That keeps our fingers flying in hate and love,       30
If we could cut off,
If we could unmake
What we were made to make:

But that we then should lose
Our loss,                                           35
Our kingdom's crown,
And to great Nothing toss
Our last left jewel down,
The light that long before us was,
The land we did not own,                            40
The choice we could not choose.
For once we played upon that other hill,
And from that house we come.
There is a line around it still
And all inside is home.                             45
Once there we pored on every stone and tree
In a long dream through the unsetting day,
And looking up could nothing see
But the right way on every way.
And lost it after,                                  50
No foot knows where,
To find this mourning air,
Commemorative laughter,
The mask, the doom
Written backwards,                                  55
The illegible tomb
Pointing backwards,
The reverse side
Where strength is weakness,
The body, pride,                                    60
The soul, a sickness.

Yet from that missing heaven outspread
Here all we read.


## THE THREEFOLD PLACE

This is the place. The autumn field is bare,
    The row lies half-cut all the afternoon,
The birds are hiding in the woods, the air
    Dreams fitfully outworn with waiting.
                                    Soon        5

Out of the russet woods in amber mail
  Heroes come walking through the yellow sheaves,
Walk on and meet. And then a silent gale
  Scatters them on the field like autumn leaves.

Yet not a feathered stalk has stirred, and all      10
  Is still again, but for the birds that call
On every warrior's head and breast and shield.
  Sweet cries and horror on the field.

One field. I look again and there are three:
  One where the heroes fell to rest,      15
One where birds make of iron limbs a tree,
  Helms for a nest,
  And one where grain stands up like armies drest.


## THE ORIGINAL PLACE

*This is your native land.*
*By ancient inheritance*
*Your lives are free, though a hand*
*Strange to you set you here,*
*Ordained this liberty*      5
*And gave you hope and fear*
*And the turning maze of chance.*

To weave our tale of Time
Rhyme is knit to rhyme
So close, it's like a proof      10
That nothing else can be
But this one tapestry
Where gleams under the woof
A giant Fate half-grown,
Imprisoned and its own.      15

*To your unquestioned rule*
*No bound is set. You were*
*Made for this work alone.*
*This is your native air.*
*You could not leave these fields.*      20
*And when Time is grown*

*Beneath your countless hands*
*They say this kingdom shall*
*Be stable and beautiful.*

But at its centre stands                    25
A stronghold never taken,
Stormed at hourly in vain,
Held by a force unknown
That neither answers nor yields.
There our arms are shaken,                  30
There the hero was slain
That bleeds upon our shields.


## THE SUFFICIENT PLACE

See, all the silver roads wind in, lead in
To this still place like evening. See, they come
Like messengers bearing gifts to this little house,
And this great hill worn down to a patient mound,
And these tall trees whose motionless branches bear    5
An aeon's summer foliage, leaves so thick
They seem to have robbed a world of shade, and kept
No room for all these birds that line the boughs
With heavier riches, leaf and bird and leaf.
Within the doorway stand                              10
Two figures, Man and Woman, simple and clear
As a child's first images. Their manners are
Such as were known before the earliest fashion
Taught the Heavens guile. The room inside is like
A thought that needed thus much space to write on,    15
Thus much, no more. Here all's sufficient. None
That comes complains, and all the world comes here,
Comes, and goes out again, and comes again.
This is the Pattern, these the Archetypes,
Sufficient, strong, and peaceful. All outside          20
From end to end of the world is tumult. Yet
These roads do not turn in here but writhe on
Round the wild earth for ever. If a man
Should chance to find this place three times in time
His eyes are changed and make a summer silence          25
Amid the tumult, seeing the roads wind in
To their still home, the house and the leaves and birds.

## THE DREAMT-OF PLACE

I saw two towering birds cleaving the air
And thought they were Paolo and Francesca
Leading the lost, whose wings like silver billows
Rippled the azure sky from shore to shore,
They were so many. The nightmare god was gone   5
Who roofed their pain, the ghastly glen lay open,
The hissing lake was still, the fiends were fled,
And only some few headless, footless mists
Crawled out and in the iron-hearted caves.
Like light's unearthly eyes the lost looked down,   10
And heaven was filled and moving. Every height
On earth was thronged and all that lived stared upward.
I thought, This is the reconciliation,
This is the day after the Last Day,
The lost world lies dreaming within its coils,   15
Grass grows upon the surly sides of Hell,
Time has caught time and holds it fast for ever.
And then I thought, Where is the knife, the butcher,
The victim? Are they all here in their places?
Hid in this harmony? But there was no answer.   20

# *The Narrow Place*

## *1943*

# THE NARROW PLACE

## TO J. F. H. (1897–1934)

Shot from the sling into the perilous road,
The hundred mile long hurtling bowling alley,
To-day I saw you pass full tilt for the jack.
Or it seemed a race beyond time's gate you rode,
Trussed to the motor cycle, shoulder and head       5
Fastened to flying fate, so that your back
Left nothing but a widening wake of dumb
Scornful oblivion. It was you, yet some
Soft finger somewhere turned a different day,
The day I left you in that narrow valley,          10
Close to my foot, but already far away;
And I remembered you were seven years dead.

Yet you were there so clearly, I could not tell
For a moment in the hot still afternoon
What world I walked in, since it held us two,      15
A dead and a living man. Had I cracked the shell
That hides the secret souls, had I fallen through,
I idly wondered, and in so falling found
The land where life's untraceable truants run
Hunting a halting stage? Was this the ground       20
That stretched beyond the span-wide world-wide ditch,
So like the ground I knew, yet so unlike,
Because it said 'Again', all this again,
The flying road, the motionless house again,
And, stretched between, the tension of your face –  25
As you ran in dust the burning comet's race
Athirst for the ease of ash – the eating itch
To be elsewhere, nowhere, the driving pain
Clamping the shoulders back? Was death's low dike
So easy to leap as this and so commonplace,        30
A jump from here through here straight into here,
An operation to make you what you were
Before, no better or worse? And yet the fear?

95

The clock-hand moved, the street slipped into its place,
Two cars went by. A chance face flying past          35
Had started it all and made a hole in space,
The hole you looked through always. I knew at last
The sight you saw there, the terror and mystery
Of unrepeatable life so plainly given
To you half wrapped still in eternity,               40
Who had come by such a simple road from heaven;
So that you did not need to have the story
Retold, or bid the heavy world turn again,
But felt the terror of the trysting place,
The crowning test, the treachery and the glory.     45


## THE WAYSIDE STATION

Here at the wayside station, as many a morning,
I watch the smoke torn from the fumy engine
Crawling across the field in serpent sorrow.
Flat in the east, held down by stolid clouds,
The struggling day is born and shines already       5
On its warm hearth far off. Yet something here
Glimmers along the ground to show the seagulls
White on the furrows' black unturning waves.

But now the light has broadened.
I watch the farmstead on the little hill,            10
That seems to mutter: 'Here is day again'
Unwillingly. Now the sad cattle wake
In every byre and stall,
The ploughboy stirs in the loft, the farmer groans
And feels the day like a familiar ache              15
Deep in his body, though the house is dark.
The lovers part
Now in the bedroom where the pillows gleam
Great and mysterious as deep hills of snow,
An inaccessible land. The wood stands waiting       20
While the bright snare slips coil by coil around it,
Dark silver on every branch. The lonely stream
That rode through darkness leaps the gap of light,
Its voice grown loud, and starts its winding journey
Through the day and time and war and history.       25

96

## THE RIVER

The silent stream flows on and in its glass
Shows the trained terrors, the well-practised partings,
The old woman standing at the cottage gate,
Her hand upon her grandson's shoulder. He,
A bundle of clouts creased as with tribulations,    5
Bristling with spikes and spits and bolts of steel,
Bound in with belts, the rifle's snub-nosed horn
Peering above his shoulder, looks across
From this new world to hers and tries to find
Some ordinary words that share her sorrow.    10
The stream flows on
And shows a blackened field, a burning wood,
A bridge that stops half-way, a hill split open
With scraps of houses clinging to its sides,
Stones, planks and tiles and chips of glass and china    15
Strewn on the slope as by a wrecking wave
Among the grass and wild-flowers. Darkness falls,
The stream flows through the city. In its mirror
Great oes and capitals and flourishes,
Pillars and towers and fans and gathered sheaves    20
Hold harvest-home and Judgment Day of fire.
The houses stir and pluck their roofs and walls
Apart as if in play and fling their stones
Against the sky to make a common arc
And fall again. The conflagrations raise    25
Their mountainous precipices. Living eyes
Glaze instantly in crystal change. The stream
Runs on into the day of time and Europe,
Past the familiar walls and friendly roads,
Now thronged with dumb migrations, gods and altars    30
That travel towards no destination. Then
The disciplined soldiers come to conquer nothing,
March upon emptiness and do not know
Why all is dead and life has hidden itself.
The enormous winding frontier walls fall down,    35
Leaving anonymous stone and vacant grass.
The stream flows on into what land, what peace,
Far past the other side of the burning world?

## THEN

There were no men and women then at all,
But the flesh lying alone,
And angry shadows fighting on a wall
That now and then sent out a groan
Buried in lime and stone,                                    5
And sweated now and then like tortured wood
Big drops that looked yet did not look like blood.

And yet as each drop came a shadow faded
And left the wall.
There was a lull                                            10
Until another in its shadow arrayed it,
Came, fought and left a blood-mark on the wall;
And that was all; the blood was all.

If there had been women there they might have wept
For the poor blood, unowned, unwanted,                     15
Blank as forgotten script.
The wall was haunted
By mute maternal presences whose sighing
Fluttered the fighting shadows and shook the wall
As if that fury of death itself were dying.                20

## THE REFUGEES

A crack ran through our hearthstone long ago,
And from the fissure we watched gently grow
The tame domesticated danger,
Yet lived in comfort in our haunted rooms.
Till came the Stranger                                      5
And the great and the little dooms.

We saw the homeless waiting in the street
Year after year,
The always homeless,
Nationless and nameless,                                   10
To whose bare roof-trees never come
Peace and the house martin to make a home.
We did not fear
A wrong so dull and old,
So patiently told and patiently retold,                   15

While we sat by the fire or in the window-seat.
Oh what these suffered in dumb animal patience,
That we now suffer,
While the world's brow grows darker and the world's
   hand rougher.
We bear the lot of nations,                 20
Of times and races,
Because we watched the wrong
Last too long
With non-committal faces.
Until from Europe's sunset hill           25
We saw our houses falling
Wall after wall behind us.
What could blind us
To such self-evident ill
And all the sorrows from their caverns calling?   30

This is our punishment. We came
Here without blame, yet with blame,
Dark blame of others, but our blame also.
This stroke was bound to fall,
Though not to fall so.                 35
A few years did not waste
The heaped up world. The central pillar fell
Moved by no living hand. The good fields sickened
By long infection. Oh this is the taste
Of evil done long since and always, quickened   40
No one knows how
While the red fruit hung ripe upon the bough
And fell at last and rotted where it fell.

For such things homelessness is ours
And shall be others'. Tenement roofs and towers   45
Will fall upon the kind and the unkind
Without election,
For deaf and blind
Is rejection bred by rejection
Breeding rejection,               50
And where no counsel is what will be will be.
We must shape here a new philosophy.

## SCOTLAND 1941

We were a tribe, a family, a people.
Wallace and Bruce guard now a painted field,
And all may read the folio of our fable,
Peruse the sword, the sceptre and the shield.
A simple sky roofed in that rustic day,                    5
The busy corn-fields and the haunted holms,
The green road winding up the ferny brae.
But Knox and Melville clapped their preaching palms
And bundled all the harvesters away,
Hoodicrow Peden in the blighted corn                      10
Hacked with his rusty beak the starving haulms.
Out of that desolation we were born.

Courage beyond the point and obdurate pride
Made us a nation, robbed us of a nation.
Defiance absolute and myriad-eyed                         15
That could not pluck the palm plucked our damnation.
We with such courage and the bitter wit
To fell the ancient oak of loyalty,
And strip the peopled hill and the altar bare,
And crush the poet with an iron text,                     20
How could we read our souls and learn to be?
Here a dull drove of faces harsh and vexed,
We watch our cities burning in their pit,
To salve our souls grinding dull lucre out,
We, fanatics of the frustrate and the half,               25
Who once set Purgatory Hill in doubt.
Now smoke and dearth and money everywhere,
Mean heirlooms of each fainter generation,
And mummied housegods in their musty niches,
Burns and Scott, sham bards of a sham nation,             30
And spiritual defeat wrapped warm in riches,
No pride but pride of pelf. Long since the young
Fought in great bloody battles to carve out
This towering pulpit of the Golden Calf,
Montrose, Mackail, Argyle, perverse and brave,            35
Twisted the stream, unhooped the ancestral hill.
Never had Dee or Don or Yarrow or Till
Huddled such thriftless honour in a grave.

Such wasted bravery idle as a song,
Such hard-won ill might prove Time's verdict wrong,    40
And melt to pity the annalist's iron tongue.


## THE LETTER

Tried friendship must go down perforce
Before the outward eating rage
And murderous heart of middle age,
Killing kind memory at its source,
If it were not for mortality,                               5
The thought of that which levels all
And coldly pillows side by side
The tried friend and the too much tried.

Then think of that which will have made
Us and all else contemporary.                             10
Look long enough and you will see
The dead fighting with the dead.
Now's the last hour for chivalry,
And we can still escape the shame
Of striking the unanswering head,                        15
Before we are changed put off the blame.

But should this seem a niggardly
And ominous reconcilation,
Look again until you see,
Fixed in the body's final station,                       20
The features of immortality.
Try to pursue this quarrel then.
You cannot. This is less than man
And more. That more is our salvation.
Now let us seize it. Now we can.                         25


## THE HUMAN FOLD

Here penned within the human fold
No longer now we shake the bars,
Although the ever-moving stars
Night after night in order rolled
Rebuke this stationary farce.                             5
There's no alternative here but love,

So far as genuine love can be
Where there's no genuine liberty
To give or take, to lose or have,
And having rots with wrong, and loss          10
Itself has no security
Except in the well-managed grave,
And all we do is done to prove
Content and discontent both are gross.
Yet sometimes here we still can see           15
The dragon with his tears of gold,
The bat-browed sphinx
Shake loose her wings
That have no hold and fan no air,
All struck dead by her stare.                 20
Hell shoots its avalanche at our feet,
In heaven the souls go up and down,
And we can see from this our seat
The heavenly and the hellish town,
The green cross growing in a wood             25
Close by old Eden's crumbling wall,
And God Himself in full manhood
Riding against the Fall.
All this; but here our sight is bound
By ten dull faces in a round,                 30
Each with a made-to-measure glance
That is in misery till it's found.
Yet looking at each countenance
I read this burden in them all:
'I lean my cheek from eternity                35
For time to slap, for time to slap.
I gather my bones from the bottomless clay
To lay my head in the light's lap.'

By what long way, by what dark way,
From what unpredetermined place,              40
Did we creep severally to this hole
And bring no memory and no grace
To furnish evidence of the soul,
Though come of an ancient race?
All gone, where now we cannot say,            45
Altar and shrine and boundary stone,
And of the legends of our day
This one remains alone:
'They loved and might have loved for ever,

But public trouble and private care                50
Faith and hope and love can sever
And strip the bed and the altar bare'.
Forward our towering shadows fall
Upon the naked nicheless wall,
And all we see is that shadow-dance.               55
Yet looking at each countenance
I read this burden in them all
'I lean my cheek from eternity
For time to slap, for time to slap.
I gather my bones from the bottomless clay         60
To lay my head in the light's lap'.


## THE NARROW PLACE

How all the roads creep in.
This place has grown so narrow,
You could not swing a javelin,
And if you shot an arrow,
It would skim this meagre mountain wall            5
And in some other country
Like a lost meteor fall.
When first this company
Took root here no one knows,
For nothing comes and goes                         10
But the bleak mountain wind,
That so our blood has thinned
And sharpened so our faces –
Unanswerably grave
As long-forsaken places –                          15
They have lost all look of hate or love
And keep but what they have.
The cloud has drawn so close,
This small much-trodden mound
Must, must be very high                            20
And no road goes by.
The parsimonious ground
That at its best will bear
A few thin blades as fine as hair
Can anywhere be found,                             25
Yet is so proud and niggardly

And envious, it will trust
Only one little wild half-leafless tree
To straggle from the dust.

Yet under it we sometimes feel such ease          30
As if it were ten thousand trees
And for its foliage had
Robbed half the world of shade.
All the woods in grief
Bowed down by leaf and bird and leaf          35
From all their branches could not weep
A sleep such as that sleep.

Sleep underneath the tree.
It is your murdering eyes that make
The sterile hill, the standing lake,          40
And the leaf-breaking wind.
Then shut your eyes and see,
Sleep on and do not wake
Till there is movement in the lake,
And the club-headed water-serpents break          45
In emerald lightnings through the slime,
Making a mark on Time.


## THE RECURRENCE

All things return, Nietzsche said,
The ancient wheel revolves again,
Rise, take up your numbered fate;
The cradle and the bridal bed,
Life and the coffin wait.          5
All has been that ever can be,
And this sole eternity
Cannot cancel, cannot add
One to your delights or tears,
Or a million million years          10
Tear the nightmare from the mad.

Have no fear then. You will miss
Achievement by the self-same inch,
When the great occasion comes
And they watch you, you will flinch,          15
Lose the moment, be for bliss

A footlength short. All done before.
Love's agonies, victory's drums
Cannot huddle the Cross away
Planted on its future hill.                                    20
The secret on the appointed day
Will be made known, the ship once more
Hit upon the waiting rock
Or come safely to the shore,
Careless under the deadly tree                                 25
The victim drowse, the urgent warning
Come too late, the dagger strike,
Strike and strike through eternity,
And worlds hence the prison clock
Will toll on execution morning,                                30
What is ill be always ill,
Wretches die behind a dike,
And the happy be happy still.

But the heart makes reply:
This is only what the eye                                      35
From its tower on the turning field
Sees and sees and cannot tell why,
Quarterings on the turning shield.
The great non-stop heraldic show.
And the heart and the mind know,                               40
What has been can never return,
What is not will surely be
In the changed unchanging reign,
Else the Actor on the Tree
Would loll at ease, miming pain,                               45
And counterfeit mortality.


## THE GOOD MAN IN HELL

If a good man were ever housed in Hell
    By needful error of the qualities,
Perhaps to prove the rule or shame the devil,
    Or speak the truth only a stranger sees,

Would he, surrendering to obvious hate,                        5
    Fill half eternity with cries and tears,
Or watch beside Hell's little wicket gate
    In patience for the first ten thousand years,

Feeling the curse climb slowly to his throat
    That, uttered, dooms him to rescindless ill,     10
Forcing his praying tongue to run by rote,
    Eternity entire before him still?

Would he at last, grown faithful in his station,
    Kindle a little hope in hopeless Hell,
And sow among the damned doubts of damnation,   15
    Since here someone could live and could live well?

One doubt of evil would bring down such a grace,
    Open such a gate, all Eden would enter in,
Hell be a place like any other place,
    And love and hate and life and death begin.     20


## THE WHEEL

How can I turn this wheel that turns my life,
Create another hand to move this hand
Not moved by me, who am not the mover,
Nor, though I love and hate, the lover,
The hater? Loves and hates are thrust     5
Upon me by the acrimonious dead,
The buried thesis, long since rusted knife,
Revengeful dust.
A stony or obstreperous head,
Though slain so squarely, can usurp my will     10
As I walk above it on the sunny hill.

Then how do I stand?
How can I here remake what there made me
And makes and remakes me still?
Set a new mark? Circumvent history?     15
Nothing can come of history but history,
The stationary storm that cannot bate
Its neutral violence,
The transitory solution that cannot wait,
The indecisive victory     20
That is like loss read backwards and cannot bring
Relief to you and me,
The jangling
Of all the voices of plant and beast and man
That have not made a harmony     25

Since first the great controversy began,
And cannot sink to silence
Unless a grace
Come of itself to wrap our souls in peace
Between the turning leaves of history and make     30
Ourselves ourselves, winnow the grudging grain,
And take
From that which made us that which will make us again.


## THE FACE

See me with all the terrors on my roads,
The crusted shipwrecks rotting in my seas,
And the untroubled oval of my face
That alters idly with the moonlike modes
And is unfathomably framed to please              5
And deck the angular bone with passing grace.

I should have worn a terror-mask, should be
A sight to frighten hope and faith away,
Half charnel field, half battle and rutting ground.
Instead I am a smiling summer sea                 10
That sleeps while underneath from bound to bound
The sun- and star-shaped killers gorge and play.


## THE LAW

O you my Law
Which I serve not,
O you my Good
Which I prize not,
O you my Truth                                    5
Which I seek not:

Where grace is beyond desert
Thanks must be thanklessness;
Where duty is past performance
Disservice is only service;                       10
Where truth is unsearchable
All seeking is straying.

If I could know ingratitude's
Bounds I should know gratitude;
And disservice done                                15
Would show me the law of service;
And the wanderer at last
Learns his long error.

If I could hold complete
The reverse side of the pattern,                   20
The wrong side of Heaven,
O then I should know in not knowing
My truth in my error.


## THE CITY

Day after day we kept the dusty road,
    And nearer came small-towered Jerusalem,
Nearer and nearer. Lightened of the goad,
    Our beasts went on as if the air wafted them.

We saw the other troops with music move           5
    Between the mountain meadows, far and clear,
Onwards towards the city, and above
    The ridge the fresh young firmament looked near.

All stood so silent in the silent air,
    The little houses set on every hill,           10
A tree before each house. The people were
    Tranquil, not sad nor glad. How they could till

Their simple fields, here, almost at the end,
    Perplexed us. We were filled with dumb surprise
At wells and mills, and could not understand      15
    This was an order natural and wise.

We looked away. Yet some of us declared:
    'Let us stay here. We ask no more than this,'
Though we were now so close, we who had dared
    Half the world's spite to hit the mark of bliss.   20

So we went on to the end. But there we found
  A dead land pitted with blind whirling places,
And crowds of angry men who held their ground
  With blank blue eyes and raging rubicund faces.

We drew our swords and in our minds we saw     25
  The streets of the holy city running with blood,
And centuries of fear and power and awe,
  And all our children in the deadly wood.


## THE GROVE

There was no road at all to that high place
But through the smothering grove,
Where as we went the shadows wove
Adulterous shapes of animal hate and love.
The idol-crowded nightmare Space,     5
Wood beyond wood, tree behind tree,
And every tree an empty face
Gashed by the casual lightning mark
The first great Luciferian animal
Scored on leaf and bark.     10
This was, we knew, the heraldic ground,
And therefore now we heard our footsteps fall
With the true legendary sound,
Like secret trampling behind a wall,
As if they were saying: 'To be: to be.'     15

And oh the silence, the drugged thicket dozing
Deep in its dream of fear,
The ring closing
And coming near,
The well-bred self-sufficient animals     20
With clean rank pelts and proud and fetid breath,
Screaming their arrogant calls,
Their moonstone eyes set straight at life and death.
Did we see or dream it? And the jungle cities –
For there were cities there and civilizations     25
Deep in the forest; powers and dominations
Like shapes begotten by dreaming animals,
Proud animal dreams uplifted high,
Booted and saddled on the animal's back
And staring with the arrogant animal's eye:     30

The golden dukes, the silver earls, and gleaming black
The curvetting knights sitting their curvetting steeds,
The sweet silk-tunicked eunuchs singing ditties,
Swaying like wandering weeds,
The scarlet cardinals,                                     35
And lions high in the air on the banner's field,
Crowns, sceptres, spears and stars and moons of blood,
And sylvan wars in bronze within the shield,
All quartered in the wide world's wood,
The smothering grove where there was place for pities. 40

We trod the maze like horses in a mill,
And then passed through it
As in a dream of the will.
How could it be? There was the stifling grove,
Yet here was light; what wonder led us to it?         45
How could the blind path go
To climb the crag and top the towering hill,
And all that splendour spread? We know
There was no road except the smothering grove.


## THE GATE

We sat, two children, warm against the wall
Outside the towering stronghold of our fathers
That frowned its stern security down upon us.
We could not enter there. That fortress life,
Our safe protection, was too gross and strong       5
For our unpractised palates. Yet our guardians
Cherished our innocence with gentle hands,
(They, who had long since lost their innocence,)
And in grave play put on a childish mask
Over their tell-tale faces, as in shame         10
For the rich food that plumped their lusty bodies
And made them strange as gods. We sat that day
With that great parapet behind us, safe
As every day, yet outcast, safe and outcast
As castaways thrown upon an empty shore.        15
Before us lay the well-worn scene, a hillock
So small and smooth and green, it seemed intended
For us alone and childhood, a still pond
That opened upon no sight a quiet eye,
A little stream that tinkled down the slope.        20

But suddenly all seemed old
And dull and shrunken, shut within itself
In a sullen dream. We were outside, alone.
And then behind us the huge gate swung open.


## THE LITTLE GENERAL

Early in spring the little General came
  Across the sound, bringing the island death,
And suddenly a place without a name,
  And like the pious ritual of a faith,

Hunter and quarry in the boundless trap,                    5
  The white smoke curling from the silver gun,
The feather curling in the hunter's cap,
  And clouds of feathers floating in the sun,

While down the birds came in a deafening shower,
  Wing-hurricane, and the cattle fled in fear.            10
Up on the hill a remnant of a tower
  Had watched that single scene for many a year,

Weaving a wordless tale where all were gathered
  (Hunter and quarry and watcher and fabulous field)
A sylvan war half human and half feathered,             15
  Perennial emblem painted on the shield

Held up to cow a never-conquered land
Fast in the little General's fragile hand.


## THE PRIZE

Did we come here, drawn by some fatal thing,
Fly from eternity's immaculate bow
Straight to the heart of time's great turning ring,
That we might win the prize that took us so?
Was it some ordinary sight, a flower,
The white wave falling, falling upon the shore,
The blue of the sky, the grasses' waving green?

Or was it one sole thing, a certain door
Set in a wall, a half-conjectured scene
Of men and women moving as in a play,    10
A turn in the winding road, a distant tower,
A corner of a field, a single place
Apart, a single house, a single tree,
A look upon one half-averted face
That has been once, or is, or is to be?    15

We hurried here for some such thing and now
Wander the countless roads to seek our prize,
That far within the maze serenely lies,
While all around each trivial shape exclaims:
'Here is your jewel; this is your longed for day',  20
And we forget, lost in the countless names.

## THE SHADES

The bodiless spirits waiting chill
In the ports of black Nonentity
For passage to the living land,
Without eyes strive to see,
Without ears strain to hear,    5
Stretch an unincarnate hand
In greeting to the hollow hill
Above the insubstantial sea,
The billow curving on the sand,
The bird sitting on the tree;    10
And in love and in fear
Ensnare the smile, condense the tear,
Rehearse the play of evil and good,
The comedy and the tragedy.
Until the summoned ghosts appear    15
In patterned march around the hill
Against the hoofed and horned wood.

## THE RING

Long since we were a family, a people,
The legends say; an old kind-hearted king
Was our foster father, and our life a fable.

Nature in wrath broke through the grassy ring
Where all our gathered treasures lay in sleep –      5
Many a rich and many a childish thing.

She filled with hoofs and horns the quiet keep.
Her herds beat down the turf and nosed the shrine
In bestial wonder, bull and adder and ape,

Lion and fox, all dressed by fancy fine      10
In human flesh and armed with arrows and spears;
But on the brow of each a secret sign

That haughtily put aside the sorrowful years
Or struck them down in stationary rage;
Yet they had tears that were not like our tears,      15

And new, all new, for Nature knows no age.
Fatherless, sonless, homeless haunters, they
Had never known the vow and the pilgrimage,

Poured from one fount into the faithless day.
We are their sons, but long ago we heard      20
Our fathers or our fathers' fathers say

Out of their dream the long-forgotten word
That rounded again the ring where sleeping lay
Our treasures, still unrusted and unmarred.

E

# POSTSCRIPT

## * ISAIAH

Isaiah from his ledge could see
Angel and man and animal
At their everlasting play.

He saw the crack in the palace wall
Open and shut like a mouth jerking,                    5
Spitting out teeth of stone.
He and the Three were all alone
With Time and with Time's working.

The Three were one, the One was three,
For his eyes could never see                           10
This or that, so quick its passing.
But the triple shadows crossing
Framed an image in their fall,
A shape against the breaking wall.

## THE RETURN OF ODYSSEUS

The doors flapped open in Odysseus' house,
The lolling latches gave to every hand,
Let traitor, babbler, tout and bargainer in.
The rooms and passages resounded
With ease and chaos of a public market,                5
The walls mere walls to lean on as you talked,
Spat on the floor, surveyed some newcomer
With an absent eye. There you could be yourself.
Dust in the nooks, weeds nodding in the yard,
The thick walls crumbling. Even the cattle came        10
About the doors with mild familiar stare
As if this were their place.
All round the island stretched the clean blue sea.

Sole at the house's heart Penelope
Sat at her chosen task, endless undoing                    15
Of endless doing, endless weaving, unweaving,
In the clean chamber. Still her loom ran empty
Day after day. She thought: 'Here I do nothing
Or less than nothing, making an emptiness
Amid disorder, weaving, unweaving the lie               20
The day demands. Odysseus, this is duty,
To do and undo, to keep a vacant gate
Where order and right and hope and peace can enter.
Oh will you ever return? Or are you dead,
And this wrought emptiness my ultimate emptiness?' 25

She wove and unwove and wove and did not know
That even then Odysseus on the long
And winding road of the world was on his way.


## ROBERT THE BRUCE

*To Douglas in Dying:*

'My life is done, yet all remains,
    The breath has gone, the image not,
The furious shapes once forged in heat
    Live on though now no longer hot.

'Steadily the shining swords                              5
    In order rise, in order fall,
In order on the beaten field
    The faithful trumpets call.

'The women weeping for the dead
    Are not sad now but dutiful,                          10
The dead men stiffening in their place
    Proclaim the ancient rule.

'Great Wallace's body hewn in four,
    So altered, stays as it must be.
O Douglas do not leave me now,                            15
    For past your head I see

'My dagger sheathed in Comyn's heart
　　And nothing there to praise or blame,
Nothing but order which must be
　　Itself and still the same.　　　　　　　　　　20

'But that Christ hung upon the Cross,
　　Comyn would rot until time's end
And bury my sin in boundless dust,
　　For there is no amend

'In order; yet in order run　　　　　　　　　　25
　　All things by unreturning ways.
If Christ live not, nothing is there
　　For sorrow or for praise.'

So the King spoke to Douglas once
　　A little while before his death,　　　　　　　30
Having outfaced three English kings
　　And kept a people's faith.


## THE TROPHY

The wise king dowered with blessings on his throne,
The rebel raising the flag in the market place,
Haunt me like figures on an ancient stone
The ponderous light of history beats upon,
Or the enigma of a single face　　　　　　　　5
Handed unguessed, unread from father to son,
As if it dreamed within itself alone.

Regent and rebel clash in horror and blood
Here on the blindfold battlefield. But there,
Motionless in the grove of evil and good　　　10
They grow together and their roots are twined
In deep confederacy far from the air,
Sharing the secret trophy each with other;
And king and rebel are like brother and brother,
Or father and son, co-princes of one mind,　　15
Irreconcilables, their treaty signed.

## THE ANNUNCIATION

Now in this iron reign
I sing the liberty
Where each asks from each
What each most wants to give
And each awakes in each                    5
What else would never be,
Summoning so the rare
Spirit to breathe and live.

Then let us empty out
Our hearts until we find                   10
The last least trifling toy,
Since now all turns to gold,
And everything we have
Is wealth of heart and mind,
That squandered thus in turn               15
Grows with us manifold.

Giving, I'd give you next
Some more than mortal grace,
But that you deifying
Myself I might deify,                       20
Forgetting love was born
Here in a time and place,
And robbing by such praise
This life we magnify.

Whether the soul at first,                  25
This pilgrimage began,
Or the shy body leading
Conducted soul to soul
Who knows? This is the most
That soul and body can,                     30
To make us each for each
And in our spirit whole.


## THE CONFIRMATION

Yes, yours, my love, is the right human face.
I in my mind had waited for this long,
Seeing the false and searching for the true,

117

Then found you as a traveller finds a place
Of welcome suddenly amid the wrong                    5
Valleys and rocks and twisting roads. But you,
What shall I call you? A fountain in a waste,
A well of water in a country dry,
Or anything that's honest and good, an eye
That makes the whole world bright. Your open heart, 10
Simple with giving, gives the primal deed,
The first good world, the blossom, the blowing seed,
The hearth, the steadfast land, the wandering sea,
Not beautiful or rare in every part,
But like yourself, as they were meant to be.          15


## THE COMMEMORATION

I wish I could proclaim
My faith enshrined in you
And spread among a few
Our high but hidden fame,
That we new life have spun                    5
Past all that's thought and done,
And someone or no one
Might tell both did the same.

Material things will pass
And we have seen the flower                    10
And the slow falling tower
Lie gently in the grass,
But meantime we have stored
Riches past bed and board
And nursed another hoard                       15
Than callow lad and lass.

Invisible virtue now
Expands upon the air
Although no fruit appear
Nor weight bend down the bough,                20
And harvests truly grown
For someone or no one
Are stored and safely won
In hollow heart and brow.

How can one thing remain        25
Except the invisible,
The echo of a bell
Long rusted in the rain?
This strand we weave into
Our monologue of two,        30
And time cannot undo
That strong and subtle chain.


## THE OLD GODS

Old gods and goddesses who have lived so long
Through time and never found eternity,
Fettered by wasting wood and hollowing hill,

You should have fled our ever-dying song.
The mound, the well, and the green trysting tree,    5
They are forgotten, yet you linger still.

Goddess of caverned breast and channelled brow
And cheeks slow hollowed by millenial tears,
Forests of autumns fading in your eyes,

Eternity marvels at your counted years    10
And kingdoms lost in time, and wonders how
There could be thoughts so bountiful and wise

As yours beneath the ever-breaking bough,
And vast compassion curving like the skies.


## THE BIRD

Adventurous bird walking upon the air,
Like a schoolboy running and loitering, leaping and springing,
Pensively pausing, suddenly changing your mind
To turn at ease on the heel of a wing-tip. Where
In all the crystalline world was there to find    5
For your so delicate walking and airy winging
A floor so perfect, so firm and so fair,
And where a ceiling and walls so sweetly ringing,
Whenever you sing, to your clear singing?

The wide-winged soul itself can ask no more     10
Than such a pure, resilient and endless floor
For its strong-pinioned plunging and soaring and upward and
    upward springing.

## THE GUESS

We buried them beneath the deep green hill –
A little Ark full, women, men and cattle,
Children and household pets, engrossed by war.
And then one morning they were back again
And held as once before their little reign.     5
All joys and sorrows but the last were there:
That day erased: no pit or mound of battle.
They lay as by some happy chance reborn
An hour or two before the birth of ill,
And ere ill came they'd be away again.     10
Quick leave and brief reward, so lightly worn.

I watched them move between sleep and awake.
It was a dream and could not be fulfilled,
For all these ghosts were blessed. Yet there seemed
Nothing more natural than blessedness,     15
Nor any life as true as this I dreamed,
So that I did not feel that I had willed
These forms, but that a long forgotten guess
Had shown, past chaos, the natural shape we take.

## THE SWIMMER'S DEATH

He lay outstretched upon the sunny wave,
That turned and broke into eternity.
The light showed nothing but a glassy grave
Among the trackless tumuli of the sea.
Then over his buried brow and eyes and lips     5
From every side flocked in the homing ships.

## THE QUESTION

Will you, sometime, who have sought so long and seek
Still in the slowly darkening hunting ground,
Catch sight some ordinary month or week
Of that strange quarry you scarcely thought you sought –
Yourself, the gatherer gathered, the finder found,   5
The buyer, who would buy all, in bounty bought –
And perch in pride on the princely hand, at home,
And there, the long hunt over, rest and roam?

## THE DAY

If, in the mind of God or book of fate,
This day that's all to live lies lived and done,
And there already like Griseldas wait
My apprentice thoughts and actions, still untried;
If, where I travel, some thing or some one   5
Has gone before me sounding through the wide
Immensity of nothingness to make
A region and a road where road was none,
Nor shape, nor shaping hand; if for my sake
The elected joy grows there and the chosen pain   10
In the field of good and ill, in surety sown:
Oh give me clarity and love that now
The way I walk may truly trace again
The in eternity written and hidden way;
Make pure my heart and will, and me allow   15
The acceptance and revolt, the yea and nay,
The denial and the blessing that are my own.

# *The Voyage*

## *and other poems*

### TO LUMIR AND CATRIONA

---

## *1946*

## THE RETURN OF THE GREEKS

The veteran Greeks came home
Sleepwandering from the war.
We saw the galleys come
Blundering over the bar.
Each soldier with his scar                          5
In rags and tatters came home.

Reading the wall of Troy
Ten years without a change
Was such intense employ
(Just out of the arrows' range),                    10
All the world was strange
After ten years of Troy.

Their eyes knew every stone
In the huge heartbreaking wall
Year after year grown                               15
Till there was nothing at all
But an alley steep and small,
Tramped earth and towering stone.

Now even the hills seemed low
In the boundless sea and land,                      20
Weakened by distance so.
How could they understand
Space empty on every hand
And the hillocks squat and low?

And when they arrived at last                       25
They found a childish scene
Embosomed in the past,
And the war lying between—
A child's preoccupied scene
When they came home at last.                        30

But everything trite and strange,
The peace, the parcelled ground,
The vinerows—never a change!

The past and the present bound
In one oblivious round                              35
Past thinking trite and strange.

But for their grey-haired wives
And their sons grown shy and tall
They would have given their lives
To raise the battered wall                          40
Again, if this was all
In spite of their sons and wives.

Penelope in her tower
Looked down upon the show
And saw within an hour                              45
Each man to his wife go,
Hesitant, sure and slow:
She, alone in her tower.


## THE ESCAPE

Escaping from the enemy's hand
    Into the enemy's vast domain,
I sought by many a devious path,
    Having got in, to get out again.

The endless trap lay everywhere,                    5
    And all the roads ran in a maze
Hither and thither, like a web
    To catch the careless days.

The great farmhouses sunk in time
    Rose up out of another land;                    10
Here only the empty harvest-home
    Where Caliban waved his wand.

There was no promise in the bud,
    No comfort in the blossoming tree,
The waving yellow harvests were                     15
    Worse than sterility.

Yet all seemed true. The family group
   Still gathered round the dying hearth,
The old men droned the ancient saws,
   And the young mother still gave birth.    20

But this I saw there. In the church
   In rows the stabled horses stood,
And the cottar's threshold stone
   Was mired with earth and blood.

And when I reached the line between    25
   The Occupied and Unoccupied,
It was as hard as death to cross,
   Yet no change on the other side.

All false, all one. The enemy
   These days was scarcely visible;    30
Only his work was everythwere,
   Ill work contrived so well

That he could smile and turn his back,
   Let brute indifference overawe
The longing flesh and leaping heart    35
   And grind to dust the ancient law.

A land of bright delusion where
   Shape scarce disturbed the emptiness
Yet troubled the sight that strove to make
   Of every shape a shape the less.    40

There the perpetual question ran,
   What is escape? and What is flight?
Like dialogue in a dismal dream
   Where right is wrong and wrong is right.

But at the very frontier line,    45
   Beyond the region of desire,
There runs a wall of towering flame:
   The battle is there of blood and fire.

I must pass through that fiery wall,
   Emerge into the battle place,    50
And there at last, lifting my eyes,
   I'll see the enemy's face.

## THE CASTLE

All through that summer at ease we lay,
And daily from the turret wall
We watched the mowers in the hay
And the enemy half a mile away.
They seemed no threat to us at all.                    5

For what, we thought, had we to fear
With our arms and provender, load on load,
Our towering battlements, tier on tier,
And friendly allies drawing near
On every leafy summer road.                            10

Our gates were strong, our walls were thick,
So smooth and high, no man could win
A foothold there, no clever trick
Could take us, have us dead or quick.
Only a bird could have got in.                         15

What could they offer us for bait?
Our captain was brave and we were true . . .
There was a little private gate,
A little wicked wicket gate.
The wizened warder let them through.                   20

Oh then our maze of tunnelled stone
Grew thin and treacherous as air.
The cause was lost without a groan,
The famous citadel overthrown,
And all its secret galleries bare.                     25

How can this shameful tale be told?
I will maintain until my death
We could do nothing, being sold;
Our only enemy was gold,
And we had no arms to fight it with.                   30

## MOSES

He left us there, went up to Pisgah hill,
And saw the holiday land, the sabbath land,
The mild prophetic beasts, millennial herds,
The sacred lintel, over-arching tree,
The vineyards glittering on the southern slopes,          5
And in the midst the shining vein of water,
The river turning, turning towards its home.
Promised to us. The dream rose in his nostrils
With homely smell of wine and corn and cattle,
Byre, barn and stall, sweat-sanctified smell of peace.     10
He saw the tribes arrayed beside the river,
White robes and sabbath stillness, still light falling
On dark heads whitened by the desert wave,
The Sabbath of Sabbaths come and Canaan their home.
All this he saw in dreaming. But we who dream             15
Such common dreams and see so little saw
The battle for the land, the massacres,
The vineyards drenched in aboriginal blood,
The settlement, unsatisfactory order,
The petty wars and neighbouring jealousies               20
And local troubles. But we did not see,
We did not see and Moses did not see,
The great disaster, exile, diaspora,
The holy bread of the land crumbled and broken
In Babylon, Caesarea, Alexandria                          25
As on a splendid dish, or gnawed as offal.
Nor did we see, beyond, the ghetto rising,
Toledo, Cracow, Vienna, Budapesth,
Nor, had we seen, would we have known our people
In the wild disguises of fantastic time,                  30
Packed in dense cities, wandering countless roads,
And not a road in the world to lead them home.
How could we have seen such things? How could we have seen
That plot of ground pledged by the God of Moses
Trampled by sequent tribes, seized and forgotten          35
As a child seizes and forgets a toy,
Strange languages, strange gods and customs borne
Over it and away with the light migrations,
Stirring each century ancestral dust.
All this was settled while we stood by Jordan             40
That first great day, could not be otherwise.

Moses saw that day only; we did not see it;
But now it stands becalmed in time for ever:
White robes and sabbath peace, the snow-white emblem.


## SAPPHO

Sappho, Sappho's pitiless murderess,
Strides in judgment through the end of night
To circumvent the round blue trap of day
(That soon will lock its jail of miseries),
Drives her victim to the penal rock,                              5
Angry, abrupt, broken-off edge of time.
Pursuer and pursued
Tied each to each by such a sullen knot
No arrowy thought of immaterial god
Can slip between and ease the torment crying:          10
'All my life cries out against all my life,
My love against all my love. I'll carry Phaon
Until I drop or leap the final crag
Where all is left behind, things and their names.
For if a single name should follow there          15
I must reiterate this death and leap
Precipice after precipice of death
Till name of wood and hill and night and day
And all that summons Phaon is stripped off.'

Now the dumb hulks of being rise around her:          20
Beast, rock and tree, illegible figures, stare
At her in destitution as on the day
Before the first day broke, when all was nameless,
Nameless earth, water, firmament, and nameless
Woman and man. Till on the utmost edge          25
She leans above the unanswering shapes of life,
Cries once and leaps, and battered on the stones,
Batters love, Phaon and all the misery out.


## THE COVENANT

The covenant of god and animal,
The frieze of fabulous creatures winged and crowned,
And in the midst the woman and the man—

Lost long ago in fields beyond the Fall—
Keep faith in sleep-walled night and there are found 5
On our long journey back where we began.

Then the heraldic crest of nature lost
Shines out again until the weariless wave
Roofs with its sliding horror all that realm.

What jealousy, what rage could overwhelm    10
The golden lion and lamb and vault a grave
For innocence, innocence past defence or cost?


## THOUGHT AND IMAGE

Past time and space the shaping Thought
    Was born in freedom and in play;
The Image then on earth was wrought
    Of water and of clay.

And when the embodied Soul would know    5
    Itself and be to itself revealed,
For its instruction it must go
    To the beast that roams the field.

Thenceforth the Soul grew intimate
    With beast and herb and stone, and passed    10
Into the elements to mate
    With the dull earth at last.

It's said that to reverse its doom
    And save the entangled Soul, to earth
God came and entered in the womb
    And passed through the gate of birth;

Was born a Child in body bound
    Among the cattle in a byre.
The clamorous world was all around,
    Beast, insect, plant, earth, water, fire.    20

On bread and wine his flesh grew tall,
    The round sun helped him on his way,
Wood, iron, herb and animal
    His friends were till the testing day.

Then braced by iron and by wood,                                      25
   Engrafted on a tree he died,
And little dogs lapped up the blood
   That spurted from his broken side.

The great bull gored him with his horns,
   And stinging flies were everywhere,                      30
The sun beat on him, clinging thorns
   Writhed in and out among his hair.

His body next was locked in stone,
   By steel preserved in sterile trust,
And with the earth was left alone,                                    35
   And, dust, lay with the dust.

There all at last with all was done,
   The great knot loosened, flesh unmade
Beyond the kingdom of the sun,
   In the invincible shade.

All that had waited for his birth
   Were round him then in dusty night,
The creatures of the swarming earth,
   The souls and angels in the height.

## TWICE-DONE, ONCE-DONE

Nothing yet was ever done
   Till it was done again,
And no man was ever one
   Except through dead men.

I could neither rise nor fall                                         5
   But that Adam fell.
Had he fallen once for all
   There'd be nothing to tell.

Unless in me my fathers live
   I can never show
I am myself—ignorant if                                               10
   I'm a ghost or no.

Father Adam and Mother Eve,
  Make this pact with me:
Teach me, teach me to believe,          15
  For to believe's to be.

Many a woman since Eve was made
  Has seen the world is young,
Many and many a time obeyed
  The legend-making tongue.          20

Abolish the ancient custom—who
  Would mark Eve on her shelf?
Even a story to be true
  Must repeat itself.

Yet we the latest born are still          25
  The first ones and the last,
And in our little measures fill
  The oceanic past.

For first and last is every way,
  And first and last each soul,          30
And first and last the passing day,
  And first and last the goal.


\* DIALOGUE

'Now let us lover by lover lay
  And enemy now to enemy bring,
Set open the immaculate way
  Of everything to everything
  And crown our destiny king.'          5

'If lover were by lover laid,
  And enemy brought to enemy,
All that's made would be unmade
  And done would be the destiny
  Of time and eternity.          10

'But love with love can never rest,
   And hate can never bear with hate,
Each by each must be possessed,
   For, see, at every turning wait
   The enemy and the mate.'         15

## THE VOYAGE
### (*For Eric Linklater*)

That sea was greater than we knew.
Week after week the empty round
Went with us; the Unchanging grew,
And we were headed for that bound.

How we came there we could not tell.     5
Seven storms had piled us in that peace,
Put us in check and barred us well
With seven walls of seven seas.

As one may vanish in a day
In some untravelled fold of space     10
And there pursue his patient way
Yet never come to any place

Though following still by star and sun,
For every chart is rased and furled,
And he out of this world has run     15
And wanders now another world,

So we by line and compass steered
And conned the book of sun and star,
Yet where it should no sign appeared
To tell us, You are there or there,     20

Familiar landfall, slender mast:
We on the ocean were alone.
The busy lanes where fleets had passed
Showed us no sail except our own.

Still south we steered day after day          25
And only water lay around
As if the land had stolen away
Or sprawled upon the ocean ground.

The sun by day, the stars by night
Had only us to look upon,          30
Bent on us their collected light,
And followed on as we went on.

Sometimes in utter wonder lost
That loneliness like this could be
We stood and stared until almost          35
We saw no longer sky or sea,

But only the frame of time and space,
An empty floor, a vacant wall,
And on that blank no line to trace
Movement, if we moved at all.          40

What thoughts came then! Sometimes it seemed
We long had passed the living by
On other seas and only dreamed
This sea, this journey and this sky,

Or traced a ghostly parallel          45
That limned the land but could not merge,
And haven and home and harbour bell
Were just behind the horizon verge,

Or the world itself had ended so
Without a cry, and we should sail          50
To and fro, to and fro,
Long past the lightning and the gale.

O then what crowding fantasies
Poured in from empty sea and sky!
At night we heard the whispering quays,          55
Line after line, slide softly by.

Delusions in the silent noon;
Fields in the hollows of the waves;
Or spread beneath the yellow moon,
A land of harvests and of graves.          60

135

The soft sea-sounds beguiled our ear.
We thought we walked by mountain rills
Or listened half a night to hear
The spring wind hunting on the hills.

And faces, faces, faces came                    65
Across the salt sea-desert air,
And rooms in which a candle flame
Made everything renowned and rare.

The words we knew like our right hand,
Mountain and valley, meadow and grove,          70
Composed a legendary land
Rich with the broken tombs of love.

Delusion or truth? We were content
Thenceforth to sail the harmless seas
Safe past the Fate and the Accident,            75
And called a blessing on that peace.

And blessing, we ourselves were blest,
Lauded the loss that brought our gain,
Sang the tumultuous world to rest,
And wishless called it back again.               80

For loss was then our only joy,
Privation of all, fulfilled desire,
The world our treasure and our toy
In destitution clean as fire.

Our days were then—I cannot tell                85
How we were then fulfilled and crowned
With life as in a parable,
And sweetly as gods together bound.

Delusion and dream! Our captain knew
Compass and clock had never yet                 90
Failed him; the sun and stars were true.
The mark was there that we should hit.

And it rose up, a sullen stain
Flawing the crystal firmament.
A wound! We felt the familiar pain              95
And knew the place to which we were sent.

## THE FATHERS

Our fathers all were poor,
Poorer our fathers' fathers;
Beyond, we dare not look.
We, the sons, keep store
Of tarnished gold that gathers                    5
Around us from the night,
Record it in this book
That, when the line is drawn,
Credit and creditor gone,
Column and figure flown,                          10
Will open into light.

Archaic fevers shake
Our healthy flesh and blood
Plumped in the passing day
And fed with pleasant food.                        15
The fathers' anger and ache
Will not, will not away
And leave the living alone,
But on our careless brows
Faintly their furrows engrave                      20
Like veinings in a stone,
Breathe in the sunny house
Nightmare of blackened bone,
Cellar and choking cave.

Panics and furies fly                              25
Through our unhurried veins,
Heavenly lights and rains
Purify heart and eye,
Past agonies purify
And lay the sullen dust.                           30
The angers will not away.
We hold our fathers' trust,
Wrong, riches, sorrow and all
Until they topple and fall,
And fallen let in the day.                         35

## THE THREE MIRRORS

I looked in the first glass
And saw the fenceless field
And like broken stones in grass
The sad towns glint and shine.
The slowly twisting vine                                    5
Scribbled with wrath the stone,
The mountain summits were sealed
In incomprehensible wrath.
The hunting roads ran on
To round the flying hill                                    10
And bring the quarry home.
But the obstinate roots ran wrong,
The lumbering fate fell wrong,
The walls were askew with ill,
Askew went every path,                                      15
The dead lay askew in the tomb.

I looked in the second glass
And saw through the twisted scroll
In virtue undefiled
And new in eternity                                         20
Father and mother and child,
The house with its single tree,
Bed and board and cross,
And the dead asleep in the knoll.
But the little blade and leaf                               25
By an angry law were bent
To shapes of terror and grief,
By a law the field was rent,
The crack ran over the floor,
The child at peace in his play                              30
Changed as he passed through a door,
Changed were the house and the tree,
Changed the dead in the knoll,
For locked in love and grief
Good with evil lay.                                         35

If I looked in the third glass
I should see evil and good
Standing side by side
In the ever standing wood,
The wise king safe on his throne,                           40

138

The rebel raising the rout,
And each so deeply grown
Into his own place
He'd be past desire or doubt.
If I could look I should see                    45
The world's house open wide,
The million million rooms
And the quick god everywhere
Glowing at work and at rest,
Tranquillity in the air,                        50
Peace of the humming looms
Weaving from east to west,
And you and myself there.


## THE RIDER VICTORY

The rider Victory reins his horse
Midway across the empty bridge
As if head-tall he had met a wall.
Yet there was nothing there at all,
No bodiless barrier, ghostly ridge            5
To check the charger in his course
So suddenly, you'd think he'd fall.

Suspended, horse and rider stare
Leaping on air and legendary.
In front the waiting kingdom lies,            10
The bridge and all the roads are free;
But halted in implacable air
Rider and horse with stony eyes
Uprear their motionless statuary.


## THE WINDOW

Within the great wall's perfect round
Bird, beast and child serenely grew
In endless change on changeless ground
That in a single pattern bound
The old perfection and the new.               5

There was a tower set in the wall
And a great window in the tower,

139

And if one looked, beyond recall
The twisting glass kept him in thrall
With changing marvels hour by hour.          10
And there one day we looked and saw
Marsh, mere and mount in anger shaken,
The world's great side, the giant flaw,
And watched the stately forests fall,
The white ships sinking in the sea,          15
The tower run toppling in the field,
The last left stronghold sacked and taken,
And earth and heaven in jeopardy.
Then turning towards you I beheld
The wrinkle writhe across your brow,          20
And felt time's cap clapped on my head,
And all within the enclosure now,
Light leaf and smiling flower, was false,
The great wall breached, the garden dead.

Across the towering window fled          25
Disasters, victories, festivals.


# THE HOUSE

The young and the lusty loll in bed
And the bent and the aged lay the fire
And sweep the floor and cook the food.
'No reason or rule is in this house,'

Sighed the little old woman, shaking her head,          5
'Where the young and the rich have their desire,
And all the reward of the poor and the good
Is to prop the walls of this thankless house.

'Yes,' she muttered '*they*'ve all they want,
But we have nothing but knowledge to chew,          10
Only that, and necessity.
These two maintain this niggardly house.

'For the young and the rich are ignorant
And never guess what they've yet to rue—
The lenten days when they will be          15
Servants like us of this tyrannous house.'

140

## THE MYTH

My childhood all a myth
Enacted in a distant isle;
Time with his hourglass and his scythe
Stood dreaming on the dial,
And did not move the whole day long        5
That immobility might save
Continually the dying song,
The flower, the falling wave.
And at each corner of the wood
In which I played the ancient play,        10
Guarding the traditional day
The faithful watchers stood.

My youth a tragi-comedy,
Ridiculous war of dreams and shames
Waged for a Pyrrhic victory                15
Of reveries and names,
Which in slow-motion rout were hurled
Before sure-footed flesh and blood
That of its hunger built a world,
Advancing rood by rood.                    20
And there in practical clay compressed
The reverie played its useful part,
Fashioning a diurnal mart
Of radiant east and west.

So manhood went. Now past the prime       25
I see this life contrived to stay
With all its works of labouring time
By time beguiled away.
Consolidated flesh and bone
And its designs grow halt and lame;        30
Unshakeable arise alone
The reverie and the name.
And at each border of the land,
Like monuments a deluge leaves,
Guarding the invisible sheaves             35
The risen watchers stand.

## ON SEEING TWO LOVERS
## IN THE STREET

You do not know
What is done with you,
Do not fear
What's done or undone:
You are not here,                                    5
You are not two
Any more, but one.

Pity these two
Who all have lost,
Envy these two                                       10
Who have paid their cost
To gain this soul
That dazzling hovered
Between them whole.
There they are lost                                  15
And their tracks are covered;
Nothing can find them
Until they awake
In themselves or take
New selves to bind them.                             15

## SONG

Why should your face so please me
That if one little line should stray
Bewilderment would seize me
And drag me down the tortuous way
Out of the noon into the night?                      5
But so, into this tranquil light
You raise me.

How could our minds so marry
That, separate, blunder to and fro,
Make for a point, miscarry,                           10
And blind as headstrong horses go?
Though now they in their promised land
At pleasure travel hand in hand
Or tarry.

This concord is an answer                             15
To questions far beyond our mind
Whose image is a dancer.
All effort is to ease refined
Here, weight is light; this is the dove
Of love and peace, not heartless love                20
The lancer.

And yet I still must wonder
That such an armistice can be
And life roll by in thunder
To leave this calm with you and me.                  25
This tranquil voice of silence, yes,
This single song of two, this is
A wonder.


## SUBURBAN DREAM

Walking the suburbs in the afternoon
In summer when the idle doors stand open
    And the air flows through the rooms
    Fanning the curtain hems,

You wander through a cool elysium                    5
Of women, schoolgirls, children, garden talks,
    With a schoolboy here and there
    Conning his history book.

The men are all away in offices,
Committee-rooms, laboratories, banks,                10
    Or pushing cotton goods
    In Wick or Ilfracombe.

The massed unanimous absence liberates
The light keys of the piano and sets free
    Chopin and everlasting youth,                    15
    Now, with the masters gone.

And all things turn to images of peace,
The boy curled over his book, the young girl poised
    On the path as if beguiled
    By the silence of a wood.                        20

It is a child's dream of a grown-up world.
But soon the brazen evening clocks will bring
   The tramp of feet and brisk
   Fanfare of motor horns
   And the masters come.          25

## READING IN WARTIME

Boswell by my bed,
Tolstoy on my table:
Though the world has bled
For four and a half years,
And wives' and mothers' tears         5
Collected would be able
To water a little field
Untouched by anger and blood,
A penitential yield
Somewhere in the world;         10
Though in each latitude
Armies like forests fall,
The iniquitous and the good
Head over heels hurled,
And confusion over all:         15
Boswell's turbulent friend
And his deafening verbal strife,
Ivan Ilych's death
Tell me more about life,
The meaning and the end         20
Of our familiar breath,
Both being personal,
Than all the carnage can,
Retrieve the shape of man,
Lost and anonymous,         25
Tell me wherever I look
That not one soul can die
Of this or any clan
Who is not one of us
And has a personal tie         30
Perhaps to someone now
Searching an ancient book,
Folk-tale or country song
In many and many a tongue,
To find the original face,         35

The individual soul,
The eye, the lip, the brow
For ever gone from their place,
And gather an image whole.


## THE LULLABY

The lullaby has crooned to sleep so many
On all the iron fields in such a clamour,
 There is astonishment
  Among the waking.

So quickly these awake were cast in slumber,  5
Full in the light, then covered thick in shadow,
 There seemed no time to shed
  Them from the others.

So deafening the clamour, soft the crooning,
So swift the change and simple the confusion,  10
 That these though side by side
  Were far asunder.

The returning and the unreturning races,
Those who took heed, and those who would not listen
 But turned straight towards the dark,  15
  So that there was nothing

To do or say, no greeting on their journey,
Farewell or words at all—these two are haunted
 For ever each by each,
  In each commingled.  20


## DEJECTION

 I do not want to be
 Here, there or anywhere;
 My melancholy
 Folds me beyond the reach of care
 As in a valley  5
 Whence long ago I tried to sally,
 But dreamt and left my dream upon the air.

And now in lunar pleasure
I watch the undreaming folk of rock and stone
Lie side by side alone     10
Enjoying their enormous leisure,
That shall continue till the day
When rock and stone are put away;
And feel no more than they the sun that burns
On this unmoving scenery,     15
Nor count nor care to count the dull returns
Of day and month and year and century
Crowding within the crowding urns.

For every eloquent voice dies in this air
Wafted from anywhere to anywhere     20
And never counted by the careful clock,
That cannot strike the hour
Of power that will dissolve this power
Until the rock rise up and split the rock.

## SONG OF PATIENCE

What use has patience,
Won with such difficulty,
Forced out in such a sigh?

The heart in its stations
Has need of patience,     5
Holding through night and day
Solitary monologue,
Systole and diastole,
Two surly words that say
Each to each in the breast:     10
'Solid flesh, fluttering soul,
Troubles and fears, troubles and fears,
Quick hope, long delay,
Where is rest? Where is rest?'
Prologue and epilogue     15
Reiterated in the breast
For thirty, forty, fifty years.
The heart in its stations
Has need of patience.

Patience wearies of itself,                              20
Impatient patience,
For itself can find no use
But to rehearse upon the shelf
Its hackneyed stations,
And so would end the long abuse,                         25
Make each breath its parting breath,
Die in pain, be born in pain,
And to love at last attain:
Love to whom all things are well,
Love that turns all things to ease,                      30
The life that fleets before the eye,
And the motionless isle of death;
That tunes the tedious miseries
And even patience makes to please;
Love to whom the sorrows tell                            35
Their abysmal dreams and cry:
'Weave the spell! Weave the spell!
Make us well.'


## * SONG

Here in this corner
Deep in the morning,
Here you will stay.

Here is the warner,
Here the warning                                          5
And here the way.

Light here is dark;
Light be your work,
And light your play.

Brightness to wrap you in,                               10
Darkness to lap you in,
No farewell to say,
You cannot away.

Keep fast your mystery;
Time has no history, 15
All things are clear,
Fear not your fear,
You cannot away.

Then wrap you and lap you within the long day,
And drop no tear 20
For the star or the sphere,
There's no anywhere
But here, but here.


## SORROW

I do not want it so,
But since things so are made,
Sorrow, sorrow,
Be you my second trade.
I'll learn the workman's skill 5
And mould the mass of ill
Until I have it so, or so,
And want it so.

I cannot have it so
Unless I frankly make 10
A pact with sorrow
For joy and sorrow's sake,
And wring from sorrow's pay
Wealth joy would toss away—
Till both are balanced, so, or so, 15
And even go.

If it were only so . . .
But right and left I find
Sorrow, sorrow,
And cannot be resigned, 20
Knowing that we were made
By joy to drive joy's trade
And not to waver to and fro,
But quickly go.

## EPITAPH

Into the grave, into the grave with him.
Quick, quick, with dust and stones this dead man cover
Who living was a flickering soul so dim
He was never truly loved nor truly a lover.

Since he was half and half, now let him be                    5
Something entire at last here in this night
Which teaches us its absolute honesty
Who stay between the light and the half-light.

He scarce had room for sorrow, even his own;
His vastest dreams were less than six feet tall;        10
Free of all joys, he crept in himself alone:
To the grave with this poor image of us all.

If now is Resurrection, then let stay
Only what's ours when this is put away.


## COMFORT IN SELF-DESPITE

When in revulsion I detest myself
Thus heartily, myself with myself appal,
And in this mortal rubbish delve and delve,
A dustman damned—perhaps the original

Virtue I'd thought so snugly buried so                    5
May yet be found, else never to be found,
And thus exhumed into the light may grow
After this cruel harrowing of the ground.

For as when I have spoken spitefully
Of this or that friend, piling ill on ill,              10
Remembrance cleans his image and I see
The pure and touching good no taunt could kill,

So I may yet recover by this bad
Research that good I scarcely dreamt I had.

149

## THE TRANSMUTATION

That all should change to ghost and glance and gleam,
And so transmuted stand beyond all change,
And we be poised between the unmoving dream
And the sole moving moment—this is strange

Past all contrivance, word, or image, or sound,     5
Or silence, to express, that we who fall
Through time's long ruin should weave this phantom ground
And in its ghostly borders gather all.

There incorruptible the child plays still,
The lover waits beside the trysting tree,     10
The good hour spans its heaven, and the ill,
Rapt in their silent immortality,

As in commemoration of a day
That having been can never pass away.


## TIME HELD IN TIME'S DESPITE

Now there is only left what time has made
Our very own in our and time's despite,
And we ourselves have nothing, but are stayed
By lonely joys and griefs and blank delight.

For this that's ours so surely could not be     5
But by the word of terror or of grace
That spoke, when all was lost, the guarantee:
'Impersonally soul and soul embrace,

And incorruptibly are bodies bound.'
The hours that melt like snowflakes one by one     10
Leave us this residue, this virgin ground
For ever fresh, this firmament and this sun.

Then let us lay unasking hand in hand,
And take our way, thus led, into our land.

# FOR ANN SCOTT-MONCRIEFF
## (1914–1943)

Dear Ann, wherever you are
Since you lately learnt to die,
You are this unsetting star
That shines unchanged in my eye;
So near, inaccessible,                                                5
Absent and present so much
Since out of the world you fell,
Fell from hearing and touch—
So near. But your mortal tongue
Used for immortal use,                                               10
The grace of a woman young,
The air of an early muse,
The wealth of the chambered brow
And soaring flight of your eyes:
These are no longer now.                                             15
Death has a princely prize.

You who were Ann much more
Than others are that or this,
Extravagant over the score
To be what only is,                                                  20
Would you not still say now
What you once used to say
Of the great Why and How,
On that or the other day?
For though of your heritage                                          25
The minority here began,
Now you have come of age
And are entirely Ann.

Under the years' assaults,
In the storm of good and bad,                                       30
You too had the faults
That Emily Brontë had,
Ills of body and soul,
Of sinner and saint and all
Who strive to make themselves whole,                               35
Smashed to bits by the Fall.
Yet 'the world is a pleasant place'

151

I can hear your voice repeat,
While the sun shone in your face
Last summer in Princes Street.          40


## A BIRTHDAY

I never felt so much
Since I have felt at all
The tingling smell and touch
Of dogrose and sweet briar,
Nettles against the wall,          5
All sours and sweets that grow
Together or apart
In hedge or marsh or ditch.
I gather to my heart
Beast, insect, flower, earth, water, fire,          10
In absolute desire,
As fifty years ago.

Acceptance, gratitude:
The first look and the last
When all between has passed          15
Restore ingenuous good
That seeks no personal end,
Nor strives to mar or mend.
Before I touched the food
Sweetness ensnared my tongue;          20
Before I saw the wood
I loved each nook and bend,
The track going right and wrong;
Before I took the road
Direction ravished my soul.          25
Now that I can discern
It whole or almost whole,
Acceptance and gratitude
Like travellers return
And stand where first they stood.          30

## ALL WE

All we who make
Things transitory and good
Cannot but take
When walking in a wood
Pleasure in everything                    5
And the maker's solicitude,
Knowing the delicacy
Of bringing shape to birth.
To fashion the transitory
We gave and took the ring              10
And pledged ourselves to the earth.


## IN LOVE FOR LONG

I've been in love for long
With what I cannot tell
And will contrive a song
For the intangible
That has no mould or shape,              5
From which there's no escape.

It is not even a name,
Yet is all constancy;
Tried or untried, the same,
It cannot part from me;                    10
A breath, yet as still
As the established hill.

It is not any thing,
And yet all being is;
Being, being, being,                        15
Its burden and its bliss.
How can I ever prove
What it is I love?

This happy happy love
Is sieged with crying sorrows,             20
Crushed beneath and above
Between to-days and morrows;
A little paradise
Held in the world's vice.

And there it is content                    25
And careless as a child,
And in imprisonment
Flourishes sweet and wild;
In wrong, beyond wrong,
All the world's day long.                  30

This love a moment known
For what I do not know
And in a moment gone
Is like the happy doe
That keeps its perfect laws                 35
Between the tiger's paws
And vindicates its cause.

# *The Labyrinth*

## *1949*

## TOO MUCH

No, no, I did not bargain for so much
When I set out upon the famous way
My fathers praised so fondly—such and such
The road, the errand, the prize, the part to play.

For everything is different. Hour and place          5
Are huddled awry, at random teased and tossed,
Too much piled on too much, no track or trace,
And north and south and road and traveller lost.

Then suddenly again I watch the old
Worn saga write across my years and find,          10
Scene after scene, the tale my fathers told,
But I in the middle blind, as Homer blind,

Dark on the highway, groping in the light,
Threading my dazzling way within my night.


## THE LABYRINTH

Since I emerged that day from the labyrinth,
Dazed with the tall and echoing passages,
The swift recoils, so many I almost feared
I'd meet myself returning at some smooth corner,
Myself or my ghost, for all there was unreal          5
After the straw ceased rustling and the bull
Lay dead upon the straw and I remained,
Blood-splashed, if dead or alive I could not tell
In the twilight nothingness (I might have been
A spirit seeking his body through the roads          10
Of intricate Hades)—ever since I came out
To the world, the still fields swift with flowers, the trees
All bright with blossom, the little green hills, the sea,
The sky and all in movement under it,
Shepherds and flocks and birds and the young and old,   15
(I stared in wonder at the young and the old,
For in the maze time had not been with me;
I had strayed, it seemed, past sun and season and change,
Past rest and motion, for I could not tell

At last if I moved or stayed; the maze itself          20
Revolved around me on its hidden axis
And swept me smoothly to its enemy,
The lovely world)—since I came out that day,
There have been times when I have heard my footsteps
Still echoing in the maze, and all the roads          25
That run through the noisy world, deceiving streets
That meet and part and meet, and rooms that open
Into each other—and never a final room—
Stairways and corridors and antechambers
That vacantly wait for some great audience,          30
The smooth sea-tracks that open and close again,
Tracks undiscoverable, indecipherable,
Paths on the earth and tunnels underground,
And bird-tracks in the air—all seemed a part
Of the great labyrinth. And then I'd stumble          35
In sudden blindness, hasten, almost run,
As if the maze itself were after me
And soon must catch me up. But taking thought,
I'd tell myself, 'You need not hurry. This
Is the firm good earth. All roads lie free before you.'  40
But my bad spirit would sneer, 'No, do not hurry.
No need to hurry. Haste and delay are equal
In this one world, for there's no exit, none,
No place to come to, and you'll end where you are,
Deep in the centre of the endless maze.'          45

I could not live if this were not illusion.
It is a world, perhaps; but there's another.
For once in a dream or trance I saw the gods
Each sitting on the top of his mountain-isle,
While down below the little ships sailed by,          50
Toy multitudes swarmed in the harbours, shepherds drove
Their tiny flocks to the pastures, marriage feasts
Went on below, small birthdays and holidays,
Ploughing and harvesting and life and death,
And all permissible, all acceptable,          55
Clear and secure as in a limpid dream.
But they, the gods, as large and bright as clouds,
Conversed across the sounds in tranquil voices
High in the sky above the untroubled sea,
And their eternal dialogue was peace          60
Where all these things were woven, and this our life

Was as a chord deep in that dialogue,
As easy utterance of harmonious words,
Spontaneous syllables bodying forth a world.

That was the real world; I have touched it once,    65
And now shall know it always. But the lie,
The maze, the wild-wood waste of falsehood, roads
That run and run and never reach an end,
Embowered in error—I'd be prisoned there
But that my soul has birdwings to fly free.    70

Oh these deceits are strong almost as life.
Last night I dreamt I was in the labyrinth,
And woke far on. I did not know the place.


## THE WAY

Friend, I have lost the way.
*The way leads on.*
Is there another way?
*The way is one.*
I must retrace the track.    5
*It's lost and gone.*
Back, I must travel back!
*None goes there, none.*
Then I'll make here my place,
(*The road runs on*),    10
Stand still and set my face,
(*The road leaps on*),
Stay here, for ever stay.
*None stays here, none.*
I cannot find the way.    15
*The way leads on.*
Oh places I have passed!
*That journey's done.*
And what will come at last?
*The road leads on.*    20

## THE RETURN

I see myself sometimes, an old old man
Who has walked so long with time as time's true servant,
That he's grown strange to me—who was once myself—
Almost as strange as time, and yet familiar
With old man's staff and legendary cloak,                       5
For see, it is I, it is I. And I return
So altered, so adopted, to the house
Of my own life. There all the doors stand open
Perpetually, and the rooms ring with sweet voices,
And there my long life's seasons sound their changes,   10
Childhood and youth and manhood all together,
And welcome waits, and not a room but is
My own, beloved and longed for. And the voices,
Sweeter than any sound dreamt of or known,
Call me, recall me. I draw near at last,                        15
An old old man, and scan the ancient walls
Rounded and softened by the compassionate years,
The old and heavy and long-leaved trees that watch
This my inheritance in friendly darkness.
And yet I cannot enter, for all within                          20
Rises before me there, rises against me,
A sweet and terrible labyrinth of longing,
So that I turn aside and take the road
That always, early or late, runs on before.


## THE WEST

We followed them into the west,
And left them there, and said good-bye. For now
We could go no farther, could not step one step
Beyond the little earthen mound that hid
Their traces from us; for this was an end.               5
It was as if the west had ended there.
And yet we knew another west ran on,
A west beyond the west, and towards it travelled
Those we had followed to this stopping place.
So we returned by the east and north and south      10
To our own homes, remembering sometimes there,
Sometimes forgetting, thinking yet not thinking,
Bound by the ancient custom of our country.

But from the east newcomers constantly
Pour in among us, mix with us, pass through us,                     15
And travel towards the west; and that migration
Has been from the beginning, it is said,
And long before men's memory it was woven
Into the tranquil pattern of our lives.
And that great movement like a quiet river,                          20
Which always flowing yet is always the same,
Begets a stillness. So that when we look
Out at our life we see a changeless landscape,
And all disposed there in its due proportion,
The young and old, the good and bad, the wise and foolish,  25
All these are there as if they had been for ever,
And motionless as statues, prototypes
Set beyond time, for whom the sun stands still.
And each day says in its passing, 'This is all.'—
While the unhurrying progress goes its way,                          30
And we upon it, year by year by year,
Led through the endless stations of the sun.
There are no aborigines in our country,
But all came hither so, and shall leave so,
Even as these friends we followed to their west.                     35

And yet this is a land, and we say 'Now',
Say 'Now' and 'Here', and are in our own house.


## THE JOURNEY BACK

### I

I take my journey back to seek my kindred,
Old founts dried up whose rivers run far on
Through you and me. Behind, the water-beds
Stone-white with drought; in front the riverless future
Through which our myriad tributaries will wander            5
When this live patchwork land of green and brown
With all its load of corn and weeds is withered.
But here, but here the water, clear or muddied.

Seek the beginnings, learn from whence you came,
And know the various earth of which you are made.      10
So I set out on this calm summer evening
From this my house and my father's. Looking back

I see that all behind is pined and shrunken,
The great trees small again, the good walls gone,
The road grown narrow and poor, wild heath and thorn  15
Where comfortable houses spread their gardens.
Only the sea and sky the same. But quiet
Deeper than I had breathed. Yet in this place,
Most strange and most familiar, my heart says
In a friend's voice, 'I beat in surety;'  20
My hands grow firm, my father's farmer hands,
And open and shut on surety while I walk
In patient trust. This is my father's gift
Left here for me at the first friendly station
On the long road.  25
            But past it all is strange.
I must in other lives with many a leap
Blindfold, must lodge in dark and narrow skulls
With a few thoughts that pad from wall to wall
And never get out, must moulder in dusty hearts,  30
Inhabit many a dark or a sunny room,
Be in all things. And now I'm locked inside
The savage keep, the grim rectangular tower
From which the fanatic neighbour-hater scowls;
There all is emptiness and dirt and envy,  35
Dry rubbish of a life in anguish guarded
By mad and watchful eyes. From which I fall
To gasp and choke in the cramped miser's body
That winds its tightening winch to squeeze the soul
In a dry wooden box with slits for eyes.  40
And when I'm strangling there I flutter out
To drift like gossamer on the sunny wind,
A golden thistledown fool blown here and there,
Who for a lifetime scarcely knows a grief
Or thinks a thought. Then gasp in the hero's breast  45
That like a spring day in the northern seas
Is storm and shine and thunder all commingled,
A long-linked chain of lightning quenched in night.
Perhaps a murderer next, I watch those hands
That shall be always with me, serve my ends,  50
Button, unbutton for my body's needs,
Are intimate with me, the officious tools
That wash my face, push food into my mouth
Loathed servants fed from my averted heart.

So I usurp, grown avid for the end,                    55
Body on body, am both father and child,
Causer and actor, spoiler and despoiled,
Robbing myself, myself, grinding the face
Of the poor, I poorest, who am both rich and poor,
Victor and victim, hapless Many in One.                60

In all these lives I have lodged, and each a prison.
I fly this prison to seek this other prison,
Impatient for the end—or the beginning
Before the walls were raised, the thick doors fastened,
And there was nothing but the breathing air,          65
Sun and soft grass, and sweet and vacant ease.
But there's no end, and I could break my journey
Now, here, without a loss, but that some day
I know I shall find a man who has done good
His long lifelong and is                               70
Image of man from whom all have diverged.
The rest is hearsay. So I hie me back
To my sole starting-point, my random self
That in these rags and tatters clothes the soul.


                        2

            Through countless wanderings,             75
            Hastenings, lingerings,
            From far I come,
            And pass from place to place
            In a sleep-wandering pace
            To seek my home.                          80

            I wear the silver scars
            Of blanched and dying stars
            Forgotten long,
            Whose consternations spread
            Terror among the dead                     85
            And touched my song.

            The well-bred animal
            With coat of seemly mail
            Was then my guide.


                        163

I trembled in my den                              90
With all my kindred when
The dragon died.

Through forests wide and deep
I passed and as a sleep
My wandering was.                                 95
Before the word was said
With animal bowed head
I kept the laws.

I thread the shining day;
The mountains as in play                          100
Dizzily turn
My wild road round and round.
No one has seen the ground
For which I burn.

Through countless wanderings,                     105
Hastenings, lingerings,
Nearer I come,
In a sleep-wandering pace
To find the secret place
Where is my home.                                 110


3

And I remember in the bright light's maze
While poring on a red and rusted arrow
How once I laid my dead self in the barrow,
Closed my blank eyes and smoothed my face,
And stood aside, a third within that place,       115
And watched these two at their strange ritual,
And grieved for that day's deed so often done
When the poor child of man, leaving the sun,
Walks out into the sun and goes his way,
Not knowing the resurrection and the life,        120
Shut in his simple recurring day,
Familiar happiness and ordinary pain.
And while he lives content with child and wife
A million leaves, a million destinies fall,
And over and over again                           125
The red rose blooms and moulders by the wall.

4

And sometimes through the air descends a dust
Blown from the scentless desert of dead time
That whispers: Do not put your trust
In the fed flesh, or colour, or sense, or shape.                    130
This that I am you cannot gather in rhyme.
For once I was all
That you can name, a child, a woman, a flower,
And here escape
From all that was to all,                                          135
Lost beyond loss.
So in the air I toss
Remembrance and rememberer all confused
In a light fume, the last power used,
The last form found,                                               140
And child and woman and flower
Invisibly fall through the air on the living ground.


5

I have stood and watched where many have stood
And seen the calamities of an age
Where good seemed evil and evil good                               145
And half the world ran mad to wage
War with an eager heart for the wrong,
War with a bitter heart for the right,
And many, many killed in the fight.

In those days was heard a song:                                    150
Blessing upon this time and place,
Blessing upon the disfigured face
And on the cracked and withered tongue
That mouthing a blessing cannot bless,
Blessing upon our helplessness                                     155
That, wild for prophecy, is dumb.
Without the blessing cannot the kingdom come.

6

They walk high in their mountainland in light
On winding roads by many a grassy mound
And paths that wander for their own delight.          160

There they like planets pace their tranquil round
That has no end, whose end is everywhere,
And tread as to a music underground,

An ever-winding and unwinding air
That moves their feet though they in silence go,          165
For music's self itself has buried there,

And all its tongues in silence overflow
That movement only should be melody.
This is the other road, not that we know.

This is the place of peace, content to be.          170
All we have seen it; while we look we are
There truly, and even now in memory,

Here on this road, following a falling star.

7

Yet in this journey back
If I should reach the end, if end there was          175
Before the ever-running roads began
And race and track and runner all were there
Suddenly, always, the great revolving way
Deep in its trance;—if there was ever a place
Where one might say, 'Here is the starting-point,'          180
And yet not say it, or say it as in a dream,
In idle speculation, imagination,
Reclined at ease, dreaming a life, a way,
And then awaken in the hurtling track,
The great race in full swing far from the start,          185
No memory of beginning, sign of the end,
And I the dreamer there, a frenzied runner;—
If I should reach that place, how could I come
To where I am but by that deafening road,
Life-wide, world-wide, by which all come to all,          190

The strong with the weak, the swift with the stationary,
For mountain and man, hunter and quarry there
In tarrying do not tarry, nor hastening hasten,
But all with no division strongly come
For ever to their steady mark, the moment,                195
And the tumultuous world slips softly home
To its perpetual end and flawless bourne.
How could we be if all were not in all?
Borne hither on all and carried hence with all,
We and the world and that unending thought              200
Which has elsewhere its end and is for us
Begotten in a dream deep in this dream
Beyond the place of getting and of spending.
There's no prize in this race; the prize is elsewhere,
Here only to be run for. There's no harvest,            205
Though all around the fields are white with harvest.
There is our journey's ground; we pass unseeing.
But we have watched against the evening sky,
Tranquil and bright, the golden harvester.


## THE BRIDGE OF DREAD

But when you reach the Bridge of Dread
Your flesh will huddle into its nest
For refuge and your naked head
Creep in the casement of your breast,

And your great bulk grow thin and small              5
And cower within its cage of bone,
While dazed you watch your footsteps crawl
Toadlike across the leagues of stone.

If they come, you will not feel
About your feet the adders slide,                    10
For still your head's demented wheel
Whirls on your neck from side to side

Searching for danger. Nothing there.
And yet your breath will whistle and beat
As on you push the stagnant air                      15
That breaks in rings about your feet

167

Like dirty suds. If there should come
Some bodily terror to that place,
Great knotted serpents dread and dumb,
You would accept it as a grace.                    20

Until you see a burning wire
Shoot from the ground. As in a dream
You'll wonder at that flower of fire,
That weed caught in a burning beam.

And you are past. Remember then,                   25
Fix deep within your dreaming head
Year, hour or endless moment when
You reached and crossed the Bridge of Dread.


## THE HELMET

The helmet on his head
Has melted flesh and bone
And forged a mask instead
That always is alone.

War has rased its brow                             5
Without a single scar
And left a silent vow
Upon it, like a star.

Its space-devouring eyes
Pass me and hurry on,                              10
Quick as the bullet flies
Until the target's won.

Just now I do not know
What worlds its musings kill . . .
Rivers of sweetness flow                           15
From every little hill;

And we are walking there,
And we are sitting here,
Waiting for what we were
To speak and to appear.                            20

168

But he can never come home,
Nor I get to the place
Where, tame, the terrors roam
Whose shadows fill his face.


## THE CHILD DYING

Unfriendly friendly universe,
I pack your stars into my purse,
And bid you, bid you so farewell.
That I can leave you, quite go out,
Go out, go out beyond all doubt,          5
My father says, is the miracle.

You are so great, and I so small:
I am nothing, you are all:
Being nothing, I can take this way.
Oh I need neither rise nor fall,          10
For when I do not move at all
I shall be out of all your day.

It's said some memory will remain
In the other place, grass in the rain,
Light on the land, sun on the sea,        15
A flitting grace, a phantom face,
But the world is out. There is no place
Where it and its ghost can ever be.

Father, father, I dread this air
Blown from the far side of despair,       20
The cold cold corner. What house, what hold,
What hand is there? I look and see
Nothing-filled eternity,
And the great round world grows weak and old.

Hold my hand, oh hold it fast—            25
I am changing!—until at last
My hand in yours no more will change,
Though yours change on. You here, I there,
So hand in hand, twin-leafed despair—
I did not know death was so strange.      30


169

# THE COMBAT

It was not meant for human eyes,
That combat on the shabby patch
Of clods and trampled turf that lies
Somewhere beneath the sodden skies
For eye of toad or adder to catch.                    5

And having seen it I accuse
The crested animal in his pride,
Arrayed in all the royal hues
Which hide the claws he well can use
To tear the heart out of the side.                    10

Body of leopard, eagle's head
And whetted beak, and lion's mane,
And frost-grey hedge of feathers spread
Behind—he seemed of all things bred.
I shall not see his like again.                       15

As for his enemy, there came in
A soft round beast as brown as clay;
All rent and patched his wretched skin;
A battered bag he might have been,
Some old used thing to throw away.                    20

Yet he awaited face to face
The furious beast and the swift attack.
Soon over and done. That was no place
Or time for chivalry or for grace.
The fury had him on his back.                         25

And two small paws like hands flew out
To right and left as the trees stood by.
One would have said beyond a doubt
This was the very end of the bout,
But that the creature would not die.                  30

For ere the death-stroke he was gone,
Writhed, whirled, huddled into his den,
Safe somehow there. The fight was done,
And he had lost who had all but won.
But oh his deadly fury then.                          35

A while the place lay blank, forlorn,
Drowsing as in relief from pain.
The cricket chirped, the grating thorn
Stirred, and a little sound was born.
The champions took their posts again.          40

And all began. The stealthy paw
Slashed out and in. Could nothing save
These rags and tatters from the claw?
Nothing. And yet I never saw
A beast so helpless and so brave.          45

And now, while the trees stand watching, still
The unequal battle rages there.
The killing beast that cannot kill
Swells and swells in his fury till
You'd almost think it was despair.          50


## THE INTERCEPTER

Whatever I do, wherever I go,
This is my everlasting care:
The Intercepter haunts my ways
And checks me everywhere.

I leave him at the end of the street          5
And wander careless through the lands.
Right in the middle of the road
The Intercepter stands.

When dreaming on the dreaming hills,
I let my thoughts roam far and wide,          10
The Intercepter lifts his hand
And closes up my side.

Asleep, awake, at work or play,
Whatever I do, wherever I go,
The Intercepter bars my way,          15
And to my 'Yes' says 'No'.

Is he my friend or my enemy,
Betrayer, saviour from disgrace?
The Intercepter frowns at me
With my own frowning face.                    20


## HEAD AND HEART

Our tears have mingled with the rain,
Our cries have vanished on the wind,
Time has carried away our pain.

These are our houses, calm and blind
With permanence of polished stone             5
That paints indifference on the mind.

Beyond their walls outlawed, alone,
Our muted sorrows smoulder and start,
The lonely tear, the silent groan.

How well they keep themselves apart!          10
Oh, what we know and what we see
Are separate as head and heart,

And all our sorrow a memory.


## THE INTERROGATION

We could have crossed the road but hesitated,
And then came the patrol;
The leader conscientious and intent,
The men surly, indifferent.
While we stood by and waited                  5
The interrogation began. He says the whole
Must come out now, who, what we are,
Where we have come from, with what purpose, whose
Country or camp we plot for or betray.
Question on question.                         10
We have stood and answered through the standing day
And watched across the road beyond the hedge
The careless lovers in pairs go by,
Hand linked in hand, wandering another star,
So near we could shout to them. We cannot choose 15

Answer or action here,
Though still the careless lovers saunter by
And the thoughtless field is near.
We are on the very edge,
Endurance almost done,                                    20
And still the interrogation is going on.


## THE BORDER

What shall avail me
When I reach the border?
This staff will fail me,
This pass all in order.

These words I have learned                                5
Will not help me then,
These honours hard earned,
And applause of men.

My harp truly set
Will break string by string;                              10
I shall quite forget
That once I could sing.

Absence pure and cold
Of sense and memory
Lightly will hold                                          15
All that is me.

All, all will fail me,
Tongue, foot and hand.
Strange I shall hale me
To that strange land.                                      20


## THE GOOD TOWN

Look at it well. This was the good town once,
Known everywhere, with streets of friendly neighbours,
Street friend to street and house to house. In summer
All day the doors stood open; lock and key
Were quaint antiquities fit for museums                   5
With gyves and rusty chains. The ivy grew

From post to post across the prison door.
The yard behind was sweet with grass and flowers,
A place where grave philosophers loved to walk.
Old Time that promises and keeps his promise      10
Was our sole lord indulgent and severe,
Who gave and took away with gradual hand
That never hurried, never tarried, still
Adding, substracting. These our houses had
Long fallen into decay but that we knew      15
Kindness and courage can repair time's faults,
And serving him breeds patience and courtesy
In us, light sojourners and passing subjects.
There is a virtue in tranquillity
That makes all fitting, childhood and youth and age, 20
Each in its place.

                    Look well. These mounds of rubble,
And shattered piers, half-windows, broken arches
And groping arms were once inwoven in walls
Covered with saints and angels, bore the roof,      25
Shot up the towering spire. These gaping bridges
Once spanned the quiet river which you see
Beyond that patch of raw and angry earth
Where the new concrete houses sit and stare.
Walk with me by the river. See, the poplars      30
Still gather quiet gazing on the stream.
The white road winds across the small green hill
And then is lost. These few things still remain.
Some of our houses too, though not what once
Lived there and drew a strength from memory.      35
Our people have been scattered, or have come
As strangers back to mingle with the strangers
Who occupy our rooms where none can find
The place he knew but settles where he can.
No family now sits at the evening table;      40
Father and son, mother and child are *out*,
A quaint and obsolete fashion. In our houses
Invaders speak their foreign tongues, informers
Appear and disappear, chance whores, officials
Humble or high, frightened, obsequious,      45
Sit carefully in corners. My old friends
(Friends ere these great disasters) are dispersed
In parties, armies, camps, conspiracies.
We avoid each other. If you see a man

Who smiles good-day or waves a lordly greeting   50
Be sure he's a policeman or a spy.
We know them by their free and candid air.

It was not time that brought these things upon us,
But these two wars that trampled on us twice,
Advancing and withdrawing, like a herd   55
Of clumsy-footed beasts on a stupid errand
Unknown to them or us. Pure chance, pure malice,
Or so it seemed. And when, the first war over,
The armies left and our own men came back
From every point by many a turning road,   60
Maimed, crippled, changed in body or in mind,
It was a sight to see the cripples come
Out on the fields. The land looked all awry,
The roads ran crooked and the light fell wrong.
Our fields were like a pack of cheating cards   65
Dealt out at random—all we had to play
In the bad game for the good stake, our life.
We played; a little shrewdness scraped us through.
Then came the second war, passed and repassed,
And now you see our town, the fine new prison,   70
The house-doors shut and barred, the frightened faces
Peeping round corners, secret police, informers,
And all afraid of all.

                    How did it come?
From outside, so it seemed, an endless source,   75
Disorder inexhaustible, strange to us,
Incomprehensible. Yet sometimes now
We ask ourselves, we the old citizens:
'Could it have come from us? Was our peace peace?
Our goodness goodness? That old life was easy   80
And kind and comfortable; but evil is restless
And gives no rest to the cruel or the kind.
How could our town grow wicked in a moment?
What is the answer? Perhaps no more than this,
That once the good men swayed our lives, and those   85
Who copied them took a while the hue of goodness,
A passing loan; while now the bad are up,
And we, poor ordinary neutral stuff,
Not good nor bad, must ape them as we can,
In sullen rage or vile obsequiousness.   90
Say there's a balance between good and evil

In things, and it's so mathematical,
So finely reckoned that a jot of either,
A bare preponderance will do all you need,
Make a town good, or make it what you see.    95
But then, you'll say, only that jot is wanting,
That grain of virtue. No: when evil comes
All things turn adverse, and we must begin
At the beginning, heave the groaning world
Back in its place again, and clamp it there.    100
Then all is hard and hazardous. We have seen
Good men made evil wrangling with the evil,
Straight minds grown crooked fighting crooked minds.
Our peace betrayed us; we betrayed our peace.
Look at it well. This was the good town once.'    105

These thoughts we have, walking among our ruins.


## THE USURPERS

There is no answer. We do here what we will
And there is no answer. This our liberty
No one has known before, nor could have borne,
For it is rooted in this deepening silence
That is our work and has become our kingdom.    5
If there were an answer, how could we be free?
It was not hard to still the ancestral voices:
A careless thought, less than a thought could do it.
And the old garrulous ghosts died easily,
The friendly and unfriendly, and are not missed    10
That once were such proud masters. In this air
Our thoughts are deeds; we dare do all we think,
Since there's no one to check us, here or elsewhere.
All round us stretches nothing; we move through nothing,
Nothing but nothing world without end. We are    15
Self-guided, self-impelled and self-sustained,
Archer and bow and burning arrow sped
On its wild flight through nothing to tumble down
At last on nothing, our home and cure for all.
Around us is alternate light and darkness.    20
We live in light and darkness. When night comes
We drop like stones plumb to its ocean ground,
While dreams stream past us upward to the place
Where light meets darkness, place of images,

176

Forest of ghosts, thicket of muttering voices. 25
We never seek that place; we are for the day
And for the night alone, at home in both.
But each has its device, and this is night's:
To hide in the very heart of night from night,
Black in its blackness. 30
                For these fluttering dreams,
They'd trouble us if we were credulous,
For all the ghosts that frightened frightened men
Long since were bred in that pale territory.
These we can hold in check, but not forget, 35
Not quite forget, they're so inconsequent.
Sometimes we've heard in sleep tongues talking so:
'I lean my face far out from eternity
For time to work its work on: time, oh time,
What have you done?' These fancies trouble us. 40
The day itself sometimes works spells upon us
And then the trees look unfamiliar. Yet
It is a lie that they are witnesses,
That the mountains judge us, brooks tell tales about us.
We have thought sometimes the rocks looked strangely on us, 45
Have fancied that the waves were angry with us,
Heard dark runes murmuring in the autumn wind,
Muttering and murmuring like old toothless women
That prophesied against us in ancient tongues.

These are imaginations. We are free. 50


## THE BARGAIN

I knew it! yes, before time told on time
For the first time, or ever I knew time was.
I saw the effect before I marked the cause,
I bore the charge and did not know the crime.

Innocent of deceit, I felt the change, 5
Perplexed what change could be; my mind and heart
That knew the whole saw part disowned by part
And creep into itself, forlorn and strange.

G

Time gave and took away. This life it gave;
And life is quick and warm, and death is cold.          10
It took the story that never can be told,
The unfading light and the unbreaking wave.

I strike the bargain, since time's hand is there;
But having done, this clause I here declare.


## OEDIPUS

I, Oedipus, the club-foot, made to stumble,
Who long in the light have walked the world in darkness,
And once in the darkness did that which the light
Found and disowned—too well I have loved the light,
Too dearly have rued the darkness. I am one          5
Who as in innocent play sought out his guilt,
And now through guilt seeks other innocence,
Beset by evil thoughts, led by the gods.

There was a room, a bed of darkness, once
Known to me, now to all. Yet in that darkness,          10
Before the light struck, she and I who lay
There without thought of sin and knew each other
Too well, yet were to each other quite unknown
Though fastened mouth to mouth and breast to breast—
Strangers laid on one bed, as children blind,          15
Clear-eyed and blind as children—did we sin
Then on that bed before the light came on us,
Desiring good to each other, bringing, we thought,
Great good to each other? But neither guilt nor death.

Yet if that darkness had been darker yet,          20
Buried in endless dark past reach of light
Or eye of the gods, a kingdom of solid darkness
Impregnable and immortal, would we have sinned,
Or lived like the gods in deathless innocence?
For sin is born in the light; therefore we cower          25
Before the face of the light that none can meet
And all must seek. And when in memory now,
Woven of light and darkness, a stifling web,
I call her back, dear, dreaded, who lay with me,

I see guilt, only guilt, my nostrils choke          30
With the smell of guilt, and I can scarcely breathe
Here in the guiltless guilt-evoking sun.

And when young Oedipus—for it was Oedipus
And not another—on that long vanished night
Far in my night, at that predestined point          35
Where three paths like three fates crossed one another,
Tracing the evil figure—when I met
The stranger who menaced me, and flung the stone
That brought him death and me this that I carry,
It was not him but fear I sought to kill,          40
Fear that, the wise men say, is father of evil,
And was my father in flesh and blood, yet fear,
Fear only, father and fear in one dense body,
So that there was no division, no way past:
Did I sin then, by the gods admonished to sin,          45
By men enjoined to sin? For it is duty
Of god and man to kill the shapes of fear.

These thoughts recur, vain thoughts. The gods see all,
And will what must be willed, which guards us here.
Their will in them was anger, in me was terror          50
Long since, but now is peace. For I am led
By them in darkness; light is all about me;
My way lies in the light; they know it; I
Am theirs to guide and hold. And I have learned,
Though blind, to see with something of their sight,  55
Can look into that other world and watch
King Oedipus the just, crowned and discrowned,
As one may see oneself rise in a dream,
Distant and strange. Even so I see
The meeting at the place where three roads crossed,  60
And who was there and why, and what was done
That had to be done and paid for. Innocent
The deed that brought the guilt of father-murder. Pure
The embrace on the bed of darkness. Innocent
And guilty. I have wrought and thought in darkness, 65
And stand here now, an innocent mark of shame,
That so men's guilt might be made manifest
In such a walking riddle—their guilt and mine,
For I've but acted out this fable. I have judged
Myself, obedient to the gods' high judgment,          70
And seen myself with their pure eyes, have learnt

That all must bear a portion of the wrong
That is driven deep into our fathomless hearts
Past sight or thought; that bearing it we may ease
The immortal burden of the gods who keep     75
Our natural steps and the earth and skies from harm.

## CIRCLE AND SQUARE

'I give you half of me;
No more, lest I should make
A ground for perjury.
For your sake, for my sake,
Half will you take?'     5

'Half I'll not take nor give,
For he who gives gives all.
By halves you cannot live;
Then let the barrier fall,
In one circle have all.'     10

'A wise and ancient scorner
Said to me once: Beware
The road that has no corner
Where you can linger and stare.
Choose the square.     15

'And let the circle run
Its dull and fevered race.
You, my dear, are one;
Show your soul in your face;
Maintain your place.     20

'Give, but have something to give.
No man can want you all.
Live, and learn to live.
When all the barriers fall
You are nothing at all.'     25

## LOVE'S REMORSE

I feel remorse for all that time has done
To you, my love, as if myself, not time,
Had set on you the never-resting sun
And the little deadly days, to work this crime.

For not to guard what by such grace was given,     5
But leave it for the idle hours to take,
Let autumn bury away our summer heaven:
To such a charge what answer can I make

But the old saw still by the heart retold,
'Love is exempt from time.' And that is true.     10
But we, the loved and the lover, we grow old;
Only the truth, the truth is always new:

'Eternity alone our wrong can right,
That makes all young again in time's despite.'


## LOVE IN TIME'S DESPITE

You who are given to me to time were given
Before through time I stretched my hand to catch
Yours in the flying race. Oh we were driven
By rivalry of him who has no match.

For that cold conqueror, unfeeling lover,     5
Who robs your deep heart's treasuries as in play,
Trampling your tender harvests over and over,
Where no door is at case can find his way.

His light embrace is subtle and keen as thought;
Yet, perfect careful lover, he has no care     10
For you at all, is naught and leaves you naught.

And we who love and love again can dare
To keep in his despite our summer still,
Which flowered, but shall not wither, at his will.

## SOLILOQUY

I have seen Alexandria, imperial Rome,
And the sultry backlanes of Jerusalem
One late spring evening thirty years ago
Trouble me still. It was a holy day:
The inns and taverns packed to the very door,     5
Goods, cattle, families, fellowships, clans;
And some time after a man was crucified,
So it is said, who died for love of the world.
Strange deeds, strange scenes. I have passed through war and peace,
Watched populations driven along the roads     10
To emptiness, movements like bird-migrations
Of races and great families, bare at the last,
Equal in destitution. I have felt
Fear in my throat and fury in my heart,
Dreaded the shadow of the waving palm,     15
The rustling of the lizard, have been caught
In battles where armies shouted foreign cries,
Fought for strange purposes; and in an eddy
Deep in the slaughter once I watched
A madman sitting happy in the sand,     20
Rapt in his world. I have seen more than I know.
I was a brisk young merchant, brazen as youth
When youth is brazen. Now I am old and wait
Here in my country house in quiet Greece.
What have I gathered?     25
                  I have picked up wisdom lying
Disused about the world, available still,
Employable still, small odds and scraps of wisdom,
A miscellaneous lot that yet makes up
A something that is genuine, with a body,     30
A shape, a character, more than half Platonic
(Greek, should I say?), and yet of practical use.
I have learnt a host of little things, and one
Too great for thinking, scarcely to be borne:
That there's a watershed in human life,     35
A natural mountain which we have to scale;
And once at the top, our journey all lies downward,
Down the long slope to age and sleep and the end,
(Sadder but easier than the hills of youth,
And sometimes shot with gleams of sunset light).     40
Oh the air is different on this side of the hill,
The sunset side. And when I breathed it first

I felt dismay so deep and yet so quiet,
It was a silence rather, a sea of silence.
This is my trouble, the common trouble.                    45

                              I have seen
Troy's harbour deep in the fields with turf grown over
And poppies nodding on the rustic quays;
And temples and curious caverns in the rocks
Scrawled thick with suns and birds and animals,    50
Fruit, fire and feast, flower-garlanded underworld;
Past reading.

                    I have learned another lesson
When life's half done you must give quality
To the other half, else you lose both, lose all.      55
Select, select: make an anthology
Of what's been given you by bold casual time.
Revise, omit; keep what's significant.
Fill, fill deserted time. Oh there's no comfort
In the wastes of empty time. Provide for age.        60
Life must be lived; then live. And so I turn
To past experience, watch it being shaped,
But never to its own true shape. However,
I have fitted this or that into the pattern,
Caught sight sometimes of the original              65
That is myself—should rather be myself—
The soul past price bartered at any price
The moment bids, cheap as the cheapest moment.
I have had such glimpses, made such tentative
Essays to shape my life, have had successes,         70
Whether real or apparent time may tell,
Though there's no bargain you can drive with time.
All this is insufficient.

                              I have watched
In cheering ports the great fleets setting out,       75
And on another and a darker day
Returning with disaster at the helm,
Death at the prow—and then the punishments,
The crucifixions on the burning hills,
Hour-long day-long slow death. And once I came 80
Upon the gaunt-ribbed skeleton of a wreck

183

Black underneath the toothed black promontory;
Nothing but these to comfort one another,
And the spray and grinding sea.

I have seen such things.   85
I have begotten life and taken away
Life lent to others. I have thought of death,
And followed Plato to eternity,
Walked in his radiant world; have trod the fields
My fathers' sins have trampled richly down,   90
Loam warmed by a sun that burns at the world's heart,
Sol of the underworld. My heart is steady,
Beats in my breast and cannot burn or break,
Systole and diastole for seventy years.

Set up the bleak worn day to show our sins,   95
Old and still ageing, like a flat squat herd
Crawling like sun on wall to the rim of time,
Up the long slope for ever.

Light and praise,
Love and atonement, harmony and peace,   100
Touch me, assail me; break and make my heart.


## THE ABSENT

They are not here. And we, we are the Others
Who walk by ourselves unquestioned in the sun
Which shines for us and only for us.
For They are not here.
And are made known to us in this great absence   5
That lies upon us and is between us
Since They are not here.
Now, in this kingdom of summer idleness
Where slowly we the sun-tranced multitudes dream and wander
In deep oblivion of brightness   10
And breathe ourselves out, out into the air—
It is absence that receives us;
We do not touch, our souls go out in the absence
That lies between us and is about us.
For we are the Others,   15
And so we sorrow for These that are not with us,
Not knowing we sorrow or that this is our sorrow,

Since it is long past thought or memory or device of mourning,
Sorrow for loss of that which we never possessed,
The unknown, the nameless,                                    20
The ever-present that in their absence are with us
(With us the inheritors, the usurpers claiming
The sun and the kingdom of the sun) that sorrow
And loneliness might bring a blessing upon us.


## THE VISITOR

No, no, do not beguile me, do not come
Between me and my ghost, that cannot move
Till you are gone,
And while you gossip must be dumb.
Do not believe I do not want your love,          5
Brother and sister, wife and son.
But I would be alone
Now, now and let him in,
Lest while I speak he is already flown,
Offended by the din                               10
Of this half-uttered scarcely whispered plea
(So delicate is he).
No more, no more.
Let the great tidings stay unsaid,
For I must to the door,                           15
And oh I dread
He may even now be gone
Or, when I open, will not enter in.


## THE TRANSFIGURATION

So from the ground we felt that virtue branch
Through all our veins till we were whole, our wrists
As fresh and pure as water from a well,
Our hands made new to handle holy things,
The source of all our seeing rinsed and cleansed  5
Till earth and light and water entering there
Gave back to us the clear unfallen world.
We would have thrown our clothes away for lightness,
But that even they, though sour and travel stained,
Seemed, like our flesh, made of immortal substance, 10
And the soiled flax and wool lay light upon us

Like friendly wonders, flower and flock entwined
As in a morning field. Was it a vision?
Or did we see that day the unseeable
One glory of the everlasting world                                    15
Perpetually at work, though never seen
Since Eden locked the gate that's everywhere
And nowhere? Was the change in us alone,
And the enormous earth still left forlorn,
An exile or a prisoner? Yet the world                                 20
We saw that day made this unreal, for all
Was in its place. The painted animals
Assembled there in gentle congregations,
Or sought apart their leafy oratories,
Or walked in peace, the wild and tame together,                       25
As if, also for them, the day had come.
The shepherds' hovels shone, for underneath
The soot we saw the stone clean at the heart
As on the starting-day. The refuse heaps
Were grained with that fine dust that made the world;   30
For he had said, 'To the pure all things are pure.'
And when we went into the town, he with us,
The lurkers under doorways, murderers,
With rags tied round their feet for silence, came
Out of themselves to us and were with us,                             35
And those who hide within the labyrinth
Of their own loneliness and greatness came,
And those entangled in their own devices,
The silent and the garrulous liars, all
Stepped out of their dungeons and were free.                          40
Reality or vision, this we have seen.
If it had lasted but another moment
It might have held for ever! But the world
Rolled back into its place, and we are here,
And all that radiant kingdom lies forlorn,                            45
As if it had never stirred; no human voice
Is heard among its meadows, but it speaks
To itself alone, alone it flowers and shines
And blossoms for itself while time runs on.

But he will come again, it's said, though not            50
Unwanted and unsummoned; for all things,
Beasts of the field, and woods, and rocks, and seas,
And all mankind from end to end of the earth
Will call him with one voice. In our own time,

Some say, or at a time when time is ripe.                55
Then he will come, Christ the uncrucified,
Christ the discrucified, his death undone,
His agony unmade, his cross dismantled—
Glad to be so—and the tormented wood
Will cure its hurt and grow into a tree                  60
In a green springing corner of young Eden,
And Judas damned take his long journey backward
From darkness into light and be a child
Beside his mother's knee, and the betrayal
Be quite undone and never more be done.                  65


## THE DEBTOR

I am debtor to all, to all am I bounden,
Fellowman and beast, season and solstice, darkness and light,
And life and death. On the backs of the dead,
See, I am borne, on lost errands led,
By spent harvests nourished. Forgotten prayers            5
To gods forgotten bring blessings upon me.
Rusted arrow and broken bow, look, they preserve me
Here in this place. The never-won stronghold
That sank in the ground as the years into time,
Slowly with all its men steadfast and watching,          10
Keeps me safe now. The ancient waters
Cleanse me, revive me. Victor and vanquished
Give me their passion, their peace and the field.
The meadows of Lethe shed twilight around me.
The dead in their silences keep me in memory,            15
Have me in hold. To all I am bounden.


## SONG

Sunset ends the day,
The years shift their place,
Under the sun's sway
Times from times fall;
Mind fighting mind                                        5
The secret cords unwind
No power can replace:
Love gathers all.


187

The living and the dead
Centuries separate,                            10
Man from himself is led
Through mazes past recall,
Distraction can disguise
The wastrel and the wise
Till neither knows his state:                  15
Love gathers all.

Father at odds with son
Breeds ageless enmity,
Friendships undone
Build up a topless wall;                       20
Achilles and Hector slain
Fight, fight and fight again
In measureless memory:
Love gathers all.

The quarrel from the start,                    25
Long past and never past,
The war of mind and heart,
The great war and the small
That tumbles the hovel down
And topples town on town                       30
Come to one place at last:
Love gathers all.


## THE TOY HORSE

See him, the gentle Bible beast,
With lacquered hoofs and curling mane,
His wondering journey from the East
Half done, between the rock and plain,

His little kingdom at his feet                  5
Through which the silver rivulets flow,
For while his hoofs in silence beat
Beside him Eden and Canaan go.

The great leaves turn and then are still.
Page after page through deepening day          10
He steps, and from each morning hill
Beholds his stationary way.

His lifted foot commands the West,
And, lingering, halts the turning sun;
Endless departure, endless rest,                    15
End and beginning here are one.

Dumb wooden idol, you have led
Millions on your calm pilgrimage
Between the living and the dead,
And shine yet in your golden age.                   20

# *One Foot in Eden*

## TO WILLA

## *1956*

# PART I

## MILTON

Milton, his face set fair for Paradise,
And knowing that he and Paradise were lost
In separate desolation, bravely crossed
Into his second night and paid his price.
There towards the end he to the dark tower came     5
Set square in the gate, a mass of blackened stone
Crowned with vermilion fiends like streamers blown
From a great funnel filled with roaring flame.

Shut in his darkness, these he could not see,
But heard the steely clamour known too well     10
On Saturday nights in every street in Hell.
Where, past the devilish din, could Paradise be?
A footstep more, and his unblinded eyes
Saw far and near the fields of Paradise.

## THE ANIMALS

They do not live in the world,
Are not in time and space.
From birth to death hurled
No word do they have, not one
To plant a foot upon,     5
Were never in any place.

For with names the world was called
Out of the empty air,
With names was built and walled,
Line and circle and square,     10
Dust and emerald;
Snatched from deceiving death
By the articulate breath.

193

But these have never trod
Twice the familiar track,                    15
Never never turned back
Into the memoried day.
All is new and near
In the unchanging Here
Of the fifth great day of God,               20
That shall remain the same,
Never shall pass away.

On the sixth day we came.


## THE DAYS

Issuing from the Word
The seven days came,
Each in its own place,
Its own name.
And the first long days                      5
A hard and rocky spring,
Inhuman burgeoning,
And nothing there for claw or hand,
Vast loneliness ere loneliness began,
Where the blank seasons in their journeying  10
Saw water at play with water and sand with sand.
The waters stirred
And from the doors were cast
Wild lights and shadows on the formless face
Of the flood of chaos, vast                   15
Lengthening and dwindling image of earth and heaven.
The forest's green shadow
Softly over the water driven,
As if the earth's green wonder, endless meadow
Floated and sank within its own green light.  20
In water and night
Sudden appeared the lion's violent head,
Raging and burning in its watery cave.
The stallion's tread
Soundlessly fell on the flood, and the animals poured 25
Onward, flowing across the flowing wave.
Then on the waters fell
The shadow of man, and earth and the heavens scrawled

194

With names, as if each pebble and leaf would tell
The tale untellable. And the Lord called                              30
The seventh day forth and the glory of the Lord.

And now we see in the sun
The mountains standing clear in the third day
(Where they shall always stay)
And thence a river run,                                               35
Threading, clear cord of water, all to all:
The wooded hill and the cattle in the meadow,
The tall wave breaking on the high sea-wall,
The people at evening walking,
The crescent shadow                                                  40
Of the light-built bridge, the hunter stalking
The flying quarry, each in a different morning,
The fish in the billow's heart, the man with the net,
The hungry swords crossed in the cross of warning,
The lion set                                                         45
High on the banner, leaping into the sky,
The seasons playing
Their game of sun and moon and east and west,
The animal watching man and bird go by,
The women praying                                                    50
For the passing of this fragmentary day
Into the day where all are gathered together,
Things and their names, in the storm's and the lightning's nest,
The seventh great day and the clear eternal weather.

## ADAM'S DREAM

They say the first dream Adam our father had
After his agelong daydream in the Garden
When heaven and sun woke in his wakening mind,
The earth with all its hills and woods and waters,
The friendly tribes of trees and animals,                            5
And earth's last wonder Eve (the first great dream
Which is the ground of every dream since then)—
They say he dreamt lying on the naked ground,
The gates shut fast behind him as he lay
Fallen in Eve's fallen arms, his terror drowned                     10
In her engulfing terror, in the abyss
Whence there's no further fall, and comfort is—
That he was standing on a rocky ledge

195

High on the mountainside, bare crag behind,
In front a plain as far as eye could reach,                15
And on the plain a few small figures running
That were like men and women, yet were so far away
He could not see their faces. On they ran,
And fell, and rose again, and ran, and fell,
And rising were the same yet not the same,                20
Identical or interchangeable,
Different in indifference. As he looked
Still there were more of them, the plain was filling
As by an alien arithmetical magic
Unknown in Eden, a mechanical                              25
Addition without meaning, joining only
Number to number in no mode or order,
Weaving no pattern. For these creatures moved
Towards no fixed mark even when in growing bands
They clashed against each other and clashing fell         30
In mounds of bodies. For they rose again,
Identical or interchangeable,
And went their way that was not like a way;
Some back and forward, back and forward, some
In a closed circle, wide or narrow, others                35
In zigzags on the sand. Yet all were busy,
And tense with purpose as they cut the air
Which seemed to press them back. Sometimes they paused
While one stopped one—fortuitous assignations
In the disorder, whereafter two by two                    40
They ran awhile,
Then parted and again were single. Some
Ran straight against the frontier of the plain
Till the horizon drove them back. A few
Stood still and never moved. Then Adam cried              45
Out of his dream, 'What are you doing there?'
And the crag answered 'Are you doing there?'
'What are you doing there?'—'you doing there?'
The animals had withdrawn and from the caves
And woods stared out in fear or condemnation,             50
Like outlaws or like judges. All at once
Dreaming or half-remembering, 'This is time',
Thought Adam in his dream, and time was strange
To one lately in Eden. 'I must see',
He cried, 'the faces. Where are the faces? Who            55
Are you all out there?' Then in his changing dream
He was a little nearer, and he saw

They were about some business strange to him
That had a form and sequence past their knowledge;
And that was why they ran so frenziedly.          60
Yet all, it seemed, made up a story, illustrated
By these the living, the unknowing, cast
Each singly for his part. But Adam longed
For more, not this mere moving pattern, not
This illustrated storybook of mankind             65
Always a-making, improvised on nothing.
At that he was among them, and saw each face
Was like his face, so that he would have hailed them
As sons of God but that something restrained him.
And he remembered all, Eden, the Fall,            70
The Promise, and his place, and took their hands
That were his hands, his and his children's hands,
Cried out and was at peace, and turned again
In love and grief in Eve's encircling arms.


OUTSIDE EDEN

A few lead in their harvest still
By the ruined wall and broken gate.
Far inland shines the radiant hill.
Inviolable the empty gate,
Impassable the gaping wall;                        5
And the mountain over all.

Such is the country of this clan,
Haunted by guilt and innocence.
There is a sweetness in the air
That bloomed as soon as time began,              10
But now is dying everywhere.
This people guard in reverence
Their proud and famous family tree
Sprung from a glorious king who once
Lived in such boundless liberty                   15
As never a one among the great
Has known in all the kingdoms since;
For death was barred from his estate.
Lost long ago, the histories say,
He and his consort lost it all.                   20
Guiltiest and least guilty, they
In innocence discovered sin

Round a lost corner of the day,
And fell and fell through all the fall
That hurled them headlong over the wall.    25
Their children live where then they lay.

Guilt is next door to innocence.
So here this people choose to live
And never think to travel hence,
Nor learn to be inquisitive,    30
Nor browse in sin's great library,
The single never-ending book
That fills the shelves of all the earth.
There the learned enquirers look
And blind themselves to see their face.    35
But these live in the land of birth
And count all else an idle grace.

The simple have long memories.
Memory makes simple all that is.
So these the lawless world can love    40
At ease, the thickets running wild,
The thorny waste, the flourishing grove.
Their knotted landscape, wrong and clear
As the crude drawings of a child,
Is to them become more dear    45
Than geometrical symmetry.
Their griefs are all in memory grown
As natural as a weathered stone.
Their troubles are a tribute given
Freely while gazing at the hill.    50
Such is their simplicity,
Standing on earth, looking at heaven.


# PROMETHEUS

The careless seasons pass and leave me here.
The forests rise like ghosts and fade like dreams.
All has its term; flowers flicker on the ground
A summer moment, and the rock is bare.
Alone the animals trace their changeless figure,    5
Embodying change. Agelong I watch the leopard
Glaring at something past the end of time,
And the wild goat immobile on his rock,

Lost in a trance of roaming through the skies:
I look and he is there. But pilgrim man                    10
Travels foreknowing to his stopping place,
Awareness on his lips, which have tasted sorrow,
Foretasted death. These strangers do not know
Their happiness is in that which leads their sorrow
Round to an end. My hope is not like theirs.             15
I pray for the end of all things and this pain
Which makes me cry: Move faster, sun and stars,
And bear these chains and bear this body away
Into your flying circuit; freedom waits
There in the blessed nothingness that follows            20
The charging onset of the centaur-stars,
Trampling time out. For when these clamorous races
Lie silent in the ground from which they came,
And all the earth is quiet, a hush may fall
Even in the house of heaven, and the heedless gods       25
May raise their eyes to look and bid me come
Again among them, then when the feud is over
And fire and those in whom it blazed and died
Are strewn in ashes on the ashen hills.

What shall I say to the gods? Heaven will be strange,    30
And strange those scars inscribed in distant time.
Who will give answer to the earth's dark story?
Zeus with the ponderous glory of the bull,
Or the boy Eros with his fretful quiver?
What expectation there except at most                    35
That this my knowledge will be an aeon's gossip?

The shrines are emptying and the peoples changing.
It may be I should find Olympus vacant
If I should return. For I have heard a wonder:
Lands without gods; nothing but earth and water;         40
Words without mystery; and the only creed
An iron text to beat the round skulls flat
And fit them for the cap of a buried master.
Strange ritual. Now time's storm is rising, sweeping
The sons of man into an emptier room,                    45
Vast as a continent, bare as a desert,
Where the dust takes man's lifetime to revolve
Around the walls, harried by peevish gusts
And little spiteful eddies; nothing standing
But the cast-iron cities and rubbish mountains.          50

At the world's end to whom shall I tell the story?
A god came down, they say, from another heaven
Not in rebellion but in pity and love,
Was born a son of woman, lived and died,
And rose again with all the spoils of time          55
Back to his home, where now they are transmuted
Into bright toys and various frames of glory;
And time itself is there a world of marvels.
If I could find that god, he would hear and answer.


## THE GRAVE OF PROMETHEUS

No one comes here now, neither god nor man.
For long the animals have kept away,
Scared by immortal cries and the scream of vultures;
Now by this silence. The heavenly thief who stole
Heaven's dangerous treasure turned to common earth 5
When that great company forsook Olympus.
The fire was out, and he became his barrow.
Ten yards long there he lay outstretched, and grass
Grew over him: all else in a breath forgotten.
Yet there you still may see a tongue of stone,          10
Shaped like a calloused hand where no hand should be,
Extended from the sward as if for alms,
Its palm all licked and blackened as with fire.
A mineral change made cool his fiery bed,
And made his burning body a quiet mound,          15
And his great face a vacant ring of daisies.


## ORPHEUS' DREAM

And she was there. The little boat
Coasting the perilous isles of sleep,
Zones of oblivion and despair,
Stopped, for Eurydice was there.
The foundering skiff could scarcely keep          5
All that felicity afloat.

As if we had left earth's frontier wood
Long since and from this sea had won
The lost original of the soul,

The moment gave us pure and whole          10
Each back to each, and swept us on
Past every choice to boundless good.

Forgiveness, truth, atonement, all
Our love at once—till we could dare
At last to turn our heads and see          15
The poor ghost of Eurydice
Still sitting in her silver chair,
Alone in Hades' empty hall.


## THE OTHER OEDIPUS

Remembered on the Peloponnesian roads,
He and his serving-boy and his concubine,
White-headed and light-hearted, their true wits gone
Past the last stroke of time into a day
Without a yesterday or a to-morrow,          5
A brightness laid like a blue lake around them,
Or endless field to play or linger in.
They were so gay and innocent, you'd have thought
A god had won a glorious prize for them
In some celestial field, and the odds were gone,          10
Fate sent on holiday, the earth and heaven
Thenceforth in endless friendly talk together.
They were quite storyless and had clean forgotten
That memory burning in another world;
But they too leaf-light now for any story.          15
If anyone spoke a word of other guilt
By chance before them, then they stamped their feet
In rage and gnashed their teeth like peevish children.
But then forgot. The road their welcoming home.
They would not stay in a house or let a door          20
Be shut on them. The surly Spartan farmers
Were kind to them, pitying their happiness.


## THE CHARM

There was a drug that Helen knew.
Dropped in the wine-cup it could take
All memory and all grief away,
And while the drinker, wide awake,

Sat in his chair, indifference grew 5
Around him in the estranging day.
He saw the colours shine and flow,
The giant lineaments break and change,
But all storyless, all strange.
The crystal spheres on Helen's brow 10
Took and gave back the coloured world,
Yet only seemed to smile or glare
At nothing but the empty air.
The serving women crossed the floor,
Swept by a silent tempest, whirled 15
Into the light and through the door.
This he saw and nothing more,
While all the charities, unborn,
Slept soundly in his burdened breast
As he took his heavy rest, 20
Careless, thoughtless and forlorn.

So strong the enchantment, Homer says,
That if this man's own son had died,
Killed at his feet, his dreaming gaze
(Like a false-hearted summer day 25
Watching the hunter and his prey
At ease) would not have changed at all,
Nor his heart knocked against his side.
But far within him something cried
For the great tragedy to start, 30
The pang in lingering mercy fall,
And sorrow break upon his heart.


## TELEMACHOS REMEMBERS

Twenty years, every day,
The figures in the web she wove
Came and stood and went away.
Her fingers in their pitiless play
Beat downward as the shuttle drove. 5

Slowly, slowly did they come,
With horse and chariot, spear and bow,
Half-finished heroes sad and mum,
Came slowly to the shuttle's hum.
Time itself was not so slow. 10

And what at last was there to see?
A horse's head, a trunkless man,
Mere odds and ends about to be,
And the thin line of augury
Where through the web the shuttle ran.                    15

How could she bear the mounting load,
Dare once again her ghosts to rouse?
Far away Odysseus trod
The treadmill of the turning road
That did not bring him to his house.                       20

The weary loom, the weary loom,
The task grown sick from morn to night,
From year to year. The treadle's boom
Made a low thunder in the room.
The woven phantoms mazed her sight.                        25

If she had pushed it to the end,
Followed the shuttle's cunning song
So far she had no thought to rend
In time the web from end to end,
She would have worked a matchless wrong.                   30

Instead, that jumble of heads and spears,
Forlorn scraps of her treasure trove.
I wet them with my childish tears
Not knowing she wove into her fears
Pride and fidelity and love.                               35

## THE HEROES

When these in all their bravery took the knock
And like obedient children swaddled and bound
Were born to sleep within the chambered rock,
A splendour broke from that impervious ground,
Which they would never know. Whence came that greatness? 5
No fiery chariot whirled them heavenwards, they
Saw no Elysium opening, but the straitness
Of full submission bound them where they lay.

What could that greatness be? It was not fame.
Yet now they seemed to grow as they grew less,            10

203

And where they lay were more than where they had stood.
They did not go to any beatitude.
They were stripped clean of feature, presence, name,
When that strange glory broke from namelessness.


## ABRAHAM

The rivulet-loving wanderer Abraham
Through waterless wastes tracing his fields of pasture
Led his Chaldean herds and fattening flocks
With the meandering art of wavering water
That seeks and finds, yet does not know its way.          5
He came, rested and prospered, and went on,
Scattering behind him little pastoral kingdoms,
And over each one its own particular sky,
Not the great rounded sky through which he journeyed,
That went with him but when he rested changed.          10
His mind was full of names
Learned from strange peoples speaking alien tongues,
And all that was theirs one day he would inherit.
He died content and full of years, though still
The Promise had not come, and left his bones,          15
Far from his father's house, in alien Canaan.


## THE SUCCESSION

Legendary Abraham,
The old Chaldean wanderer,
First among these peoples came,
Cruising above them like a star
That is in love with distances          5
And has through age to calmness grown,
Patient in the wilderness
And untarrying in the sown.
At last approached his setting mark.
Thence he sent his twin star out,          10
Isaac, to revolve alone.
For two great stars that through an age
Play in their corner of the sky,
Separate go into the dark,
And ere they end their roundabout          15
One must live and one must die.

204

Isaac in his tutelage
Wheeled around the father light.
Then began his pilgrimage
Through another day and night,                    20
Other peoples, other lands.
Where the father could not go
There is gone the careless son.
He can never miss his way.
By strangers' hands to strangers' hands          25
He is carried where he will.
Free, he must the powers obey,
Serve, be served by good and ill,
Safe through all the hazards run.
All shall watch him come and go                   30
Until his quittance he has won;
And Jacob wheels into the day.

We through the generations came
Here by a way we do not know
From the fields of Abraham,                        35
And still the road is scarce begun.
To hazard and to danger go
The sallying generations all
Where the imperial highways run.
And our songs and legends call                     40
The hazard and the danger good;
For our fathers understood
That danger was by hope begot
And hazard by revolving chance
Since first we drew the enormous lot.              45


## THE ROAD

The great road stretched before them, clear and still,
Then from in front one cried: 'Turn back! Turn back!'
Yet they had never seen so fine a track,
Honest and frank past any thought of ill.
But when they glanced behind, how strange, how strange,   5
These wild demented windings in and out—
Traced by some devil of mischief or of doubt?—
That was the road they had come by. Could it change?

How could they penetrate that perilous maze
Backwards, again, climb backwards down the scree            10
From the wrong side, slither among the dead?
Yet as they travelled on, for many days
These words rang in their ears as if they said,
'There was another road you did not see.'


# THE ANNUNCIATION

The angel and the girl are met.
Earth was the only meeting place.
For the embodied never yet
Travelled beyond the shore of space.
The eternal spirits in freedom go.                                   5

See, they have come together, see,
While the destroying minutes flow,
Each reflects the other's face
Till heaven in hers and earth in his
Shine steady there. He's come to her                            10
From far beyond the farthest star,
Feathered through time. Immediacy
Of strangest strangeness is the bliss
That from their limbs all movement takes.
Yet the increasing rapture brings                                  15
So great a wonder that it makes
Each feather tremble on his wings.

Outside the window footsteps fall
Into the ordinary day
And with the sun along the wall                                    20
Pursue their unreturning way.
Sound's perpetual roundabout
Rolls its numbered octaves out
And hoarsely grinds its battered tune.

But through the endless afternoon                                 25
These neither speak nor movement make,
But stare into their deepening trance
As if their gaze would never break.

## * THE CHRISTMAS

Now Christmas comes. The menial earth
  Lays by its worn and sweaty gear
And strews with emblems of rebirth
  The burial of the solar year.

Midnight strikes. One star awake       5
  Watches the Mother and the Child
Who with his little hands will make
  Spring blossom in the winter wild.

This star that left the ordered throng
  Caused no confusion in the night,      10
Nor strayed to prove his brothers wrong,
  But told that all the stars were right.

Three little days with lengthening glow
  Sets the great year upon its way;
An infant's cry across the snow       15
  Rouses the never-setting day.

A Child, a God, he will respire
  Obediently time's mortal breath,
Freely work out his double hire,
  Endless enact a Birth, a Death,      20

Accomplishing the miracle,
  The marriage feast of heaven and earth,
Of which on earth we cannot tell
  Save in such words: a Death, a Birth.

The childish starlight glimmers near      25
  In the green firmament of the tree,
And the soft dreaming of the year
  Leads in Judaea and Galilee.

## * THE SON

This hungry flesh and bone
That white and black and brown
Share was shared by One
Once who to death went down.

Son of God and of Man,                                   5
He breathed as ours his breath,
And in this body ran
The crooked road to death.

Night and day and night
Wheeled him through time and space,     10
Whose hour was changeless light,
Infinity his place.

Time's essential heat
Bound him inside the womb
And in his arteries beat                                  15
The proud march to the tomb.

He from eternity
Stared now through a little eye,
That God and Man might see
The good and the wicked die.                              20

Born, his babbling tongue
Told infancy's helplessness,
Disgrace of being young,
Adolescent distress,

Till manhood's brutal force                               25
Through all his veins rolled on
Wild as a headstrong horse,
Though he was Heaven's son.

Thirst like a rusty knife,
Dry hunger he withstood,                                  30
Who had the water of life
And the immortal food.

The skill of the carpenter,
The sailor's dauntless heart
He learned, lest he should mar,                    35
A God, his second part.

Happiness not of Heaven,
And unimmortal sorrows
He chose, talk in the evening,
And the wild mounting morrows                       40

That wound in narrowing rings
Up to the waiting Tree
Through treachery of things
And men's treachery.

Till only despair was left;                         45
'Me why hast Thou forsaken?'
God of God bereft
Down from the tree was taken,

That so the Light shine through
The first to the last pain,                         50
And all be made new
Down to the last grain.

Ordinary men
Saw him take his fall.
All is changed since then;                          55
He is joined with all.


## THE KILLING

That was the day they killed the Son of God
On a squat hill-top by Jerusalem.
Zion was bare, her children from their maze
Sucked by the demon curiosity
Clean through the gates. The very halt and blind     5
Had somehow got themselves up to the hill.

After the ceremonial preparation,
The scourging, nailing, nailing against the wood,
Erection of the main-trees with their burden,
While from the hill rose an orchestral wailing,     10

209

H

They were there at last, high up in the soft spring day.
We watched the writhings, heard the moanings, saw
The three heads turning on their separate axles
Like broken wheels left spinning. Round *his* head
Was loosely bound a crown of plaited thorn                      15
That hurt at random, stinging temple and brow
As the pain swung into its envious circle.
In front the wreath was gathered in a knot
That as he gazed looked like the last stump left
Of a death-wounded deer's great antlers. Some          20
Who came to stare grew silent as they looked,
Indignant or sorry. But the hardened old
And the hard-hearted young, although at odds
From the first morning, cursed him with one curse,
Having prayed for a Rabbi or an armed Messiah        25
And found the Son of God. What use to them
Was a God or a Son of God? Of what avail
For purposes such as theirs? Beside the cross-foot,
Alone, four women stood and did not move
All day. The sun revolved, the shadow wheeled,         30
The evening fell. His head lay on his breast,
But in his breast they watched his heart move on
By itself alone, accomplishing its journey.
Their taunts grew louder, sharpened by the knowledge
That he was walking in the park of death,                    35
Far from their rage. Yet all grew stale at last,
Spite, curiosity, envy, hate itself.
They waited only for death and death was slow
And came so quietly they scarce could mark it.
They were angry then with death and death's deceit.      40

I was a stranger, could not read these people
Or this outlandish deity. Did a God
Indeed in dying cross my life that day
By chance, he on his road and I on mine?


## * LOST AND FOUND

That by which we have lost and still shall lose
Even what we win (but never fully win,)
It gave the choice without the skill to choose,
The rough-cast world, the broken Eden within,
Taught us the narrow miss and the accident,          5

The countless odds and the predestined plot,
Action and thought to every bias bent,
And chance, the winning and the losing lot.

It gave us time, and time gave us the story,
Beginning and end in one wild largesse spent,          10
Inexplicable. Until the heavenly Glory
Took on our flesh and wrought the meaning. Since,
Sons, daughters, brothers, sisters of that Prince
Are we, by grace, although in banishment.


## ANTICHRIST

He walks, the enchanter, on his sea of glass,
Poring upon his blue inverted heaven
Where a false sun revolves from west to east.
If he could raise his eyes he would see his hell.
He is no spirit, nor a spirit's shadow,                 5
But a mere toy shaped by ingenious devils
To bring discomfiture on credulous man.
He's the false copy where each feature's wrong,
Yet so disposed the whole gives a resemblance.
When he's in anguish smiles writhe on his lips          10
And will not stop. His imperturbable brow
Is carved by rage not his but theirs that made him,
For he's a nothing where they move in freedom,
Knowing that nothing's there. When he forgives
It is for love of sin not of the sinner.                15
He takes sin for his province, knows sin only,
Nothing but sin from end to end of the world.
He heals the sick to show his conjuring skill,
Vexed only by the cure; and turns his cheek
To goad the furious to more deadly fury,                20
And damn by a juggling trick the ingenuous sinner.
He brings men from the dead to tell the living
That their undoing is a common fetch.
Ingeniously he postures on the Tree
(His crowning jest), an actor miming death,             25
While his indifferent mind is idly pleased
That treason should run on through time for ever.
His vast indulgence is so free and ample,

You well might think it universal love,
For all seems goodness, sweetness, harmony.                    30
He is the Lie; one true thought, and he's gone.


## * THE LORD

They could not tell me who should be my lord,
But I could read from every word they said
The common thought: Perhaps that lord was dead,
And only a story now and a wandering word.
How could I follow a word or serve a fable,         5
They asked me. 'Here are lords a-plenty. Take
Service with one, if only for your sake;
Yet better be your own master if you're able.'

I would rather scour the roads, a masterless dog,
Than take such service, be a public fool,           10
Obstreperous or tongue-tied, a good rogue,
Than be with those, the clever and the dull,
Who say that lord is dead; when I can hear
Daily his dying whisper in my ear.


## ONE FOOT IN EDEN

One foot in Eden still, I stand
And look across the other land.
The world's great day is growing late,
Yet strange these fields that we have planted
So long with crops of love and hate.               5
Time's handiworks by time are haunted,
And nothing now can separate
The corn and tares compactly grown.
The armorial weed in stillness bound
About the stalk; these are our own.                 10
Evil and good stand thick around
In the fields of charity and sin
Where we shall lead our harvest in.

Yet still from Eden springs the root
As clean as on the starting day.                    15
Time takes the foliage and the fruit
And burns the archetypal leaf

To shapes of terror and of grief
Scattered along the winter way.
But famished field and blackened tree                    20
Bear flowers in Eden never known.
Blossoms of grief and charity
Bloom in these darkened fields alone.
What had Eden ever to say
Of hope and faith and pity and love                      25
Until was buried all its day
And memory found its treasure trove?
Strange blessings never in Paradise
Fall from these beclouded skies.


## THE INCARNATE ONE

The windless northern surge, the sea-gull's scream,
And Calvin's kirk crowning the barren brae.
I think of Giotto the Tuscan shepherd's dream,
Christ, man and creature in their inner day.
How could our race betray                                5
The Image, and the Incarnate One unmake
Who chose this form and fashion for our sake?

The Word made flesh here is made word again,
A word made word in flourish and arrogant crook.
See there King Calvin with his iron pen,                 10
And God three angry letters in a book,
And there the logical hook
On which the Mystery is impaled and bent
Into an ideological instrument.

There's better gospel in man's natural tongue,           15
And truer sight was theirs outside the Law
Who saw the far side of the Cross among
The archaic peoples in their ancient awe,
In ignorant wonder saw
The wooden cross-tree on the bare hillside,              20
Not knowing that there a God suffered and died.

The fleshless word, growing, will bring us down,
Pagan and Christian man alike will fall,
The auguries say, the white and black and brown,
The merry and sad, theorist, lover, all                  25

213

Invisibly will fall:
Abstract calamity, save for those who can
Build their cold empire on the abstract man.

A soft breeze stirs and all my thoughts are blown
Far out to sea and lost. Yet I know well                    30
The bloodless word will battle for its own
Invisibly in brain and nerve and cell.
The generations tell
Their personal tale: the One has far to go
Past the mirages and the murdering snow.                    35


## SCOTLAND'S WINTER

Now the ice lays its smooth claws on the sill,
The sun looks from the hill
Helmed in his winter casket,
And sweeps his arctic sword across the sky.
The water at the mill                                        5
Sounds more hoarse and dull.
The miller's daughter walking by
With frozen fingers soldered to her basket
Seems to be knocking
Upon a hundred leagues of floor                             10
With her light heels, and mocking
Percy and Douglas dead,
And Bruce on his burial bed,
Where he lies white as may
With wars and leprosy,                                       15
And all the kings before
This land was kingless,
And all the singers before
This land was songless,
This land that with its dead and living waits the Judgment Day. 20
But they, the powerless dead,
Listening can hear no more
Than a hard tapping on the sounding floor
A little overhead
Of common heels that do not know                            25
Whence they come or where they go
And are content
With their poor frozen life and shallow banishment.

214

## THE GREAT HOUSE

However it came, this great house has gone down
Unconquered into chaos (as you might see
A famous ship warped to a rotting quay
In miles of weeds and rubbish, once a town).
So the great house confronts the brutish air,          5
And points its turrets towards the hidden sky,
While in the dark the flags of honour fly
Where faith and hope and bravery would not dare.

Accident did not do this, nor mischance.
But so must order to disorder come                     10
At their due time, and honour take its stance
Deep in dishonour's ground. Chaos is new,
And has no past or future. Praise the few
Who built in chaos our bastion and our home.


## THE EMBLEM

I who so carefully keep in such repair
The six-inch king and the toy treasury,
Prince, poet, realm shrivelled in time's black air,
I am not, although I seem, an antiquary.
For that scant-acre kingdom is not dead,                5
Nor save in seeming shrunk. When at its gate,
Which you pass daily, you incline your head,
And enter (do not knock; it keeps no state)

You will be with space and order magistral,
And that contracted world so vast will grow            10
That this will seem a little tangled field.
For you will be in very truth with all
In their due place and honour, row on row.
For this I read the emblem on the shield.

# PART II

## TO FRANZ KAFKA

If we, the proximate damned, presumptive blest,
Were called one day to some high consultation
With the authentic ones, the worst and best
Picked from all time, how mean would be our station.
Oh we could never bear the standing shame,⁣     5
Equivocal ignominy of non-election;
We who will hardly answer to our name,
And on the road direct ignore direction.

But you, dear Franz, sad champion of the drab
And half, would watch the tell-tale shames drift in⁣    10
(As if they were troves of treausre) not aloof,
But with a famishing passion quick to grab
Meaning, and read on all the leaves of sin
Eternity's secret script, the saving proof.

## EFFIGIES

### I

His glances were directive, seemed to move
Pawns on a secret chess-board. You could fancy
You saw the pieces in their wooden dance
Leap in geometrical obedience
From square to square, or stop like broken clockwork⁣   5
When silence spoke its checkmate. Past that arena
Stretched out a winding moonlight labyrinth,
A shining limbo filled with vanishing faces,
Propitious or dangerous, to be scanned
In a passion of repulsion or desire.⁣    10
His glances knew two syllables: 'Come' and 'Go'.
When he was old and dull his eyes grew weary,
Gazing so long into the shifting maze,

And narrowed to the semi-circle before him,
The last defence. There if a stranger entered,                    15
His heart, that beat regardless far within,
Grew still, a hawk before the deadly drop,
Then beat again as his quick mind found the gambit.
All this he hardly knew. His face was like
The shining front of a rich and loveless house,                   20
The doors all shut. The windows cast such brightness
Outwards that none could see what was within,
Half-blinded by the strong repelling dazzle.
Set in the doors two little judas windows
Sometimes would catch the timid visitor's eye                     25
And he would grow aware of a nameless something,
Animal or human, watching his approach,
Like darkness out of darkness. When he was dying
The pieces sauntered freely about the board
Like lawless vagrants, and would not be controlled.               30
He would whisper 'Stop,'
Starting awake, and weep to think they were free.


2

Pity the poor betrayer in the maze
That closed about him when he set the trap
To catch his friend. Now he is there alone,
The envied and beloved quarry fled
Long since for death and freedom. And the maze                     5
Is like an odd device to marvel at
With other eyes if other eyes could see it;
As curious as an idle prince's toy.
There he is now, lost in security,
Quite, quite inside, no fissure in the walls,                     10
Nor any sign of the door that let him in;
Only the oblivious labyrinth all around.
He did not dream of the trap within the trap
In the mad moment, nor that he would long
Sometime to have the beloved victim there                         15
For the deep winding dialogue without end.
Pity him, for he cannot think the thought
Nor feel the pang that yet might set him free,
And Judas ransomed dangle from the tree.


217

### 3

Revolving in his own
Immovable danger zone,
Having killed his enemy
And betrayed his troublesome friend
To be with himself alone,                    5
He watched upon the floor
The punctual minutes crawl
Towards the remaining wall
Into eternity,
And thought, 'Here is the end.'              10
Cut off in blind desire,
From the window he would see,
Twisting in twisted glass,
The devastated street,
The houses all gone wrong,                   15
Watch hats and hurrying feet,
Wild birds and horses pass,
Think, 'All shall go up in fire,
Horse, man and city, all.'
Or dream a whole day long                    20
Of miles and miles of way
Through hills down to the sea
At peace in a distant day;
Gazing upon the floor.
No knock upon the door.                      25

### 4

We fired and fired, and yet they would not fall,
But stood on the ridge and bled,
Transfixed against the sky as on a wall,
Though they and we knew they were dead.
Then we went on,                             5
Passed through them or between;
But all our eyes could fasten upon
Was a great broken machine,
Or so it seemed. Then on the ridge ahead
We watched them rise again.                  10
I do not think we knew the dead
Were real, or really dead, till then.

5

She lived in comfort on her poor few pence
And sweetly starved to feed her swelling dream
Where all she had done came back in grievous blessing.
She had left her house and was by her lover left,
Her flying wings struck root upon his shoulders,                5
And in the self-same flight bore him away.
Her life was all an aria and an echo,
And when the aria ceased the echo led her
Gently to alight somewhere that seemed the earth.
There gradually she withered towards her harvest,              10
That grew as she grew less, until at last
She stared in grief at mounds and mounds of grain.


## THE DIFFICULT LAND

This is a difficult land. Here things miscarry
Whether we care, or do not care enough.
The grain may pine, the harlot weed grow haughty,
Sun, rain, and frost alike conspire against us:
You'd think there was malice in the very air.                  5
And the spring floods and summer droughts: our fields
Mile after mile of soft and useless dust.
On dull delusive days presaging rain
We yoke the oxen, go out harrowing,
Walk in the middle of an ochre cloud,                          10
Dust rising before us and falling again behind us,
Slowly and gently settling where it lay.
These days the earth itself looks sad and senseless.
And when next day the sun mounts hot and lusty
We shake our fists and kick the ground in anger.               15
We have strange dreams: as that, in the early morning
We stand and watch the silver drift of stars
Turn suddenly to a flock of black-birds flying.
And once in a lifetime men from over the border,
In early summer, the season of fresh campaigns,                20
Come trampling down the corn, and kill our cattle.
These things we know and by good luck or guidance
Either frustrate, or, if we must, endure.
We are a people; race and speech support us,
Ancestral rite and custom, roof and tree,                      25
Our songs that tell of our triumphs and disasters

(Fleeting alike), continuance of fold and hearth,
Our names and callings, work and rest and sleep,
And something that, defeated, still endures—
These things sustain us. Yet there are times                    30
When name, identity, and our very hands,
Senselessly labouring, grow most hateful to us,
And we would gladly rid us of these burdens,
Enter our darkness through the doors of wheat
And the light veil of grass (leaving behind                    35
Name, body, country, speech, vocation, faith)
And gather into the secrecy of the earth
Furrowed by broken ploughs lost deep in time.

We have such hours, but are drawn back again
By faces of goodness, faithful masks of sorrow,               40
Honesty, kindness, courage, fidelity,
The love that lasts a life's time. And the fields,
Homestead and stall and barn, springtime and autumn.
(For we can love even the wandering seasons
In their inhuman circuit.) And the dead                        45
Who lodge in us so strangely, unremembered,
Yet in their place. For how can we reject
The long last look on the ever-dying face
Turned backward from the other side of time?
And how offend the dead and shame the living                  50
By these despairs? And how refrain from love?
This is a difficult country, and our home.


## NOTHING THERE BUT FAITH

Nothing, it seemed, between them and the grave.
No, as I looked, there was nothing anywhere.
You'd think no ground could be so flat and bare:
No little ridge or hump or bush to brave
The horizon. Yet they called that land their land,            5
Without a single thought drank in that air
As simple and equivocal as despair.
This, this was what I could not understand.

The reason was, there was nothing there but faith.
Faith made the whole, yes all they could see or hear          10
Or touch or think, and arched its break of day

220

Within them and around them every way.
They looked: all was transfigured far and near,
And the great world rolled between them and death.


## DOUBLE ABSENCE

The rust-red moon above the rose-red cloud,
Ethereal gifts of the absconding sun
That now is shining full on other lands
And soon will draw its track a hundred miles
Across the quiet breast of the hushed Atlantic.                5
The smoke grows up, solid, an ashen tree
From the high Abbey chimney. A sycamore
Holds on its topmost tip a singing thrush,
Its breast turned towards the sign of the buried sun.
Chance only brings such rare felicities                       10
Beyond contrivance of the adventuring mind,
Strange past all meaning, set in their place alone.
Now the moon rises clear and fever pale
Out from the cloud's dissolving drift of ashes,
While in my mind, in double absence, hangs                    15
The rust-red moon above the rose-red cloud.


## DAY AND NIGHT

I wrap the blanket of the night
About me, fold on fold on fold—
And remember how as a child
Lost in the newness of the light
I first discovered what is old                                 5
From the night and the soft night wind.
For in the daytime all was new,
Moving in light and in the mind
All at once, thought, shape and hue.
Extravagant novelty too wild                                  10
For the new eyes of a child.

The night, the night alone is old
And showed me only what I knew,
Knew, yet never had been told;
A speech that from the darkness grew                          15
Too deep for daily tongues to say,

221

Archaic dialogue of a few
Upon the sixth or the seventh day.
And shapes too simple for a place
In the day's shrill complexity                      20
Came and were more natural, more
Expected than my father's face
Smiling across the open door,
More simple than the sanded floor
In unexplained simplicity.                          25

A man now, gone with time so long—
My youth to myself grown fabulous
As an old land's memories, a song
To trouble or to pleasure us—
I try to fit that world to this,                    30
The hidden to the visible play,
Would have them both, would nothing miss,
Learn from the shepherd of the dark,
Here in the light, the paths to know
That thread the labyrinthine park,                  35
And the great Roman roads that go
Striding across the untrodden day.


## THE OTHER STORY

How for the new thing can there be a word?
How can we know
The act, the form itself, unnamed, unheard,
Or for the first time go
Again on the road that runs ere memory              5
Snares it in syllables
And rings its burial bells
In gossip or music or poetry?
Yet we would not remember, but would be.

Why should we muse                                  10
On this great world that always is no more,
Or hope to hear sometime the great lost news?
It was all before.
And we would be where we were bred,
In Eden an hour away,                               15
Though still our cheeks are red
For what is only in remembrance

222

Revolt or sin or guilt or shame,
Or some word much the same,
But was a haze of blood from foot to head,               20
Was that, and nothing said.
Innocent, knowing nothing of innocence,
We learned it from the sad memorial name
First uttered by the offence.
And now the two words seem                               25
A single, fabulous, reciprocal glory,
A dream re-enacted in another dream,
And all accomplished as we plucked the bough.

Stories we know. There is another story.
If one of you is innocent let him tell it now.           30


DREAM AND THING

This is the thing, this truly is the thing.
We dreamt it once; now it has come about.
That was the dream, but this, this is the thing.
The dream was bold and thought it could foretell
What time would bring, but time, it seems, can bring      5
Only this thing which never has had a doubt
That everything is much like everything,
And the deep family likeness will come out.
We thought the dream would spread its folded wing;
But here's a thing that's neither sick nor well,         10
Stupid nor wise, and has no story to tell,
Though every tale is about it and about.
That is the thing, that is the very thing.
Yet take another look and you may bring
From the dull mass each separate splendour out.          15
There is no trust but in the miracle.


SONG FOR A HYPOTHETICAL AGE

Grief, they say, is personal,
Else there'd be no grief at all.
We, exempt from grief and rage,
Rule here our new impersonal age.
Now while dry is every eye                                5
The last grief is passing by.

History takes its final turn
Where all's to mourn for, none to mourn.
Idle justice sits alone
In a world to order grown.                               10
Justice never shed a tear,
And if justice we would bear
We must get another face,
Find a smoother tale to tell
Where everything is in its place                         15
And happiness inevitable.


(Long, long ago, the old men say,
A famous wife, Penelope,
For twenty years the pride of Greece,
Wove and unwove a web all day                            20
That might have been a masterpiece—
If she had let it have its way—
To drive all artistry to despair
And set the sober world at play
Beyond the other side of care,                           25
And lead a fabulous era in.
But still she said, 'Where I begin
Must I return, else all is lost,
And great Odysseus tempest-tossed
Will perish, shipwrecked on my art.                      30
But so, I guide him to the shore.'
And again the web she tore,
No more divided from her heart.)


Oh here the hot heart petrifies
And the round earth to rock is grown                     35
In the winter of our eyes;
Heart and earth a single stone.
Until the stony barrier break
Grief and joy no more shall wake.

## THE YOUNG PRINCES

There was a time: we were young princelings then
In artless state, with brows as bright and clear
As morning light on a new morning land.
We gave and took with innocent hands, not knowing
If we were rich or poor, or thinking at all          5
Of yours or mine; we were newcomers still,
And to have asked the use of that or this,
Its price, commodity, profit would have been
Discourtesy to it and shame to us.
We saw the earth stretched out to us in welcome,          10
But in our hearts we were the welcomers,
And so were courteous to all that was
In high simplicity and natural pride
To be so hailed and greeted with such glory
(Like absentminded kings who are proffered all          15
And need not have a penny in their pockets).
And when the elders told the ancestral stories,
Even as they spoke we knew the characters,
The good and bad, the simple and sly, the heroes,
Each in his place, and chance that turns the tale          20
To grief or joy; we saw and accepted all.
Then in the irreversible noonday came,
Showering its darts into our open breasts,
Doubt that kills courtesy and gratitude.
Since then we have led our dull discourteous lives,          25
Heaven doubting and earth doubting. Earth and heaven
Bent to our menial use. And yet sometimes
We still, as through a dream that comes and goes,
Know what we are, remembering what we were.

## THE CLOUD

One late spring evening in Bohemia,
Driving to the Writers' House, we lost our way
In a maze of little winding roads that led
To nothing but themselves,
Weaving a rustic web for thoughtless travellers.          5
No house was near, nor sign or sound of life:
Only a chequer-board of little fields,
Crumpled and dry, neat squares of powdered dust.
At a sudden turn we saw

A young man harrowing, hidden in dust; he seemed   10
A prisoner walking in a moving cloud
Made by himself for his own purposes;
And there he grew and was as if exalted
To more than man, yet not, not glorified:
A pillar of dust moving in dust; no more.   15
The bushes by the roadside were encrusted
With a hard sheath of dust.
We looked and wondered; the dry cloud moved on
With its interior image.
                    Presently we found   20
A road that brought us to the Writers' House,
And there a preacher from Urania
(Sad land where hope each day is killed by hope)
Praised the good dust, man's ultimate salvation,
And cried that God was dead. As we drove back   25
Late to the city, still our minds were teased
By the brown barren fields, the harrowing,
The figure walking in its cloud, the message
From far Urania. This was before the change;
And in our memory cloud and message fused,   30
Image and thought condensed to a giant form
That walked the earth clothed in its earthly cloud,
Dust made sublime in dust. And yet it seemed unreal
And lonely as things not in their proper place.
And thinking of the man   35
Hid in his cloud we longed for light to break
And show that his face was the face once broken in Eden
Beloved, world-without-end lamented face;
And not a blindfold mask on a pillar of dust.

# THE HORSES

Barely a twelvemonth after
The seven days war that put the world to sleep,
Late in the evening the strange horses came.
By then we had made our covenant with silence,
But in the first few days it was so still   5
We listened to our breathing and were afraid.
On the second day
The radios failed; we turned the knobs; no answer.
On the third day a warship passed us, heading north,
Dead bodies piled on the deck. On the sixth day   10

A plane plunged over us into the sea. Thereafter
Nothing. The radios dumb;
And still they stand in corners of our kitchens,
And stand, perhaps, turned on, in a million rooms
All over the world. But now if they should speak,                    15
If on a sudden they should speak again,
If on the stroke of noon a voice should speak,
We would not listen, we would not let it bring
That old bad world that swallowed its children quick
At one great gulp. We would not have it again.                       20
Sometimes we think of the nations lying asleep,
Curled blindly in impenetrable sorrow,
And then the thought confounds us with its strangeness.

The tractors lie about our fields; at evening
They look like dank sea-monsters couched and waiting.                25
We leave them where they are and let them rust:
'They'll moulder away and be like other loam'.
We make our oxen drag our rusty ploughs,
Long laid aside. We have gone back
Far past our fathers' land.                                          30
                              And then, that evening
Late in the summer the strange horses came.
We heard a distant tapping on the road,
A deepening drumming; it stopped, went on again
And at the corner changed to hollow thunder.                         35
We saw the heads
Like a wild wave charging and were afraid.
We had sold our horses in our fathers' time
To buy new tractors. Now they were strange to us
As fabulous steeds set on an ancient shield                          40
Or illustrations in a book of knights.
We did not dare go near them. Yet they waited,
Stubborn and shy, as if they had been sent
By an old command to find our whereabouts
And that long-lost archaic companionship.                            45
In the first moment we had never a thought
That they were creatures to be owned and used.
Among them were some half-a-dozen colts
Dropped in some wilderness of the broken world,
Yet new as if they had come from their own Eden.                     50
Since then they have pulled our ploughs and borne our loads,
But that free servitude still can pierce our hearts.
Our life is changed; their coming our beginning.

## SONG

This will not pass so soon,
Dear friend, this will not pass,
Though time is out of tune
With all beneath the moon,
Man and woman and flower and grass.          5
These will not pass.
For there's a word 'Return'
That's known among the quick and the dead,
Making two realms for ever cry and mourn.
So mourns the land of darkness when          10
Into the light away the lily is led,
And so gives thanks again
When from the earth the snow-pale beauty goes
Back to her home. Persephone,
Surely all this can only be          15
A light exchange and amorous interplay
In your strange twofold immortality;
And a diversion for a summer day
The death and resurrection of the rose.


## THE ISLAND

Your arms will clasp the gathered grain
For your good time, and wield the flail
In merry fire and summer hail.
There stand the golden hills of corn
Which all the heroic clans have borne,          5
And bear the herdsmen of the plain,
The horseman in the mountain pass,
The archaic goat with silver horn,
Man, dog and flock and fruitful hearth.
Harvests of men to men give birth.          10
These the ancestral faces bred
And show as through a golden glass
Dances and temples of the dead.
Here speak through the transmuted tongue
The full grape bursting in the press,          15
The barley seething in the vat,
Which earth and man as one confess,
Babbling of what both would be at
In garrulous story and drunken song.

228

Though come a different destiny,                    20
Though fall a universal wrong
More stern than simple savagery,
Men are made of what is made,
The meat, the drink, the life, the corn,
Laid up by them, in them reborn.                    25
And self-begotten cycles close
About our way; indigenous art
And simple spells make unafraid
The haunted labyrinths of the heart,
And with our wild succession braid                  30
The resurrection of the rose.

*Sicily*


## INTO THIRTY CENTURIES BORN

Into thirty centuries born,
At home in them all but the very last,
We meet ourselves at every turn
In the long country of the past.
There the fallen are up again                        5
In mortality's second day,
There the indisputable dead
Rise in flesh more fine than clay
And the dead selves we cast away
In imperfection are perfected,                      10
And all is plain yet never found out!
Ilium burns before our eyes
For thirty centuries never put out,
And we walk the streets of Troy
And breathe in the air its fabulous name.           15
The king, the courtier and the rout
Shall never perish in that flame;
Old Priam shall become a boy
For ever changed, for ever the same.

What various sights these countries show:           20
The horses on the roundabout
Still flying round the glittering ring
That rusted fifty years ago.
The gunboat in the little bay,
A mile, and half an age away.                        25

229

Methuselah letting the years go by
While death was new and still in doubt
And only a dream the thought, 'To die'.
And round a corner you may see
Man, maid and tempter under the tree:       30
You'd think there was no sense in death.
And nothing to remedy, nothing to blame;
The dark Enchanter is your friend.
Is it fantasy or faith
That keeps intact that marvellous show       35
And saves the helpless dead from harm?—
To-morrow sounds the great alarm
That puts the histories to rout;
To-morrow after to-morrow brings
Endless beginning without end.       40

Then on this moment set your foot,
Take your road for everywhere,
And from your roving barrier shoot
Your arrow into the empty air.
Follow at a careful pace,       45
Else you may wander in despair.
Gathered at your moving post
Is all that you have but memory.
This is the place of hope and fear,
And faith that comes when hope is lost.       50
Defeat and victory both are here.
In this place where all's to be,
In this moment you are free,
And bound to all. For you shall know
Before you Troy goes up in fire,       55
And you shall walk the Trojan streets
When home are sailed the murdering fleets,
Priam shall be a little boy,
Time shall cancel time's deceits,
And you shall weep for grief and joy       60
To see the whole world perishing
Into everlasting spring,
And over and over the opening briar.

## MY OWN

There's nothing here to keep me from my own.—
The confident roads that at their ease beguile me
With the all-promising lands, the great unknown,
Can with their gilded dust blind me, defile me.
It's so. Yet never did their lies deceive me,                    5
And when, lost in the dreaming route, I say
I seek my soul, my soul does not believe me,
But from these transports turns displeased away.

But then, but then, why should I so behave me,
Willingly duped ten, twenty times an hour,                   10
But that even at my dearest cost I'd save me
From the true knowledge and the real power?
In which through all time's changeable seasons grown,
I might have stayed, unshaken, with my own.

## THE CHOICE

The prisoner wasting in the pit,
The player bending over the strings,
The wise man tangled in his wit,
The angel grafted to his wings
Are governed by necessity,                    5
Condemned to be whatever they are
Nor once from that to move away,
Each his appointed prisoner.
But the riddling sages say,
It is your prison that sets you free,           10
Else chaos would appropriate all.
Out of chaos you built this wall,
Raised this hovel of bone and clay
To be a refuge for liberty.

## IF I COULD KNOW

If I could truly know that I do know
This, and the foreshower of this show,
Who is myself, for plot and scene are mine,
They say, and the world my sign,
Man, earth and heaven, co-patterned so or so—        5
If I could know.

If I could swear that I do truly see
The real world, and all itself and free,
Not prisoned in my shallow sight's confine,
Nor mine, but to be mine,                            10
Freely sometime to come and be with me—
If I could see.

If I could tell that I do truly hear
A music, not this tumult in my ear
Of all that cries in the world, confused or fine;   15
If there were staff and sign
Pitched high above the battle of hope and fear—
If I could hear.

Make me to see and hear that I may know
This journey and the place towards which I go;       20
For a beginning and an end are mine
Surely, and have their sign
Which I and all in the earth and the heavens show.
Teach me to know.

## THE LATE WASP

You that through all the dying summer
Came every morning to our breakfast table,
A lonely bachelor mummer,
And fed on the marmalade
So deeply, all your strength was scarcely able        5
To prise you from the sweet pit you had made,—
You and the earth have now grown older,
And your blue thoroughfares have felt a change;
They have grown colder;
And it is strange                                     10
How the familiar avenues of the air

Crumble now, crumble; the good air will not hold,
All cracked and perished with the cold;
And down you dive through nothing and through despair.


## THE LATE SWALLOW

Leave, leave your well-loved nest,
Late swallow, and fly away.
Here is no rest
For hollowing heart and wearying wing.
Your comrades all have flown                          5
To seek their southern paradise
Across the great earth's downward sloping side,
And you are alone.
Why should you cling
Still to the swiftly ageing narrowing day?            10
Prepare;
Shake out your pinions long untried
That now must bear you there where you would be
Through all the heavens of ice;
Till falling down the homing air                      15
You light and perch upon the radiant tree.


## SONG

This that I give and take,
This that I keep and break,
Is and is not my own
But lives in itself alone,
Yet is between us two,                                5
Mine only in the breaking,
It all in the remaking,
Doing what I undo.

With it all must be well,
There where the invisible                             10
Loom sweetly plies its trade.
All made there is well-made.
So be it between us two;
A giving be our taking,
A making our unmaking,                                15
A doing what we undo.

233

# Last Poems

# I

## THE SONG

I was haunted all that day by memories knocking
At a disused, deaf, dead door of my mind
Sealed up for forty years by myself and time.
They could not get to me nor I to them.
And yet they knocked. And since I could not answer,   5
Since time was past for that sole assignation,
I was oppressed by the unspoken thought
That they and I were not contemporary,
For I had gone away. Yet still in dreams
Where all is changed, time, place, identity,   10
Where fables turn to beasts and beasts to fables,
And anything can be in a natural wonder,
These meetings are renewed, dead dialogues
Utter their antique speech.
                            That night I dreamed   15
That towards the end of such another day
Spent in such thoughts, but in some other place,
I was returning from a long day's work—
What work I have forgotten—and had to cross
A park lost somewhere in the world, yet now   20
Present and whole to me as I to it:
Utilitarian strip of grass and trees—
A short-cut for poor clerks to unhallowed rooms.
I stopped beside the gate—as how often before?—
When from the park poured out the resonant moaning   25
Of some great beast in anguish. Could it be
For us, I wondered dreaming, the strange beast mourned,
Or for some deed once done and done for ever
And done in vain?
                 And yet I pushed the gate—   30
As how often before?—passed through and went my way,
When on my right appeared what seemed a cliff
Newly arisen there beside the path.
Was this the park, I thought, or had I strayed

237

Into some place forgotten in old time? 35
The dream worked on; I looked again and saw
The huge hind-quarters of some giant thing;
A horse it seemed that first had been a cliff.
As heavy as earth it stood and mourned alone,
Horse, or centaur, or wide-winged Pegasus, 40
But far too strange for any fabulous name.
I thought, here is no place for pity, I cannot share
That sorrow whose only speech is dread and awe.
And then in terror lest the thing should move
And come on me, I ran to the farther gate, 45
Stood there and listened. Darkness had fallen,
But still that wonder
Sent out its moan not meant for other ears,
A long breath drawn by pain, intolerable.

I thought, now it will move. And then it moved. 50
The moaning ceased, the hoofs rose up and fell
Gently, as treading out a meditation,
Then broke in thunder; the wild thing charged the gate,
Yet could not pass—oh pity!—that simple barrier
(Subservient to any common touch), 55
Turned back again in absolute overthrow,
And beat on the ground as if for entrance there.
The dream worked on. The clamour died; the hoofs
Beat on no common ground; silence; a drumming
As of wild swans taking their highway south 60
From the murdering ice; hoofs, wings far overhead
Climbing the sky; pain raised that wonder there;
Nothing but pain. The drumming died away.

Was it these hoofs, I thought, that knocked all day
With no articulate message, but this vision 65
That had no tongue to speak its mystery?
What wound in the world's side and we unknowing
Lay open and bleeding now? What present anguish
Drew that long dirge from the earth-haunting marvel?
And why that earthly visit, unearthly pain? 70
I was not dreaming now, but thinking the dream.
Then all was quiet, the park was its own again,
And I on my road to my familiar lodgings
A world away; and all its poor own again.
Yet I woke up saying, 'The song—the song'. 75

## THE TOWER

This is the famous Babel Tower,
You'd think it had grown since yesterday.
We are the architects of that power;
Oh, that clouds would bear it away.
When our morning stint is done                    5
We watch the mannikin sentries stand
Shoulder to shoulder with the sun
(They are like tribesmen of the air)
And view the geometrical line
Of shadow cutting in two our land.                 10
What have we fashioned but a sign?
This unending quarry strewn
With rough and smooth and wicked stone
To mount that gun aimed at the sky:
What have we made but an empty sign?               15
The archaic clouds pass slowly by.
What are our masters? Who are you there?
We scarcely see you. May there come
A great wind from a stormier star,
Blow tower and shadow to kingdom come.             20

This is the old men's story. Once
Voices were there, resounding words
Of an incomprehensible tongue
Fit for great heroes and great lords,
But never spoken anywhere.                         25
And once a simple country song
Began and suddenly ended. Since
No message drops from the middle air
Except when a dead lord flutters down
Light as a frozen and mummied fly                  30
From the perpendicular town.
(They have no license there to die.)
We cannot bear to scan that face,
Cover in haste the unchristened head,
Heap dust and rubble upon the place.               35
We too die. *So* look the dead
Whose breath stopped on a different star.
Who are they? We are what we are.

# IMAGES

## I

Take one look at that face and go your way.
Regard these lines of motionless desire
Perpetually assuaged yet unappeased,
Still yearning for what still is about to be.
What you see there is something else than beauty.   5
These are your lineaments, the face of life
When it is quite alone, and you forgotten.
Look once. But do not hope to find a sentence
To tell what you have seen. Stop at the colon:
And set a silence after to speak the word   10
That you will always seek and never find,
Perhaps, if found, the good and beautiful end.
You will not reach that place. So leave the hiatus
There in the broken sentence. What is missing
You will always think of. And do not turn again   15
To scan that face lest you should leave upon it
Your personal load of trouble and desire.
You cannot add to it nor take away.
All that you think or say will be a postscript
To that imperfect mystery, limping sentence.   20
And do not forget. But look once at that face.

## II

You in imaginary fears
Threading the terrors of a wood
That has no place but in your mind;
You hunted by the ravenous years
That send their warnings through your blood   5
Where fears long conquered still affright;
You willingly gone to be with blind
Tiresias in his buried night
That opens at an idle word—
You look in wonder at the bird,   10
Round ball of appetite and fear,
That sings at ease upon the branch,
Time a long silence in its ear
That never heard of time or space;
You who hear the avalanche   15

Must fabricate a temporal tale
To bring the timeless nightingale
And swallow to your trysting place.


## III

He is the little, sly, absconding god,
Hides in the moment. Look, and he is gone,
But turn away, and there he is back again.
He is more quick than movement,
Present and gone, absent and safe in hiding,　　　5
No spell can bind him. But idle fools and children
Take him for granted, are at their ease with him,
And he's the true friend of the absentminded.
He is too agile for time's dull iambics,
Lightly dives in and out of stale duration,　　　10
Poised on the endless present. There he is free,
Having no past or future. All things know him.
And then are eased as by a heavenly chance.
The greater gods sometimes in grave amusement
Smile at his tricks, yet nod in approbation.　　　15


## THE CHURCH

This autumn day the new cross is set up
On the unfinished church, above the trees,
Bright as a new penny, tipping the tip
Of the elongated spire in the sunny breeze,
And is at ease;　　　5
Newcomer suddenly, calmly looking down
On this American university town.

Someone inside me sketches a cross—askew,
A child's—on seeing that stick crossed with a stick,
Some simple ancestor, perhaps, that knew,　　　10
Centuries ago when all were Catholic,
That this archaic trick
Brings to the heart and the fingers what was done
One spring day in Judaea to Three in One;

When God and Man in more than love's embrance,　　　15
Far from their heaven in dust and tumult died,

And the holy Dove fluttered above that place
Seeking its desolate nest in the broken side,
And Nature cried
To see Heaven doff its glory to atone                    20
For man, lest he should die in time, alone.

I think of the Church, that stretched magnificence
Housing the crib, the desert, and the tree,
And the good Lord who lived on poverty's pence
Among the fishermen of Galilee,                          25
Courting mortality,
And schooled himself to learn his human part:
A poor man skilled in dialectic art.

What reason for that splendour of blue and gold
For One so great and poor He was past all need?         30
What but impetuous love that could not hold
Its storm of spending and must scatter its seed
In blue and gold and deed,
And write its busy Books on Books of Days
To attempt and never touch the sum of praise.            35

I look at the church again, and yet again,
And think of those who house together in Hell,
Cooped by ingenious theological men
Expert to track the sour and musty smell
Of sins they know too well;                              40
Until grown proud, they crib in rusty bars
The Love that moves the sun and the other stars.

Yet fortune to the new church, and may its door
Never be shut, or yawn in empty state
To daunt the poor in spirit, the always poor.            45
Catholic, Orthodox, Protestant, may it wait
Here for its true estate.
All's still to do; roof, window and wall are bare.
I look, and do not doubt that He is there.

## AFTER A HYPOTHETICAL WAR

No rule nor ruler: only water and clay,
And the purblind peasant squatting, elbows out
To nudge his neighbour from his inch of ground
Clutched fast through flood and drought but never loved.
Avarice without meaning. There you will see           5
The soil on its perpetual death-bed; miles
Of mendicant flowers prospering on its bier,
And weeds as old as time, their roots entangled,
Murderer choking murderer in the dark,
Though here they rule and flourish. Heaven and earth  10
Give only of their worst, breeding what's bad.
Even the dust-cart meteors on their rounds
Stop here to void their refuse, leaving this
Chaotic breed of misbegotten things,
Embryos of what could never wish to be.               15
Soil and air breed crookedly here, and men
Are dumb and twisted as the envious scrub
That spreads in silent malice on the fields.
Lost lands infected by an enmity
Deeper than lust or greed, that works by stealth      20
Yet in the sun is helpless as the blindworm,
Making bad worse. The mud has sucked half in
People and cattle until they eat and breathe
Nothing but mud. Poor tribe so meanly cheated,
Their very cradle an image of the grave.              25
What rule of governance can save them now?

## COMPLAINT OF THE DYING PEASANTRY

Our old songs are lost,
Our sons are newspapermen
At the singers' cost.
There were no papers when

Sir Patrick Spens put out to sea                       5
In all the country cottages
With music and ceremony
For five centuries.

Till Scott and Hogg, the robbers, came
And nailed the singing tragedies down                    10
In dumb letters under a name
And led the bothy to the town.

Sir Patrick Spens shut in a book,
Burd Helen stretched across a page:
A few readers look                                       15
There at the effigy of our age.

The singing and the harping fled
Into the silent library;
But we are with Helen dead
And with Sir Patrick lost at sea.                        20


## SALEM, MASSACHUSETTS

They walked black Bible streets and piously tilled
The burning fields of the new Apocalypse.
With texts and guns they drove the Indians out,
Ruled young and old with stiff Hebraic rod,
The Puritan English country gentlemen;                    5
And burned young witches.
                        Their sons' grandsons
Throve on Leviathan and the China trade
And built and lived in beautiful wooden houses,
Their Jordan past.                                       10
                    You may see the Witches' Trail
Still winding through the streets to a little knoll
That looks across a tideless inland bay
In the clear New England weather. This they saw,
The women, till the fire and smoke consumed              15
Sight, breath and body while the Elders watched
That all was well and truly consumed by fire.
The House with the Seven Gables is gone, consumed by fire,
And in the evenings businessmen from Boston
Sit in the beautiful houses, mobbed by cars.             20

## THE STRANGE RETURN

Behind him Hell sank in the plain.
He saw far off the liquid glaze
Of burning somewhere. That was all.
A burning there or in his brain?
He could not tell. His was a case,      5
He thought, that put all Hell in doubt,
Though he had cause to know that place.
Had They some darker thought in mind,
Arranged his flight, inveigled him out
To walk half-way from Heaven to Hell?      10
Was where he stood a dream of stone?
No matter, he was here alone.
And then he saw the tangled skein,
His foot-prints following him behind
And stretching to the prison lock,      15
And there two towers like ears a-cock.
Would they answer to his knock,
Brush all aside, invite him in,
Crack a dry witticism on sin,
Excuse his saunter over the sand,      20
If he returned? Or understand?
But then the towers like ears a-cock.

How from that bastion could he fall
Like Lazarus backwards into life
And travel to another death?      25
And now in buried distances
There was a wakening and he heard
Word at odds with common word,
A child's voice crying, 'Let me be!'
In a world he could not touch,      30
And others saying, 'Be in time',
With such a strange anxiety
(And he himself caught here in time).
The young girl's brow, the vertical cleft
Above the eyes that saw too much      35
Too soon: how could he counter these,
Make friends with the evils, take his part,
Salute the outer and inner strife,
The bickering between doubt and faith,
Inherit the tangle he had left,      40
Outface the trembling at his heart?

Three feet away a little tree
Put out in pain a single bud
That did not fear the ultimate fire.
And in a flash he knew it all,                    45
The long-forgotten and new desire,
And looked and saw the tree was good.


AFTER 1984

Even now we speak of Eight-four
Although that world is far away.
It is not strange that children play
Their games again. . . . A random score
Of veterans still recall the day             5
That drove the murdering lies away.

The young say that necessity
Decided all should happen so;
Men did not act, but history.—
We who remember do not know,             10
And still to us the event is strange.
We cannot understand that change.

For how from nothing could come so much?
We the deprived and uncommitted,
Nothing being left us to commit,             15
Who could not even be manumitted
Because no one could see or touch
Our fetters locked so far within,
And not a key in the world to fit;
We who had been so carefully bred          20
Not to feel sorrow or be pleased—
How could we ever be released?
Turn aboout widdershins and be free?
Love and murder, pity and sin
Turned our monotone to red.                 25

The secret universe of the blind
Cannot be known. Just so we were
Shut from ourselves even in our mind;
Only a twisting chaos within
Turned on itself, not knowing where        30
The exit was, salvation gate.

Was it chaos that set us straight,
The elements that rebelled, not we?
Or the anguish never to find
Ourselves, somewhere, at last, and be?          35
We must escape, no matter where.

Accident? Miracle? Then we fought
On to this life that was before,
Only that, no less, no more,
Strangely familiar. In the Nought          40
Did we beget it in our thought?


## THE DESOLATIONS

The desolations are not the sorrows' kin.
Sorrow is gentle and sings her sons to rest.
The desolations have no word nor music,
Only an endless inarticulate cry
Inaudible to the poetry-pampered ear.          5
The desolations tell
Nothing for ever, the interminable
Civil war of earth and water and fire.
These have to do with our making.
                                   What guards us here          10
Among the established and familiar things?
The leaf, the apple and the rounded earth
Where even imagination is an O,
And only endless harvest is gathered there,
Nothing but that. Yet sometimes absently          15
We pause and murmur 'We came crying hither',
Remembering, and set up a little stage
For our indigenous formal tragedy
Where we are all the actors.
                                   The wild earth          20
Pours its hot entrails on the slopes of Aetna,
Blasting whatever's made. Yet in a while
Black house-rows like a pleasant street in Hell
Rise from the frozen slag, and safe within
The lava rooms Sicilian families          25
Follow their ancient ways; the vine-rows yield
Seven times a year, fed on earth's dearest dust.
And all forget the admonition of fire.
There, if you listen, you may hear them say,

'Love is at home, earth's joys lie all around us,    30
The vine-stock and the rose are guarded well.
The roof-tree holds, and friends come in the evening.'
What saves us from the raging desolations
And tells us we shall walk through peace to peace?


## THE VOICES

The lid flew off, and all the desolations,
As through a roaring poet's shameless throat,
Poured out their lamentations.
It seemed somewhere they were trying to take a vote
That in the hurry and din was never taken,    5
For not one wrong was shaken.
And all as stupid and sad
As a cashiered and spavined army of horse
Charging behind their false archaic neigh
At a fantastical force    10
Ten thousand miles or years away;
Or as a tribe who having lost their tongue
Could find no articulate word to say,
Having forgotten what was fresh and young:
All so debased by time it was almost mad.    15

We were assembled for some ceremony,
Compelled to this music, forced to hear.
But as we listened insidious memory,
The secret spy within the ear,
Whispered, 'This is your speech, this is the rune    20
You never read; this is your oldest tune.'
At which we cried, 'Push, push it back under the ground.
We will not listen. We
Will not endure that sound,'
And in the clamour could not hear a voice,    25
That calmly said, 'Rejoice.'


## AN ISLAND TALE

She had endured so long a grief
That from her breast we saw it grow,
Branch, leaf and flower with such a grace

We wondered at the summer place
Which set that harvest there. But oh          5
The softly, softly yellowing leaf.

She was enclosed in quietness,
Where for lost love her tears were shed.
They stopped, and she was quite alone.
Being so poor, she was our own,          10
Her lack of all our precious bread.
She had no skill to offer less.

She turned into an island song
And died. They sing her ballad yet,
But all the simple verses tell          15
Is, Love and grief became her well.
Too well; for how can we forget
Her happy face when she was young?


## THE TWO SISTERS

Her beauty was so rare,
It wore her body down
With leading through the air
That marvel not her own.
At last to set it free          5
From enmity of change
And time's incontinence
To drink from beauty's bone,
Snatching her last defence,
She locked it in the sea.          10

The other, not content
That fault of hers should bring
Grief and mismanagement
To make an end of grace
And snap the slender ring,          15
Pulled death down on her head,
Completed destiny.
So each from her own place,
These ladies put to sea
To join the intrepid dead.          20

## THREE TALES

See, they move past, linked wrist to wrist with time,
Wise man and fool, straggler and good recruit,
Enlisted in the enigma's exploration.
They cannot read its purpose, only guess
There is no turning back, no deviation,                    5
Nor resting place on the enormous road.
There are three tales of time. The first one says
The traveller in his mind created it
That there might be a theme, a great flawed story
To interrupt the unbearable trance of peace,              10
And for that gain time was a trifling fee.
The second holds that time was there already
Before we came, and that our opening eyes
Struck full upon it. This, they say, is why
We know the changing world, for all was there            15
In that first look, with no division.
The rest was Afterwards. The third tale says
That we were born into eternity,
The boundless garden, and our issuing thence
Was self-incarceration in a prison                        20
Where we act out our wishes' wild succession.
The crystal walls are scrawled with static signs,
But as we advance our towering shadows move
With our own motion, melting in multitude.
So we go forward linked with numberless shadow,          25
Invisible, inaudible close companion,
Dear friend and enemy in our flight from time.

## THE BROTHERS

Last night I watched my brothers play,
The gentle and the reckless one,
In a field two yards away.
For half a century they were gone
Beyond the other side of care                             5
To be among the peaceful dead.

Even in a dream how could I dare
Interrogate that happiness
So wildly spent yet never less?
For still they raced about the green                      10

And were like two revolving suns;
A brightness poured from head to head,
So strong I could not see their eyes
Or look into their paradise.
What were they doing, the happy ones?          15
Yet where I was they once had been.

I thought, How could I be so dull,
Twenty thousand days ago,
Not to see they were beautiful?
I asked them, Were you really so          20
As you are now, that other day?
And the dream was soon away.

For then we played for victory
And not to make each other glad.
A darkness covered every head,          25
Frowns twisted the original face,
And through that mask we could not see
The beauty and the buried grace.

I have observed in foolish awe
The dateless mid-days of the law          30
And seen indifferent justice done
By everyone on everyone.
And in a vision I have seen
My brothers playing on the green.


## THE CONQUEROR

But oh that rich encrimsoned cloud
From which rode out the armoured man.
He saw his kingdom stretched below
And thought that he need scarcely go
To take it, his ere he began.          5
You well might think that he was proud.

We waited for the advent. Then
Some hesitation held him there.
Was it the little roads that made
The simple conqueror afraid?          10
Defeat came on him in the air,
And the soft cloud drank him in again.

## DIALOGUE

Returning from the antipodes of time,
What did you find, adventurer seeking your home?
What were you doing there in the dragon's kingdom?
Did you see yourself when you were not looking,
Or take the desert lion by surprise,                          5
Entering his gaze following the antelope
To the watering place, watching the watcher, still
So far away from the unreachable beginning,
A soul seeking its soul in fell and claw?
Did you plunge in the smothering waters to peruse       10
In shell and glaucous eye your dateless scripture,
Or scan the desert with the desert's eyes,
Watching the sand-storm racing round the plain
On the vacant trace like a pack of spectral hounds?
Did they bring you comfort?                                  15
What were you doing there at the back of the world?

Returning now from the other side of time
My steps are measured and processional
In the archaic march led by the sun.
So it must be, the light leading, the foot                   20
Stepping into the world in the opening moment.
Now, passing, I see that all is in its place,
The good and the evil, equal and strange order:
Hunter and quarry, each in a separate day,
The hecatombs of slaughter upon the hills,                   25
The shepherds watching from the eastern slopes,
New gods and kings sitting upon their chairs
(I cannot read their faces),
War and peace, generation and death,
Shameful and sad concurrences of time,                       30
The uncanny stillness of the savage keep,
The blackened gorge nothing can clean again
Where thirty thousand, men and women and children,
Were slaughtered once (no one will walk there now),
The hungry waste advancing and retiring,                     35
Violent or invisible alteration,
The transmutations, child and youth and man,
Maiden and mother, maiden and mother again,
A man and a woman building their changing house
On patient mutability. And Jack and Jill                     40
And Kate and Harry, black and brown and white,

Who keep the bond when faith and beauty leave,
And are there for their own and the world's good.
And the house-dog and the cat, timeless companions,
The bird that sang one day in the dragon's bower          45
And nests beneath my eaves, a little house-god,
The cattle in the meadow, and this my home.
But now, looking again, I see wall, roof and door
Are changed, and my house looks out on foreign ground.
This is not the end of the world's road.                    50

Yet sometimes on an evening when all is still
And the bird in flight hangs tranced upon the air,
Flying and yet at rest, as if time's work were over,
And the sun burns red and still on the bole of the yew-tree,
And the workman, his day ended, stands and listens,         55
Thinking of home, yet held in the bright stillness,
I see you stand at your window and softly arrest
Tree, bird and man and the nightward hastening sun
In an endless stasis, and what was given before
You opened your eyes upon the changing earth               60
Is there, and for a moment you are at home.

That was a moment, now a memory.
I do not live in the house of memory.
For my kinsmen say: 'Long since we lost a road,
Then reached this place, on earth the first and last,       65
Neither good nor bad, the right place nor the wrong;
A house, and there we nourish a heavenly hope.
For this a great god died and all heaven mourned
That earth might, in extremity, have such fortune.
This we know. Yet in half-memory,                          70
Not in complaint and scarcely in desire,
Sometimes we say: Long since we lost a road,
And feel the ghost of an ethereal sorrow
Passing, and lighting or darkening all the house,
Lighting or darkening, which, we do not know.              75
Does that road still run somewhere in the world?
Question on question.
Hope and sorrow ethereal roof our house.'

## PENELOPE IN DOUBT

Forgotten brooch and shrivelled scar,
Were these the only guarantee
This was Odysseus? Did she go
Through twenty years of drifting snow,
Whitening that head and hers, to be                    5
Near as a wife, and yet so far?

The brooch came closer as he told—
Grown suddenly young—how he had lost
The wild doe and the raging hound
That battled in the golden round.                      10
She listened, but what shook her most
Was that these creatures made her old.

Odysseus and that idle tale—
How many things in her had died
While hound and doe shut in the ring                   15
Still fought somewhere in the world, a thing
So strange, her heart knocked on her side.
His eyes with time were bleached and pale.

A stranger, who had seen too much,
Been where she could not follow, sealed               20
In blank and smooth estranging snow
From head to foot. How could she know
What a brown scar said or concealed?
Yet now she trembled at his touch.

## SICK CALIBAN

He looked, he saw, and quickly went his way.
Should he have cried
On all the world to help that suffering thing,
Man, beast, or bestial changeling,
Or huge fish stranded choking in dry air               5
Without the sense to die?
Yet that great emerald blazing on its finger,
The proud and sneaking malice in its eye
That said, I suffer truly and yet malinger,
Long for and hate the stupid remedy.                   10
Look: I am yourself for ever stuck half way.

And then he knew
Those he would summon were a multiplied
Mere replica of himself, and all had thought
Long since, No remedy here or anywhere                    15
For that poor bag of bone
And hank of hair.

So he went on
And for a while could hear behind his back
A trifling rumour, mere imagined moan,                    20
At last nothing at all. Yet now the lack
Began to irk him and the silence grew
Into a dead weight shut within his side,
And he knew
That he must carry it now, be patient and wise            25
Until perhaps in the end time would devise
A meaning, a light and simple syllable wrought
By a chance breath.

And so he took the straight road to his death
In surly anger that was far from mourning.                30
Behind him followed hope and faith
Saying little. But something stood at that first turning
By itself, weeping. If he could keep his eyes
On that far distant mourner, would it save
Something? Would he find breath to call                   35
To the others, and all be changed, that thing, and all?

## IMPERSONAL CALAMITY

Respectable men have witnessed terrible things,
And rich and poor things extraordinary,
These murder-haunted years. Even so, even so,
Respectable men seem still respectable,
The ordinary no less ordinary,                             5
For our inherited features cannot show
More than traditional grief and happiness
That rise from old and worn and simple springs.
How can an eye or brow
Disclose the gutted towns and the millions dead?          10
They have too slight an artistry.
Between us and the things that change us
A covenant long ago was set

And is prescriptive yet.
A single grief from man or God                    15
Freely will let
Change in and bring a stern relief.
A son or daughter dead
Can bend the back or whiten the head,
Break and remould the heart,                      20
Stiffen the face into a mask of grief.
It is an ancient art.
The impersonal calamities estrange us
From our own selves, send us abroad
In desolate thoughtlessness,                      25
While far behind our hearts know what they know,
Yet cannot feel, nor ever express.


## THE LAST WAR
### I

No place at all for bravery in that war
Nor mark where one might make a stand,
Nor use for eye or hand
To discover and reach the enemy
Hidden in air.                                     5
No way to save
By our own death the young that they might die
Sometime a different death. The thought Again
That made a promise to mortality—
Gave order and distance, reason and rhyme—         10
Will walk a little before us to the grave
While we are still in time for a little time.


### II

Or shall we think only of night and day
Vacantly visiting the vacant earth
And stare in hatred at the turncoat sun            15
That shines on glittering oes where thought of birth
Will never be—till birth will be a dream
Of a quaint custom in another place,
And we shall gaze in wonder face to face?
Or shall we picture bird and tree                  20

Silently falling, and think of all the words
By which we forged earth, night and day
And ruled with such strange ease our work and play?
Now only the lexicon of a dream.
And we see our bodies buried in falling birds.                    25

### III

Shall we all die together?
Perhaps nothing at all will be there but pain,
A choking and floundering, or gigantic stupor
Of a world-wide deserted hospital ward.
There will be strange good-byes, more strange than those  ·30
That once were spoken by terrified refugees,
Our harbingers: some of them lost in shipwreck,
Spilling salt angry tears in the salt waves,
Their lives waste-water sucked through a gaping hole,
Yet all the world around them; hope and fear.              35
We thought too idly of them, not knowing we
Might founder on common earth and choke in air,
Without one witness. Will great visions come,
And life lie clear at last as it says, Good-bye,
Good-bye, I have borne with you a little while?            40
Or shall we remember shameful things concealed,
Mean coldnesses and wounds too eagerly given?

### IV

A tree thin sick and pale by a north wall,
A smile splintering a face—
I saw them today, suddenly made aware                      45
That ordinary sights appal,
So that a tree mistreated wounds the heart,
A twisted smile twists inward through the mind
Ingeniously to find
Its place and claim a lifelong tenancy there.              50
That is not strange but the most ancient art,
I thought, consummate, still and blind.

I wondered if some pure ancestral head
Kept vigil there, but thought, Our eyes are led
Through endless circles of impure reflection,              55

257

Pillaging what is not their own
In idle greed. Face mirrors face,
Mixing to generate an image sown
By casual desire or disaffection,
Assembles a common face                                60
Aped from the crowd-face and the festive room,
And waiting lost and still
In the empty glass where it presents a will
That is not ours. Imagined, then, by whom?

I thought, our help is in all that is full-grown        65
By nature, and all that is with hands well-made,
Carved in verse or stone
Or a harvest yield. There is the harmony
By which we know our own and the world's health,
The simply good, great counterpoise                     70
To blind nonentity,
Ever renewed and squandered wealth.
Yet not enough. Because we could not wait
To untwist the twisted smile and make it straight
Or render restitution to the tree.                      75
We who were wrapped so warm in foolish joys
Did not have time to call on pity
For all that is sick, and heal and remake our city.


                           V


About the well of life where we are made
Spirits of earth and heaven together lie.               80
They do not turn their bright heads at our coming,
So deep their dream of pure commingled being,
So still the air and the level beam that flows
Along the ground, shed by the flowers and waters:
All above and beneath them a deep darkness.             85
Their bodies lie in shadow or buried in earth,
Their heads shine in the light of the underworld.
Loaded with fear and crowned with every hope
The born stream past them to the longed for place.

# II

## NIGHTMARE OF PEACE

Even in a dream how were we there
Among the commissars of peace
And that meek humming in the air
From the assenting devotees?
Police disguised on every chair          5
Up on the platform. Peace was there
In hands where it would never stir.
Aloft a battle-plated dove
Throned over all in menacing love.

But why was our old friend Everyman          10
Among this false-faced company
When we knew that he was sought
Across the border a mile away
By men the living spit of these?
He smiled and whispered he was not bought,          15
Left us and said he'd soon be back;
An old acquaintance waited below.
The whole room turned to watch him go,
And the eyes said, You will not come back.
Two hours passed: he did not come back.          20

Then as in dreams a swelling fear
Begets the palpable image, we
Were suddenly climbing through the air
In some contraption old and lame
As Icarus' handiwork. We flew on          25
Searching for hapless Everyman.
Indifferent fields, nothing to see.
Then suddenly a crowd, a pack
Of players in some archaic game?
So we would make the riddle say          30
Yet could not take our eyes away
And knew we were there, had known the same

In many a nightmare. Then it came:
A slowly lengthening horrible tail
Thrust from the ambiguous monster's back,                    35
The calmly lazily waving thing
That brushes flies on a summer day.
A beast trampling as oxen tread
The annual yield, the harvest play.
For a moment: then we saw the lies                           40
Spring open, watched the rows of eyes
Break out upon the animal's back.
And all dissolved in a common ring.
At the centre, truly dead,
Lay Everyman. So both were true,                             45
Animal and human, and we knew
These were God's creatures after all
Ashamed and broken by the fall
Into the dark.
                          Then one stepped out               50
Who had been but now a hoof or horn
Or drop of sweat on the animal,
And waved and shouted: we must come down.
And the animal was reborn.
We had crossed the border, must come down,                   55
And were again in the conference hall
With Peace the Tyrant's pitiless law,
While still within our minds we saw
The beast trampling, Everyman down.


## BALLAD OF EVERYMAN
### I

Stout Everyman set out to meet
    His brothers gathered from every land,
And make a peace for all the earth
    And link the nations hand to hand.

He came into a splendid hall                                  5
    And there he saw a motionless dove
Swung from the roof, but for the rest
    Found little sign of peace or love.

Two days he listened patiently,
　　But on the third got up and swore:　　　10
'Nothing but slaves and masters here:
　　Your dove's a liar and a whore.

'Disguised police on the high seats,
　　In every corner pimps and spies.
Goodbye to you; I'd rather be　　　　　15
　　With friends in Hell or Paradise'.

The great room turned to watch him go,
　　But oh the deadly silence then.
From that day brave Everyman
　　Was never seen by friend again.　　　20


## II

Night after night I dream a dream
　　That I am flying through the air
On some contraption old and lame
　　As Icarus' unlucky chair.

And first I see the empty fields—　　　25
　　No sign of Everyman anywhere—
And then I see a playing field
　　And two great sides in combat there.

And then they change into a beast
　　With iron hoofs and scourging tail　　30
That treads a bloody harvest down
　　In readiness for the murdering flail.

And then a rash of staring eyes
　　Covers the beast, back, sides and head,
And stare as if remembering　　　　　35
　　Something that long ago was said.

And the beast is gone, and nothing's there
　　But murderers standing in a ring,
And at the centre Everyman.
　　I never saw so poor a thing.　　　　40

Curses upon the traitorous men
  Who brought our good friend Everyman down,
And murder peace to bring their peace,
  And flatter and rob the ignorant clown.


## THE POET

And in bewilderment
My tongue shall tell
What mind had never meant
Nor memory stored.
In such bewilderment                              5
Love's parable
Into the world was sent
To stammer its word.

What I shall never know
I must make known.                              10
Where traveller never went
Is my domain.
Dear disembodiment
Through which is shown
The shapes that come and go               15
And turn again.

Heaven-sent perplexity—
If thought should thieve
One word of the mystery
All would be wrong.                              20
Most faithful fantasy
That can believe
Its immortality
And make a song.


## PETROL SHORTAGE

This mild late-winter afternoon
Everything's unfamiliar;
Vacant silence as of a peace
After a fifty-year-long war.

The planes are hunted from the sky,                    5
All round me is the natural day.
I watch this empty country road
Roll half a century away.

And looking round me I recall
That here the patient ploughmen came       10
Long years ago, and so remember
What they were and what I am.

I think, the aeroplanes will pass,
Power's stupendous equipage,
And leave with simpler dynasties            15
The mute detritus of an age.

The daring pilot will come down,
Cold marble wings will mark his place,
And soft persuasion of the grass
Restrain the swiftest of his race.          20

The cycle will come round again,
Earth will repair its broken day,
And pastoral Europe dream again
Of little wars waged far away.

A week refutes a prophecy                    25
That only ages can make true.
The deafening distractions wait,
Industrious fiends, for me and you.

## THE BREAKING

Peace in the western sky,
A ploughman follows the plough,
Children come home from school:
War is preparing now.

Great-grandfather on his farm                 5
In eighteen hundred and ten
Heard of great victories
From wandering tinkermen,
Until the press-gang came,
Took son and servant away,                   10

The fields were left forlorn
And there was nothing to say.
The farmer ploughed and reaped,
Led five lean harvests in,
The young men long away:                                15
There was a great war then.

All things stand in their place
Till hatred beats them down,
Furies and fantasies
Strike flat the little town.                            20
Then all rise up again,
But heart and blood and bone,
The very stones in the street,
Roof and foundation stone,
Remember and foreknow.                                  25
Memories, prophecies,
The song the ploughman sings,
The simple dream of peace,
Dark dreams in the dead of night
And on the reckless brow                                30
Bent to let chaos in,
Tell that they shall come down,
Be broken, and rise again.


## A RIGHTEOUS MAN

This good man is accursed
By an ancestral dudgeon, stern old grudge,
Inherited from the first
Forefather of his surly race,
Which has imprinted on his brow                         5
The vehement prophet and inveterate judge.
These you will see,
Looking at him, and the wrongous dignity
Of an old, obstinate, half-sculptured stone
That will not bow                                       10
To the artist's gentle hand and be,
What it should be, a kindly human face.
The dudgeon, which is ours, we must forgive.
But why should he hand on
The wrong so ostentatiously,                            15

As if to bear that burden were to live,
And there were nothing to say
But that we must, and yet can never pay?


## TO THE FORGOTTEN DEAD

Take the great road Oblivion
That does not cross the fields of fame
And princedoms burning bright in death.
You from time have gone away
For ever, and your eternity                    5
Is too vast for story or name.
Once you stood and did not break
And were forgotten. Do not make
Your silent magnanimity
A mock at fame's importunate breath.          10


## DIALOGUE

I never saw the world until that day,
The real fabulous world newly reborn,
And celebrated and crowned on every side
With sun and sky and lands of fruit and corn,
The dull ox and the high horse glorified,      5
Red images on the red clay,
And such a race of women and men,
I thought the famous ones had never died.
I speak in truth of what he showed me then.
But you whom he loved and yet could never dare 10
To win, how was it that you did not care
For such a man as he?
                              *Oh he was dull,*
*Sick of the cheats of his phantasmal art*
*And that unending journey through no place,*   15
*He said, and asked to fly into the cool*   .
*And subterranean harbour of my heart,*
*Darker than his, more cool. He little thought*
*It was a riotous prison that he sought,*
*A place indeed, but such a place!*             20
*What could he give me, who was never his fool,*
*Nor Helen, nor Iseult, playing a harlot's part?*
*I have wondered what he read into my face.*

I knew a man, the most unlike that one,
I think the shrewdest, sweetest man                          25
I ever saw, modest and yet a king
Among his harvests, with a harvester's eye
That had forgotten to wonder why
At this or that, knowing his natural span,
And spoke of evil as 'the other thing',                      30
Judging a virtue as he judged the weather,
Endured, accepted all, the equal brother
Of men and chance, the good and the bad day.
And when I spoke of the high horse glorified,
He smiled and answered: 'Tell me, will it pull?             35
Or find its way in the dark? Is it on my side?
Then I'm its friend. But it must answer
To bit and rein. I do not want a dancer'.
And yet he loved a good horse as a good
Workman or field or block of seasoned wood.                 40
He was neither a plain nor a fanciful fool.
Yet that first world was beautiful
And true, stands still where first it stood.

*I have known men and horses many a day.*
*Men come and go, the wise and the fanciful.*               45
*I ride my horse and make it go my way.*

## SUNSET

Fold upon fold of light,
Half-heaven of tender fire,
Conflagration of peace,
Wide hearth of the evening world.
How can a cloud give peace,                                  5
Peace speak through bodiless fire
And still the angry world?

Yet now each bush and tree
Stands still within the fire,
And the bird sits on the tree.                              10
Three horses in a field
That yesterday ran wild
Are bridled and reined by light
As in a heavenly field.
Man, beast and tree in fire,                                15
The bright cloud showering peace.

# III

## 'THE HEART COULD NEVER SPEAK'

The heart could never speak
But that the Word was spoken.
We hear the heart break
Here with hearts unbroken.
Time, teach us the art                          5
That breaks and heals the heart.

Heart, you would be dumb
But that your word was said
In time, and the echoes come
Thronging from the dead.                         10
Time, teach us the art
That resurrects the heart.

Tongue, you can only say
Syllables, joy and pain,
Till time, having its way,                        15
Makes the word live again.
Time, merciful lord,
Grant us to learn your word.

## 'AND ONCE I KNEW'

And once I knew
A hasty man,
So small, so kind, and so perfunctory,
Of such an eager kindness
It flushed his little face with standing shame.    5

Wherever he came
He poured his alms into a single hand
That was full then empty. He could not understand.
A foolish or a blessed blindness,
Saint or fool, a better man than you.                    10


## 'OUR APPREHENSIONS GIVE'

Our apprehensions give
Us to another time, and cast
Our hapless horoscope; we did not live
Either in the present or the past.

And thus afloat upon our fears                    5
We scarcely lived, and dread to be.
Straight on the reckless pilot sheers;
Our sons are born upon the sea,

And in the waves will live and die,
Not drift to the murderous strand                    10
But reading for portents in the sky,
Knowing too well, too well, the land.


## 'I SEE THE IMAGE'

I see the image of a naked man,
He stoops and picks a smooth stone from the ground,
Turns round and in a wide arc flings it backward
Towards the beginning. What will catch it,
Hand, or paw, or gullet of sea-monster?                    5
He stoops again, turns round and flings a stone
Straight on before him. I listen for its fall,
And hear a ringing on some hidden place
As if against the wall of an iron tower.

## THE DAY BEFORE THE LAST DAY

If it could come to pass, and all kill all
And in a day or a week we could destroy
Ourselves, that is the beginning only
Of the destruction, for so we murder all
That ever has been, all species and forms,     5
Man and woman and child, beast and bird,
Tree, flower and herb, and that by which they were known,
Sight and hearing and touch, feeling and thought,
And memory of our friends among the dead.
If there were only a single ear that listening heard     10
A footstep coming nearer, it would bring
Annunciation of the world's resurrection.
A sound! We would not know even the silence
Where all was now as if it had never been.

Mechanical parody of the Judgment Day     15
That does not judge but only deals damnation.
Let us essay a hypothetical picture:
'All these and all alone in death's last day.
Before them stretches the indifferent ocean
Where no wave lifts its head and stagnant water     20
Lies spent against the shore. Yet as they wait
A wan light from the east falls on their faces
And they cannot bear the light, and hide in the ground,
Yet have no comfort there, for all are alone.
And there awaken the dark ancestral dreams.     25
They dream that the grave and the sea give up their dead
In wonder at the news of the death of death,
Hearing that death itself is balked by death.
And those who were drowned a year or a thousand years
Come out with staring eyes, foam on their faces,     30
And quaint sea-creatures fixed like jewelled worms
Upon their salt-white brows, sea-tangle breasts,
That they, the once dead, might know the second death.
And then a stir and rumour break their dream,
As men and women at the point of death     35
Rise from their beds and clasp the ground in hope
Imploring sanctuary from grass and root
That never failed them yet and seemed immortal;
And women faint with child-birth lay their babes
Beside them on the earth and turn away,     40
And lovers two by two estranged for ever

Lie each in place without a parting look;
And the dying awakened know
That the generous do not try to help their neighbours,
Nor the feeble and greedy ask for succour,                          45
Nor the fastidious complain of their company,
Nor the ambitious dream of a great chance lost,
Nor the preacher try to save one soul. For all
Think only of themselves and curse the faithless earth.
The sun rises above the sea, and they look and think:              50
"We shall not watch its setting". And all get up
And stare at the sun. But they hear no great voice crying:
"There shall be no more time, nor death, nor change,
Nor fear, nor hope, nor longing, nor offence,
Nor need, nor shame". But all are silent, thinking:                55
"Choose! Choose again, you who have chosen this!
Too late! Too late!"
And then: "Where and by whom shall we be remembered?"'

Imaginary picture of a stationary fear.

# IV

## 'THERE'S NOTHING HERE'

There's nothing here I can take into my hands.
Oh, for the plough stilts and the horse's reins,
And the furrows running free behind me.
The clay still clings to me here, and the heavy smell
Of peat and dung and cattle, and the taste of the dram          5
In my mouth, the last of all.
These things are what I was made for. Send me back.
There is not even a shadow here. How can I live
Without substance and shadow? Am I here
Because I duly read the Bible on Sundays                        10
And drowsed through the minister's sermon? I knew my duty.
But in the evening
I led the young lads to the orra lasses
Across the sound to the other islands. Summer!
How can I live without summer? And the harvest moon           15
And the stooks that looked like little yellow graves, so bonny
And sad and strange, while I walked through them
For a crack with Jock at the bothy: old-farrant stories
He had, I could tell you some queer stories. And then we
    would dander
Among the farms to visit the lasses, climb                     20
Through many a window till morning. But that's no talk
For this place. And then I think of the evenings
After the long day's work . . .

## 'THE REFUGEES BORN FOR A LAND UNKNOWN'

The refugees born for a land unknown
We have dismissed their wrongs, now dull and old,
And little judgment days lost in the dark . . .

'I have fled through land and sea, blank land and sea,
Because my house is besieged by murderers,                    5
And I was wrecked in the ocean, crushed and swept,
Spilling salt angry tears in the salt waves,
My life waste water drawn down through a hole,
Yet lived. And now with alien eyes I see
The flowering trees on the unreal hills,                     10
And in an English garden all afternoon
I watch the bees among the lavender.
Bees are at home, and think they have their place,
And I outside' . . .

'Footsteps on the stairs, two heavy, two light,             15
The door opens. Since then I know nothing
But this room in a place where no doors open.
I think the world died many years ago' . . .

Sometimes they think of the childrens' children left
In the dark [?] kingdom, among their memories.              20

## DIALOGUE

I have heard you cry:
'Oh that the impression of mortality
Could ease its hold and set me free!'
Your workaday face lined with immortal cares,
As if you feared that unawares                               5
The indestructible flowers of Paradise
Might suddenly droop and wither
In a brief thoughtless intermission of your eyes,
And all your journey thither
End in consummate vacancy.                                  10
And you reply: 'All else shall fade but they'.
But I:
'In a long afternoon, long, long ago,
I Adam woke in the one and only eve
Of my sunsetting and beginning                             15
And the first unending of evening.
How can I mourn for what I chose to leave?'
And you: 'Chose you to leave?'
And I: 'Or how deny
The starting point of this my only road                     20
Where other flowers and other pleasures gem

And all my kindred come and go,
Or find a different face from this one face
Twisted with tears and laughter,
On which I read: "All [?] is before and after",                    25
And strong resolve: "To be, to be"?
Then since you are here, off with you, go abroad'.
And you: 'Death also says: "To be".'
And I, impatiently:
'Good man, you are here, not there.                                 30
Here you are not at ease, but must prefer
What you were born for, this your place,
Where all moves towards infinity
At a snail's or a bullet's pace,
Plods, hurries, dawdles: finding, choosing its rhyme,  35
Science gathering gossip of what's so small
And great, no eye can see it.
You must make friends with all
Then wait awhile; how can all things be done in time?
And you are in time'.                                               40
And you: 'I am a footstep from eternity
And cannot lift my foot'.
And I:
'You have denied the root
And think there is nothing here but night and day,     45
Sun and moon, man and star,
And death will take them all away.
But I say
That these great nothings, man and sun and star,
Will say through nothingness: "We are, we are" .'       50
And you: 'I know too well the dupes of time.
Have you not heard them say:
"Do be in time. Be sure you are in time",
With such a strange anxiety?
And once or twice these words: "Oh, let me be,         55
Do let me be",
As if drab [?] Penury [?] itself were trying to say
Through these poor lips . . .'

## 'I HAVE BEEN TAUGHT'

I have been taught by dreams and fantasies
Learned from the friendly and the darker phantoms
And got great knowledge and courtesy from the dead
Kinsmen and kinswomen, ancestors and friends
But from two mainly                                                   5
Who gave me birth.

Have learned and drunk from that unspending good
These founts whose learned windings keep
My feet from straying
To the deadly path                                                   10

That leads into the sultry labyrinth
Where all is bright and the flare
Consumed and shrivels
The moist fruit.

Have drawn at last from time which takes away               15
And taking leaves all things in their right place
An image of forever,
The One and whole.

And now that time grows shorter, I perceive
That Plato's is the truest poetry,                               20
And that these shadows
Are cast by the true.

# *Appendices*

# I

## UNCOLLECTED POEMS

### TO A DREAM

Silent you rise out of your far, dim source,
  Shadowy dream,
Like a white fountain that self-shrouding pours
  Its broken, vaporous stream,
Fettered in its own wings spread helplessly          5
  Like a great butterfly
That a sad memory chains to one lone spot,
In its own trancéd passion deep forgot.

So self-exiled, self-lost, accusing thing,
  You sway still quivering,                          10
Until a sudden tempest shakes
Your tresses, and your murmuring breaks
Into a sound more doleful than the sighs
  Of sightless Hope with ever straining eyes.
O then my palsied spirit lies in deep despite,      15
And my immutable will cries in affright,
  And my accuséd flesh
Knows its dark, mortal pang, and shudders in its mesh!

O snowy bird entangled in my shame,
  O lovely star from which I shroud                  20
  My face in a cold, alien cloud,
O regal, realmless ghost without a name,
  O pure, eternal Me
From whom forever through blind paths I flee,
  O Wrong deep-set and set immortally,               25
O timeless Truth which makes all Time a liar,
  O Heaven-forged Enemy,
O hallowed, stolen Fire,

279

O Beauty deep entombed in heavy flesh,
O Freedom captured in my spirit's mesh                    30
Yet still uncapturable, O bright sea
   Around and over me,
I fly always and can but fly to thee!

I cannot turn away my face from thine,
   Defeated, starry thing,                              35
Thy fingers loose with gentle touch divine
   The abyss-begotten, earth-forged ring
     Of things immense and small
     To which our soul is thrall,
And spread around us deep infinity.                        40
   Yet I can never know thee, evermore
     Must seek to follow where thy light path is,
   On wings of my own helplessness to soar
     Through the forbidden, fire-girt gates of bliss
      Wide open implacably.                          45
But still is conflict left, in heavenly pain
To seek, to seek, and never to attain,
Until from dissolution's dreadful sea
I rise in a new immortality.

Our life is like an ocean of dim night                     50
   In which thy star-engendered radiance falls
To lave its fire-bewildered lovely light
   Until wide morning calls
     From the far, lonely deep,
     And up the mounting, fire-upbuilded steep     55
Thou climb'st serene and fair,
And tak'st thy seat on the blue mount of air.


# BALLAD OF THE BLACK DOUGLAS

The king lay on his dowie bed,
   The may was on the tree:
'O ride ye for the Black Douglás,
   For I maun swiftly dee.

'O ride ye for the Black Douglás                           5
   Ere I hae quit my pain,
My laithly body wearies me
   And I wad sune be gane.'

They rade a' night, and wan at last
    The Douglas castle wa',              10
They've brought him in the morning mirk
    Into the royal ha'.

'O what is this that lies sae white?
    Is't may plucked frae the tree?'
'It's the king's body that's covered a',      15
    Wi' the white leprosy.'

Black Douglas knelt by the king's bed
    And kissed his snaw-white cheek,
He turned awa' and grat fu' sair,
    But nae word could he speak.        20

'O it's mony battles hae we focht,
    Gane mony gates together,
But ere thou lie where I am laid
    We still maun try anither.

'Thou'lt close my heart when it is cauld     25
    In a gowd casket fine,
Thou'lt carry it across the sea
    Till thou come to Palestine.

'And when thou see'st Jerusalem
    Set in a leafy den,             30
Light doon and mak' a grave for me,
    And turn thee hame again.

'Aft hae I langed, Jerusalem,
    To walk thy winding braes,
But sune I'll walk the earth nae mair,     35
    For death has closed all ways.'

The king has ta'en his true knight's hand,
    And turned him tae the wa'.
Black Douglas felt his fingers twine
    In the last deathly thraw.       40

'O I will close thy hameless heart
    In a gowd casket fine,
But weel I ken thy last journéy
    Will siccarly be mine.'

Black Douglas went beyond the sea,     45
  His lance within his hand,
But he never cam' wi' his gude men
  Into the Holy Land.

He never saw Jerusalem's
  Green shaws and flowery braes.     50
His king and he lie side by side
  In a far lanely place.


## PASTORAL

Scottish cattle are sleek and proud,
  Through flowery fields at ease they range.
The unemployed must show themselves
  Each morning at the Labour Exchange.

The Scottish pulpits are as full     5
  As a drove of fatted stirks.
The unemployed are empty as
  The Sunday sermons and the kirks.

Scottish adultery de luxe,
  Reported, is devoid of grace.     10
The unemployed cannot afford
  Marriage lines to save their face.

A Scottish bullock has a look
  About him that you will not see
In workless men shuffling their feet     15
  Outside some public W.C.

A Scottish bullock ends his days
  Slain by a skilled hygienic hand.
God looks after the unemployed
  When they can neither walk nor stand.     20

Our stirks shall yet sing Scots Wha Hae
  In kilts. Our lustier bulls and stallions
We'll educate at Balliol.
  The rest shall swell the Kirk's battalions.

Praise God from whom all blessings flow,    25
Praise Him all bullocks here below,
Praise him in chief the Scottish Kirk,
For He is kind to stot and stirk.

## INDUSTRIAL SCENE

The women talk, tea-drinking by the fire
   In the back parlour. The rose afternoon
Stiffens out in the street to fog and mire.
   The blood-red bullying West confronts the moon.

The house-tops, sharpening, saw into the sky.    5
   Factory sirens wail and Rest is born,
A clockwork centipede that lumbering by
   Decorates heaven with silhouettes of horn.

Incandescent burners' arctic glare
   Strikes dead a thousand families as they sit    10
At high tea in the tenements. The air
   Takes at the tidal corner of the street

The hundred-horse-power pub's wave-shouldering boom
   And thickened voices babbling Judgement Day.
At the big house the Owner waits his doom    15
   While his Rhine-maiden daughters sit and play

Wagner and Strauss. Beneath the railway bridge
   In patient waxwork line the lovers stand.
Venus weeps overhead. Poised on the ridge
   The unemployed regard the Promised Land.    20

## TIME SONG

If I were blind I still could hold
This globe of emerald and of gold,
This world to rich oblivion sold,
In the round heaven of my mind
As safe as in the other's mould.    5
But Time, Time, Time is blind,
What he has lost who else can find?
The world's hill, the day's tower

283

A glance, a breath, a sigh ago
He's swept away in a glittering stour.                    10
And there's no wizard's wand can show
The sleeping bride shut in her bower,
The day wreathed in its mound of snow
That, melting, leaves no trace behind,
For as he passes Time is blind.                           15

Could Time bring back that glance, that breath
This little and the other death
Would be no more. One stride would take
Him to the passion-weaving Tree
From which the spool was all unwound        20
Whose spinning is the only sound
Since then. Or if he'd turn his head
One glance would draw Eurydice
Obediently from the dead,
And he, false Orpheus, that could make      25
Eden's dream into a brake,
From coursing shades would turn and find his Shade.

There is a saying that if Time were
To turn again he would not find
The sight so beautiful or so rare           30
That looking would delight his mind
More than a glance, a breath, a sigh,
But that at last he'll end his race
At the same point where first he stayed,
Which done, his wanderings will trace       35
The circle of Eternity,
And all unmade will be new-made
While Time rests on forever by
The starting and the finishing tree.

## 'NO MORE OF THIS TRAPPED GAZING'

No more of this trapped gazing. These sights are not
For your deciphering. So might Agamemnon
Have pored upon the Grecian tents one night,
Had they been Time and Troy Eternity.
And next day came the battle.                            5
                                        If a look
Could change the thing it looked on, this device

Might serve all purposes.
                                        Odysseus
Knew one untroubled hour of musing when          10
He sat outside the town beside the well
While Nausicaa went on into the evening
To tell of his approach. (But when he rose
There was no change in the stormy sea behind
And stormy fate ahead.)                          15
                            If you could hold
Complete in one great glance this reverse pattern
(That's all you'll see) you'd be a god, although
On the wrong side of Heaven.
                                    Mad Hölderlin  20
Praised God and Man, cut off from God and Man
In a bright twisted world.
                                Beethoven lived
In such a world as your one.
                                    Caesar died   25
On a small hill like any other hill.

You are immortal and you have been given
Mortality as well. Hence this possession.


## 'IT MIGHT BE THE DAY AFTER
## THE LAST DAY'

It might be the day after the last day,
The trumpets still, the nations gone away,
The visiting deities left in a crowd,
And the sun itself wrapped in a single cloud.
Even a look today is like a rebirth               5
Of the ill-used, bountiful, menial earth.
Forget that she is not all. Remember only
That as we sit here we two are not lonely,
That this is worth seeing, if it were only for
These men and women walking along the shore      10
In ill-cut clothes fit for our curious kindred.
O turn on them your from death uplifted head!
Then watch the wave falling and falling and falling,
Hark to the bird from the sea-castle calling,
Pore on these smooth illegible rocks that stand  15
Like quiet grazing beasts on the soft sand,
And think this is your home: air, sea and land.

## LETTERS

### I

Forgiveness now, about to be,
Shrivels and dies, and Memory
Stands in its place. Drawn and old
The offence sits where it sat that night,
Dead venom bubbles, smooth and cold,                    5
That once ran hot into the mould.
I see your tongue stretched back and tight,
Recoiling in the gathered spring,
I see the sideward sweeping sting
Striking secure at all that's mine,                    10
While round us sit the idle ring
Beneath the smooth unmoving light.
Your tongue rolled backward to the root
And then. . . . We both were destitute,
I know, that moment. A malign                          15
Power acted for us, chose alike
Me to be struck and you to strike.
It was not you. Yet how efface
The spider's web spun on your face
That instant, prise it from its place?                 20

Yes, what can we do? Tell, help me how
To untie the knot of Then and Now,
Re-enact the act, then slough it clean,
Leaving the pure essential scene,
Never touched light and hurtless air.                  25

It was not we. But we were there.
Our eyes saw. Can they see again
A different spectacle? Extricate
The fatal actors from the Fate
That moved the act? Come, let us feign                 30
A desperate reconciliation,
Rise woundless from our separate palls,
Retrieve our parts but keep our souls
Our own.
              The ever-waiting walls  35
Close in. We are there. I see the spring
Just moving.

> Now, if we can fling
> Our whole weight on it, we are free,
> And full forgiveness yet may be! 40

## THE REFUGEES

*Chorus:*
Listening in London for the Angelus,
Unthinkingly we plunge in the abyss
That opens anywhere, in a room, a street,
And destroys us and is sweet
Compared with this new world that we've made bare 5
With the salt of distance and despair.
Oh, the crystal chasm where through a storm of weeping
We watch the unchanging reapers reaping
In our own valley and the roads wind
As if they had only the sky to find, 10
Or mountain hut with its single tree,
And far within, the unbroken family.

This we must not give way to, this sweet hell,
This poison that once made us well:
Remembrance. Here no reaper reaps the lea, 15
And we have learnt a new geography:
Ourselves hurled headlong east, west, north and south
As if by some new monster's mouth
Which spews out father, mother, daughter, son
To every quarter, that, when all is done, 20
Each one, alone, denuded, rent,
Might lie like some still shuddering continent
Past latitude. This our Newfoundland, this
The map that shows us what the world's shape is.
A son's or husband's breast 25
Soars higher here than the Alps' or Andes' crest,
Carved by such storms, stripped by such expert rage
At once, as by a geological age.
This land no one but we have found,
New precipices, gulfs without a ground, 30
Deserts and quicksands and trackless caves,
And all about acres of graves
For the dead, the absentees. This we must chart
And learn our wilderness by heart,
For this is ours and, homeless, we must make 35

287

Ourselves our home, if only for home's sake.
Since home is not the corner where
We lived and worked, and only earth and air
Remain there now; since those who have come
Into our rooms, homeless at home, 40
From such a tenancy cannot create
A kind all-welcoming house-god, killing hate;
And since where we are now, others will be,
To win—who knows?—an amazed majority,
We must shape here a new philosophy. 45

*The Mother:*
The day that Heinrich died
A crack ran down the side
Of the town hill.
The pine wood moved away,
In bits the garden lay, 50
Beyond the hill
The mountains rose and sank,
Time had nothing to say,
And all the clocks were blank.
Only the sun stood still. 55
It was a hot June day.

The hill grew whole again,
The wavering wood came back,
The clocks' tick-tock, tick-tock
Startled the stumbling hours. 60
The crooked flowers
Grew straighter. Bright and doomed
The garden bloomed.
The mountains stood, the sun
Moved on, moved on. 65

*The Father:*
It came that morning,
Left without warning,
Stood at the door,
A small self-centred visitor:
Smooth urn in which the post 70
Delivered dead sons and fathers free,
A nimble host
Made to one measure,
That died in misery in a ditch

288

At death's dull leisure:                                        75
Now not a sigh, not a twitch,
Bone-ash at most.
What philosophy
Can drive that visitor from the mind
And make bereavement blind and kind?                            80

*1st Voice:*
To tremble in Liverpool or Glasgow
At the name of the Gestapo.

*2nd Voice:*
To stiffen beside a foreign lamp
Thinking of the concentration camp,
To sit in fear                                                  85
Among kind-hearted strangers,
Counting the secret list of dangers,
Cut off in safety, thinking: I am here.

*3rd Voice:*
To start awake at five each morning.
The secret police came at five each morning                     90
To search the Jewish houses in Vienna.
We rose and walked the streets, the streets were full of Jews.
We went into the country, watched the ploughmen
Stride carelessly behind their oxen, safe,
The red fox creeping through the bushes, safe,                  95
The birds busy along the hedge-rows, safe,
The white smoke rising from the farm chimneys.
At nine we went back to our rooms.
The house police kept hours, their work was finished,
Done for the day at nine. From five to nine,                    100
That was the dangerous hour. And now we start awake
At five each morning. It is not safe to sleep
After five in the morning. We shall not sleep in the morning
After five, but start awake on the stroke of five,
And hear the ploughman whistling, safe, in the field.          105

*Chorus:*
Oh Lord have pity
On this our wandering city,
That is not good or wise or witty.
And since you made us,
Don't let the airmen raid us,                                   110

The gunners cannonade us,
The germs invade us,
The U boats starve us,
And statesmen cook and carve us,
And bludgeons equalize us,                    115
And chemists carbonize us,
And great shells croak us,
And the gas choke us . . .

A crack ran through . . .
          [as 'The Refugees' in *The Narrow Place*]


## RIMBAUD

I will not dream your clumsy dreams for you,
(I know how false and true they are),
I will not make more real for you,
The hackneyed, knockabout, seesaw pair
Evil and good, and their preposterous war,          5
(I know how old and new they are).
I will not pander to your poring
On the great spectacle, poetic spectacle,
On which you glut your intellectual whoring
For genuine vicarious damnation,                    10
Mincing along the mawkish road to Hell.
I will not stop to admire
The good in the light, the wicked in the wood,
The fray and the smoking pyre.
I fight beside the good,                            15
I seek salvation.


## IN A TIME OF MORTAL SHOCKS

Live on through these and learn what is this life,
Pure spirit indwelling,
Live on through these,
And know they were not made to please
Heart, hand or eye or ear or tongue                 5
Or any member.
Then fill your solitary fife
Now in the senses' sad December
And sing your silent song.
This tale is only for your telling                  10

Who can remember
What cold flesh wreathed in its snowdrift sorrow
Has thought but never known,
And borrow
A song from the Silent One                                            15
To still the many,
Since there's not any
Tongue or syllable to express
Distress.
Be in the wound before                                                20
It gapes aghast, be nearer
Than the familiar bullet, clearer
Than pain searching the nerves in widening reaches,
Be wiser
Than learned loss that baldly teaches                                 25
Letter by letter what could have been,
Dull difficult history. Be slyer
Than Terror the Great, the gaunt ten-foot-long guiser.
Be closer
Than the tongue-shaking lie is to the liar.                           30
Lose to the loser.
Be at the root
No fear can find, the foot.
There stay secure.
There is your only place of safety. Stay                              35
There in your house and keep your day.

## TO THE CZECH LANGUAGE
## BY IVAN JELINEK

TRANSLATED BY EDWIN MUIR

When it rains in England
I hear from mothers' mouths the names of their children
And my own among them in the still-life of vowels.

When it rains in England
I hear two women tenderly speaking in Czech                            5
And the words are only another name for love.

It rains on my eyes, on the harbour, on the deck,
And fishes swim and swim round the girls' heads,
One of them with the key in its mouth, as though
It would leap the weir—longing for speech kills me.    10

When it rains in England
The drowned day crawls towards the dark, a body
Without a soul—as though myself were drowned.

When it rains in England
Two lovers should light on the banks of the Morava    15
A candle, and pray at the weir for a soul.


## THE SHRINE

There have been friendly gods about this place,
Known on the earth or nameless; you can trace
Almost their footprints and their soundless flight.

While in the sky Time's tattered pennons pass,
No shadow from them falls upon the grass    5
Walled in its drowsy Arcady of light,

Where now the heavenly ghosts with silent foot
Bless every grass down to the very root
Passing, repassing in their endless rite.

But how by them could peace be so made known,    10
Descend, settle and stay on flower and stone,
Firm as a world and fragile as a feather?

Or by some man who had grown so happy and good,
The thoughtless days and seasons caught his mood
And hung in thanks above him his own weather?    15

There have been many gods about this place.
Upon this patch of grass sometime have stood
In friendly talk a god and a man together.

## THE NORTHERN ISLANDS

In favoured summers
These islands have the sun all to themselves
And light a toy to play with, weeks on end.
The empty sky and waters are a shell
Endlessly turning, turning the wheel of light,     5
While the tranced waves run wavering up the sand.
The beasts sleep when they can, midnight or midday,
Slumbering on into unending brightness.
The green, green fields give too much, are too rank
With beautiful beasts for breeding or for slaughter.    10
The horses, glorious useless race, are leaving.
Have the old ways left with them, and the faith,
Lost in this dream too comfortable and goodly
To make room for a blessing? Where can it fall?
The old ways change in the turning, turning light,    15
Taking and giving life to life from life.

## SONNET

You will not leave us, for You cannot, Lord.
We are the inventors of disloyalty,
And every day proclaim we dare not be
Ourselves' or Yours: at every point absurd.
For this was forged the counterfeiting word    5
By which the hours beguile eternity
Or cry that You are dead Who cannot die.
So in a word You are glorified and abjured.

Yet say You died and left where once You were
Nothing at all—man, beast and plant as now    10
In semblance, yet mere obvious nature—how
Could the blind paradox, the ridiculous
Find entrance then? What would remain with us?
Nothing, nothing at all, not even despair.

## SONNET

Do not mourn still your generation's blood,
And face rubbed bare by reasonable fears,
And unintentional tears

That fall and are lost. Better to chew the cud
Of ignorant earlier days (Forgive us, time)                    5
Before experience preached the certainty
That what will be will be,
Telling us that we shall commit our crime.

Past odds and ends sustain us. We can suck
Courage from buried bravery's dear downfall,        10
Learn from forgotten fools to chance our luck
And cut our losses, piously recall
Those who believed and did not understand,
And built in faith and folly in this ancient land.

# II

# EARLY VERSIONS

## BALLAD OF ETERNAL LIFE
### I

I knew not whence my breath had streamed,
    Nor where had hid my clay,
Until my soul stood by my side
    As on my bed I lay.

It showed me Chaos and the Word,       5
    The dust, the moving Hand,
Myself, the many and the one,
    The dead, the living land.

Faintly at first I heard the sound,
    Far distant, of the sea:       10
A rushing sound – it filled my ears,
    And passéd silently.

I stood beside a dark blue shore,
    Beneath a dark blue sky.
The light came from no vanished star,       15
    The sun had not passed by.

Faintly uprist like graven mist
    A wraith upon the mere,
Burned clear, and she hung movelessly,
    Like a suspended spear.       20

O strange to see her stand so still
    Amid the wallowing sea!
With lifted hand I saw her stand
    And make a sign to me.

## II

The billows rose; down sank the land;                    25
   The sea closed in like lead;
The waves like leopards tumbled on
   Far above my head.

Slow closed the mesh, slow waxed my flesh,
   Darkly I came to birth;                    30
I rose; the sky was white as snow,
   As ashes black the earth:

The ashes of millennial fires
   Extinguished utterly!
In towering blocks the twisted rocks                    35
   Stuck up above the sea.

Blithely I swam, a moving thing,
   On the vast and moveless mere;
And headless things swam in blind swift rings
   Around. I did not fear                    40

Till, when I grasped the flame-scarred rock,
   A chill sea-creature caught
My bonéd hand with boneless hand –
   Through all a day I fought.

I struck it prone; I walked alone                    45
   In alien horizons:
The low-browed voiceless animals
   Were my companions.

Asleep, a huge forgotten brood
   Lay round like tree-stumps old:                    50
The dragons. From their eyelids fell,
   Soft-rayed, the rustling gold.

## III

What next I saw ill can I tell,
   And ill can understand;
But yet I know that once I went                    55
   Through that magic land.

296

It was a waste of jagged rock
   (Nor beast nor shrub was nigh),
Whereon a glittering palace lay
   Like ruins of the sky.           60

I crept within; I stood within.
   Far down the toppling ledge
Scaffolds of wood in order stood
   From edge to shuddering edge.

And spiders wove and silence lay      65
   On each deserted wall.
Like a wild stream from beam to beam
   I fell through that great hall.

Fell, till the last beam held me fast!
   And, swift as spouted light,     70
I sprang – each beam like air did seem –
   To the bewildered height.

In clanging words, in shattering words,
   Through all my body ran:
'I leave the blind abyss behind,     75
   I battle up to man!'

But soon the roof with final seal
   Lay full upon my head.
I beat my face like a blunted mace
   Against it, beat and bled;     80
The torrent dyed shoulder and side,
   Like a fierce fury, red.

And the dumb stone did cry and groan,
   Slow turned, and made a way!
The sky leapt up, the stars showered out,   85
   Moveless the planets lay.

## IV

Day came. The light lay cold upon
   The tarn, the watching mound.
The rushes like ranged frozen spears
   Were still. There was no sound.     90

But on the high rim of the sky
  Two clouds like phantoms fell.
They grew; they moved together like
  Two armies terrible.

They met; they broke in fire-split smoke –     95
  A red ball in the sky!
A ball of fire – it raged, and turned
  To ashes suddenly.

In the pale sky a blackened sun
  In wide blind circles whirled,     100
From which bright serpents woke, and shook
  Their fanged flames o'er the world.

Their pennon fires shot out in spires
  And split the cracking mail!
'Twas as if hell with plumes of fire     105
  Upon the air did sail.

The planet drank its fires; it stood
  In heaven immovably.
As if its fear had clamped it there,
  It stood immovably;     110

Till its fear indrawn in furious spawn
  A myriad legs gave birth:
A monstrous spider, down the air
  It clambered to the earth.

Its head was like a wooden prow     115
  Which has voyaged noiselessly
O'er the white seas of perished worlds;
  It smiled disdainfully.

Its brow was like a thin-sheathed flame;
  Its eyes were as red as blood;     120
Its lips were as thin as smirking sin;
  Its belly and feet were mud.

Like a fierce bird upflew my sword
  Into the towering sky;
I struck the beast upon the brow;     125
  It did not move nor cry;

But, like hard marble melting slow,
  It softly, softly smiled.
My body grew a storm wherethrough
  The sword in lightnings wild       130
Rove and rent; *it* sideways bent
  Meek as a wistful child.

The white sword streamed in running fire,
  The hard mail burst in two,
The white-robed, white-winged spirit up    135
  In wavering circles flew.

Hastily sank the quivering mail
  Deep, deep in the darksome ground.
Amazed I saw the trampled grass,
  The tarn, the stilly mound.       140

### V

O fair are freedom and victory!
  The sweet sky rained with wings.
I was so happy that I seemed
  Like one of those fair things.

For, as through still clear waters, fell    145
  Dissolving phantoms white,
Like wavering dreams slow shaken down
  From a great fount of light.

And sweetly, sweetly from my flesh
  I felt the fetters slip.       150
With pennons fair on the blue air
  I sailed, a white-plumed ship.

Onward I flew o'er seas so clear
  That still my wraith below,
Like a mute pilgrimaging thought,    155
  Inexorable did go.

There she who once in Chaos stood,
  In the first battling night,
Bloomed silent in the burning air,
  Like deeper light in light.      160

We linked our hands (as one they seemed),
   We rose in wavering rings;
Two plumes fell down the glittering well;
   We mounted on two wings.

Up, up we fared; the light flew back;      165
   We saw the throne of God.
We stood upon the streets of Heaven:
   Our joy rose and abode.

Then, wavering, we turned each to each,
   Looked deep, and faultering kissed.      170
The watching host were silent as
   A sea at morning whist.

## VI

These things my soul showed clear to me
   As in a trance I lay;
And I shall know them while I live,      175
   Through day and night and day.

## FROM CHORUS OF THE NEWLY DEAD
### (EARLY VERSION)

*The Harlot:*
I wake in the morning
   And comb my hair,
And think the scorning
   And guilt not there.

And sitting and seeming,      5
   I am again
A maiden dreaming
   Of love and men.

Forever and ever
   Lust in my bed,      10
And shame wherever
   I turn my head!

The mean great streets
  See where I lie.
The traffic beats;             15
  A harlot for aye!

Till the day is done
  I sit on my bed,
And watch the sun
  Roll o'er my head.          20

Then, burning, lonely,
  I walk the street;
Walk, and hear only
  My own dull feet;

Walk on and on             25
  Till far seems near.
Inscrutable One,
  Why am I here?

*The Saint:*
The sightless larvae slumbered
  Entombed in narrow clay.
Within, the night ruled changeless;
  Without, strove night and day.

Blind in a ring of splendour,     5
  It naught could hear or see;
But in its cell dawned wanly
  Form and infinity.

The day, like some great dragon,
  Spread wide its spanless wings;     10
And like prone shadows rising,
  Rose up all living things.

'All Being and all Beauty
  In my blind body are;
The immeasurable ocean,     15
  The unattainable star!'

The prisoned cosmos travailed,
  Deep, deep within the mire;
And pierced the shell with flickering
  Wings of fire.       20

'O ecstasy! O glory!
  O death-despising pain!
Infinity, infinity,
  I fly to thee again!'

*Chorus:*
We shall return no more, who once did call
  Returnless birth unto us. Now no more
Our eyes shall darken when our houses fall,
  Nor tears drop when we leave some little shore.

We knew not when, like moths from darkness turning,  5
  We flew into the bright compacted knot,
Whether dumb Fate was beckoning or spurning;
  And our lives passed, and still we knew it not.

But now like a clear-written chart we see
  Our errors and our sorrows in the sun,    10
And all that ought not and that ought to be,
  Spread there complete until the world is done.

But, long past grief, long past far-drawn desire,
  We turn with wavering steps into the gloom;
And wait in patience till a blinding fire    15
  Shall light our unimaginable doom.

# III

# REVISED VERSIONS

## THE LOST LAND

And like a thought ere morning I am gone;
My furrowing prow through silence whispers on,
I float far in through circles soft and dim,
Till a grey steeple lifts above the rim,

From which a chime falls far across the waves.          5
I see wind-lichened walls the slow tide laves,
The houses waver towards me, melt and run,
And open out in ranks, and one by one.

I see the prickly weeds, the flowers small,
The moss like magic on the creviced wall,          10
The doors wide open where the wind comes in,
Making a whispering presence, salt and thin.

And then I look again and do not know
This town where foreign people come and go,
O, this is not my country. To the roar          15
Of angered seas I wander by the shore,

Where towering cliffs hem in the thin-tongued strait,
And far below like battling dragons wait
The serpent-fangéd caves that gnash the sea,
And make a barren barking constantly;          20

And stop where in moon-blasted valleys stay
Dreadful and lovely mists at full noon-day.
I gather giant flowers, discrowned and dead,
And make a withered chaplet for my head,

And sleep upon a green embattled mound                    25
With childhood's labyrinths engirdled round,
And I have been here many times before,
And shall return hereafter many more,

While past huge mountains and across great seas
That haven lies, and my long-sought release.              30


## THE SONG

All that day I was teased by memories knocking
At some disused, stuck door of an empty room
Sealed up for forty years by myself and time.
They could not get to me nor I to them.
And yet they knocked. And since I could not answer,       5
Since where they knocked was a different door of time,
I felt I had gone away from them and myself,
As if they and I were not contemporary;
For I had gone away, my dreams left only,
Where all is changed, time, place, identity,              10
Where fables turn to beasts and beasts to fables.

However this may be, that night I dreamed
That towards the end of such another day
Spent in such thoughts, but in some other place,
I was returning from a long day's work—                   15
What work I have forgotten—and had to cross
A park lost somewhere in the world, yet now
Present and whole to me as I to it:
Utilitarian strip of grass and trees—
A short-cut for poor clerks to unhallowed rooms.          20
I stopped beside the gate—as how often before?—
When from the park poured out the resonant moaning
Of some great beast in anguish.

I was afraid, and yet I pushed the gate—
As how often before?—passed through and went my way,      25
When on my right appeared what seemed a rock.
I stood awhile, and looking again I saw
The huge hind-quarters of some giant creature.
As heavy as earth it stood and mourned alone,
Horse, or centaur, or wide-winged Pegasus,                30
But far too strange for any fabulous name.

And then in terror lest the thing should move
And come on me, I ran to the farther gate,
Stood there and listened. By then darkness had fallen,
But still that wonder                                          35
Sent out its moan not meant for others' ears,
A long breath drawn by pain.

I thought, now it will move. And then it moved.
The lamentation ceased, great hoofs rose and fell
Gently, as treading out a meditation,                         40
Then broke in a thunder clap, and charged the gate,
Yet could not pass—oh pity!—that simple barrier;
Turned back again in final overthrow,
And beat on the ground as if for entrance there.
The dream worked on. The clamour died; the hoofs    45
Beat on a different ground; silence; a drumming
As of wild swans taking their highway south
From the murdering ice; hoofs, wings far overhead
Climbing the sky; pain raised that wonder there.
The drumming died away.                                        50

Was it these hoofs, I thought, that knocked all day
With no articulate message, but this vision
That had no tongue to utter its mystery?
What wound in the world's side and we unknowing
Lay open and bleeding now? What present anguish     55
Drew that long dirge from the earth-haunting marvel?
And why that earthly visit, unearthly pain?
I was not dreaming now, but thinking the dream.
Then all was quiet, the park was its own again,
And I on my road to my familiar lodgings               60
A world away. I awoke and thought, The Song.


## THE CEREMONY

The lid flew off, and all the desolations,
As through a roaring poet's impudent throat,
Poured out their incontinent lamentations.
It seemed somewhere they were trying to take a vote
That in the hurry and din could not be taken,             5
For ground and air were shaken.
But all as stale and sad
As a cashiered and spavined army of horse

Charging behind their false archaic neigh
Against a fantastical force                                    10
Ten thousand years and a little space [?] away;
All so debased by time it was almost mad.
We were assembled for a ceremony,
Compelled by this music, forced to hear.
But as we listened spiteful memory,                           15
The secret enemy within the ear,
Said, 'This, this is your language, this the rune
You never read, this is your oldest tune'.
At which we cried, 'Push, push it back under the ground.
We will not listen. We                                        20
Will not endure that sound'.
And in the clamour could not hear a voice
That seemed to say, 'Rejoice'.

# IV

# LIST OF OTHER VERSES

*Juvenilia* (all in *The New Age* Vols. XIV–XVIII, and under pseud-
onym 'Edward Moore'):

'Salutation' XIV (6 Nov. 1913) 25–6; 'A Chronicle of Woe' XIV
(11 Dec. 1913) 185; 'A question to My Love' XIV (18 Dec. 1913)
197; 'Address to Wage Slaves' XIV (18 Dec. 1913) 216–17; 'Utopia'
XIV (16 Apr. 1914) 742; 'Sleep's Betrayals' XV (7 May 1914) 20;
'To Present-Day Critics' XV (2 Jul. 1914) 208; 'To the War Poets'
XV (8 Oct. 1914) 553; 'To the City Class' XV (22 Oct. 1914) 601;
'Metamorphosis' XVI (5 Nov. 1914) 6; 'The Forsaken Princess'
XVI (25 Feb. 1915) 463; 'Epigrams' XVIII (23 Mar. 1916) 496, (6
Apr. 1916) 544–5, (13 Apr. 1916) 568–9, (20 Apr. 1916) 595.

*Dramatic*

'Road to Fotheringay'. On life of Mary Queen of Scots. Broad-
cast on BBC Scottish Home Service 26 January 1943.
'The Return'. Short verse drama on the return of Odysseus. No
date. NLS 19653 ff. 99–114.

*Translations*

Hauptmann, Gerhart. *Dramatic Works* Vol. VIII. London and
New York 1925. Contains *Indipohdi*, *The White Saviour* and *A
Winter Ballad*, translated by Edwin and Willa Muir.
Hauptmann, Gerhart. *Dramatic Works* Vol. IX. London and
New York 1929. Contains *Veland*, translated by Edwin Muir.
Broch, Hermann. *The Sleepwalkers*. London and Boston 1932.
The third part contains verse, probably translated mainly by Willa
Muir.

# NOTES

Abbreviations

Muir's works
A—*An Autobiography*
CND—*Chorus of the Newly Dead*
CP 52—*Collected Poems 1921–1951*
CP 60—*Collected Poems 1921–1958*
CP 63/84—*Collected Poems 1963/1984*
ELS—*Essays on Literature and Society* 2nd ed. 1965
EP—*The Estate of Poetry*
FP—*First Poems*
JK—*John Knox*
JP—*Journeys and Places*
L—*The Labyrinth*
NP—*The Narrow Place*
OFE—*One Foot in Eden*
PT—*Poor Tom*
SF—*The Story and the Fable*
SJ—*Scottish Journey*
SL—*Selected Letters*
SP—*Six Poems*
TB—*The Three Brothers*
TI—*The Truth of Imagination*
V—*The Voyage*
VTT—*Variations on a Time Theme*

Libraries
BL—British Library
H—Harvard University Library
NLS—National Library of Scotland.

Periodical titles, given at the beginning of each note, are thereafter within that note normally referred to by initials.

**Textual History**

This is not a variorum edition. Those who want to see Muir's very numerous, mostly minor, revisions between periodical publication, first volume publication, *CP 52* and *CP 60* may consult Mr Robert Hollander's *A Textual and Bibliographical Study of the Poems of Edwin Muir* (1962). Here place and date of first publication, if earlier than the relevant volume, are given, and only a very selective list of significant re-visions.

## Sources

The chief repositories of papers, etc relating to Muir's poems are:

The British Library

—Add 52409 ff. 1–8 Copy of *CND* with MS amendments; ff. 9–10 Printed copy of 'The Song' with MS amendments; ff. 11–15 Sheets with drafts of late poems; ff. 16–33 Notebook with ideas for poems, drafts of late poems, etc.

—Add 52920. Letters to Sydney Schiff with TSS (ff. 213–26) of ten early poems, with variations from the printed texts.

—CUP 504 b. 13–18. Copies of *VTT*, *V*, *NP*, *OFE*, *JP* and *CP 52* with MS amendments written in by Muir during his last year, used for setting *CP 60*.

Harvard University, Lamont Library

—D 845.5.1. Tape 1. Recording, made 3 November 1955, of Muir read-ing 'Prometheus', 'The Grave of Prometheus', 'Telemachos Remembers', 'The Horses' (*OFE*), 'The Charm', 'The Late Wasp', 'The Late Swallow', 'The Tower' (spoken from memory), 'Troy', 'Merlin', 'The Recurrence', 'The Good Man in Hell', 'The Return of Odysseus', 'Oedipus'.

—MT 845.3.2. Tape 2. Recording, made not earlier than 1957, of Muir reading 'The Tower', 'After 1984', 'The Strange Return', 'The Brothers', 'Images' II and III, 'The Desolations', 'The Combat' (with comment).

Library of Congress, Recorded Sound Division

—T 2398. Recording, made 12 December 1955, of Muir reading, with commentary, 'The Animals', 'Horses' (*FP*), 'The Toy Horse', *VTT* X, 'Adam's Dream', 'One Foot in Eden', *'The Wayside Station', 'The Con-firmation', 'In Love for Long', 'The Late Wasp', *'The Late Swallow', *'The Labyrinth', *'The Combat', 'Telemachos Remembers', *'The Rider Victory', 'For Ann Scott-Moncrieff', *The Transfiguration'. A record and a cassette (PL 23) taken from the tape and not including the poems starred, is available from the Library; and application may be made to have the whole tape copied.

National Library of Scotland

—Mf Sec MSS 464. Microfilm of BL's copy of *CND* with other material now in NLS.

—MS 19651. Copy of *FP* with MS amendments.

—MS 19652. Copy of *CND* (different from BL's) with MS amendments.

—MS 19653. MS and TS drafts and fair copies, etc of poems written between 1941 and 1958; TS of 'The Return', an unpublished drama.

—MS 19657. Notebook, used at Newbattle mainly for *A*, has also drafts of poems, etc.

—MS 19663. Notebook, used at Prague 1947–8, has MS drafts of poems, etc.

—MS 19668. Diary 1937–9 records thoughts, dreams, etc. Extracts, revised, were published in *SF*, but there is much in the diary not in *SF* and some items in *SF* not in the diary.

—MS 19669. Notebook, used at Swaffham Prior 1957–8, records dreams, ideas for poems, etc.

—MS 19703 ff. 27–30. Four MS drafts of 'Orpheus Dream'.

—Tape 5.4172. Two tapes. Tape 1 has readings by Mrs Muir of 'The Transfiguration', 'The Combat', 'Song: 'Why should your face'', 'The Myth', 'The Island', 'The Animals'. Tape 2 is a copy of Harvard's Tape 1.

St Andrews University Library has a large deposit of papers relating to Mrs Muir's life and work. Some diary items give information about Muir's poems.

BBC archives in Glasgow and London contain many scripts by and about Muir, correspondence with producers, etc. Information about the location of letters is given in *SL*.

## FIRST POEMS

London: Leonard and Virginia Woolf at the Hogarth Press, April 1925; New York: B.W. Huebsch, 1925.

Probably all the poems were written abroad between late 1921 and July 1924. Early versions of most had appeared in periodicals, and TSS, now in BL, of ten had been sent to Sydney Schiff on 15 April 1924. Only a few of the many variations between these early versions and *FP* are given below.

In July 1930 Muir wrote to Woolf that he was considering the idea of a new volume, containing some of *FP* revised, *CND* revised and some new poems. In November 1935 he sent Janet Adam Smith copies of *FP* and *CND*: 'In both of them there are ghastly things: the wooden stiffness of the rhythms horrifies me now – it is as if I had sat down to write in a particularly hard and heavy overcoat. I think it must have been my interminable years in Glasgow offices, and the perpetual repression incident to them that made my first efforts at expression so stiff and awkward. Also I was deep in Coleridge and the Scottish Ballads at the time: indeed could not get much out of any other kind of poetry: and that influenced my vocabulary and metre in a way I can see clearly now. If I had only had more technical mastery at the time I might have made something really remarkable out of the Ballad of Eternal Life. As it is I can't read it still without being alternately pleased and saddened . . . (I had an idea about two years ago of bringing out a Collected Poems, and so tentatively went over these two books in pencil. I've given up the idea now.)' The idea was revived in 1936 when he offered Woolf a volume consisting of 'about 24 new poems with 16 old ones, including *Chorus of the Newly Dead*, polished up somewhat'. Woolf declined it.

A copy of *FP* in NLS contains extensive MS insertions – lists of poems, comments, amendments – written in pencil and two different inks, presumably between 1930 and 1936. The poems most favoured for inclusion in the proposed collection are probably those marked with a cross – all those, except 'Betrayal', eventually included in *CP 60*, and 'The Lost Land', 'The Enchanted Prince', 'Logos' and 'Ballad of the Monk'. Unattributed quotations in the notes are from this copy.

For *CP 52* John Hall selected six poems, and Muir added three for *CP 60* – 'October in Hellbrunn', 'Ballad of the Soul' (renamed) and 'Ballad of the Flood'. The texts were newly revised for these collections, many, but not all, the amendments in the NLS copy being incorporated, and some new ones added especially in 'Ballad of the Soul'.

Dedication. *Peerie*: little, used as an endearment, especially in Orkney and Shetland.

*Childhood. Nation and Athenaeum* XXXIV (13 Oct 1923) 54. Translated into German by Eurhythmic student Gerda Krapp at Hellerau by May 1923. The TS used by her has an extra stanza after 12, deleted by Muir:

> In sleep he stood once on a cliff so high
> That as he gazed down all was bleakly changed;
> The islands foreign and broad-backed did lie,
> And tumbling waters kept them far estranged.

cf. 'The Lost Land' and 'Remembrance'.

*The Lost Land. Scottish Nation* II (4 Dec 1923) 15. Translated into German by Gerda Krapp by May 1923. Her version (her source is lost) has an extra stanza at the beginning, translated by Howard Gaskill ('Edwin Muir in Hellerau'):

> I know a place by a forgotten lake.
> There is no storm – but constant calm.
> There are ships, like white clouds, with rolled-up sails,
> And they dream-on the echo of distant winds.

Variations between *SN* and *FP* and later extensive amendments in the NLS copy show Muir's wish to perfect this poem. See Appendix III for the amended version.

See *A* 63–4, a record of his first dream about Wyre twenty-five years after leaving. The dream goes on to take the dreamer to a chapel where he brings to life a clay image. The dream, having set out to take him back home, offers him something else. The poem stops short of this positive conclusion.

Diary May 1938: 'I am haunted by a dream of standing on a ship and watching the green hills drawing nearer and nearer across the sea: and how green they are! Have I dreamt this often, or only once? I cannot tell any longer: the picture is so vivid when it rises, and it may rise at any time, which shows that it is never away.'

*Remembrance. Nation and Athenaeum* XXXV (6 Sep 1924) 692. 'Thin, pretty bad.'

TS sent to Schiff has two stanzas at the end in place of 25–8:

> For where all form, of flesh, of soul, of mind,
> Melts – I am not those haunting shapes, nor these.
> And it is still another's face I find
> When for my own I quest through memories.

> Who are you there, and you, who smile in death?
> What vanished hopes upon your faces gleam?
> You are but dreams, and I who give you birth
> Live but in dreams, and move on but to dream.

*Horses. Nation and Athenaeum* XXXV (31 May 1924) 293. See *A* 22–3 and 206. *NA*, *FP* and the Library of Congress recording have 'so' before 'terrible' (3).

**[22]** *sight*: The reading of *NA*, *FP* and the TS sent to Schiff; 'light', the reading of *CP 52* and later *CP*'s seems to have crept in inadvertently, and is amended in MS to 'sight' in the BL copy of *CP 52*. Muir said 'sight' when recording the poem at the Library of Congress in 1955.

*Houses.* 'Very bad.'

*Maya. Nation and Athenaeum* XXXIV (12 Jan 1924) 545. 'Bad too.'
Probably written at Salzburg, where the Muirs were from October to December 1923. See *A* 215–17, and *The Marionette* 47/49 where Hans has alternating feelings of things being unreal and real.

*The Enchanted Prince.* MS amendments include deletion of third and ninth stanzas.
cf. 'The Lost Land' 33 and 'The Enchanted Knight' (*JP*).

*October at Hellbrunn. Nation and Athenaeum* XXXIV (16 Feb 1924) 701 as 'At Hellbrunn – October'.
*FP* has two extra stanzas after 12 (*N and A* has only the first of these):

> So still they stand, the statues and the trees,
>   On the brown path the leaves so moveless lie,
> My footfalls end, and motionless as these,
>   I stand self-tranced between the earth and sky.
>
> For the earth is dumb and empty, and no weight,
>   Save the shut sky, curved steep, a stone-smooth tomb,
> Weighs on it, and no ground upholds its great
>   Load of tired land and sea, save empty doom.

Other amendments for *CP* 60 include 'stone-smooth' for 'changeless' (1), 'patient' for 'close-ranked' (5), 'silent' for 'slow dumb' (13).
Hellbrunn is a seventeenth-century castle with pleasure garden, theatre and many fountains on the outskirts of Salzburg.

*Reverie. Dial* LXXV (Dec 1923) 534–5. Pencil revisions in the NLS *FP* include new line for 4 'And on the ground night's gentle palm is cool', and deletion of 23–4.

*On the Mediterranean.* 'Awful.'

*An Ancient Song.* Pencil revisions include deletion of 11–12.
John Holms wrote to Hugh Kingsmill 22 June 1925: 'Oddly enough it was written before the German business, at least before he was in the least conscious of being in love'.

*Betrayal.* 'Very bad.'

*Anatomy.* 'Bad.' Pencil revisions include an extra stanza after 8:

> My brain a radiant chamber where
>   In polished springes fast are caught
> The fluttering sprites of sun and air
>   And abstract forms of plus and nought.

*Logos.* 'No good' deleted; many revisions.
  cf. 'Ballad of Rebirth', 'Ballad of the Soul'.

*When the trees* . . .. Comma after 'clamour' (16), first omitted in *CP 63*, has been restored.

*Autumn in Prague.* Revisions for *CP 52*: 'In' for 'near' (title); 'frail' before 'cables' (17), 'great' before 'sea' (20), 'great' before 'god' (22) omitted; 'great' for 'mighty' (21).

*Salzburg November.* Many MS revisions, including deletion of 33–6. See *A* 216–17.

*Grass. Observer* No. 6938 (18 May 1924) 11.

*Ballad of Hector in Hades. Adelphi* II No. 3 (Aug 1924) 242–3. Carefully amended between *Adelphi* and *FP*, and again for *CP 52*. *Adelphi* has instead of 35–8:

> Each rut within the wagon path
> Has eyes as we pass by,
> Cold earthy eyes which shut again
> When we have passed on high.

*FP* has this stanza, slightly amended, after an early version of 35–8. Both early versions have for 43 'In dreadful distance, void and chill'.
  In *A* 42–4 Muir tells of a childhood incident and of the terror associated with it, which is got rid of in this poem; says that he 'wrote the poem down, almost complete, at one sitting'; and that his feeling about it 'is not of a suppression suddenly removed, but rather of something which had worked itself out'. The incident is used also in *TB* 48–9.
  In *Iliad* XXII Hector is chased round the walls of Troy by Achilles until tricked by Athena, disguised, into standing and confronting him; he is killed, 'and his disembodied soul took wing for the House of Hades, bewailing its lot and the youth and manhood that it left'. Muir's climax ('and do not care') is characteristically different: it is the ostensible victor who is held in the destructive circle.
  [38]  Perhaps there should be no stop at the end of this line. There is none in the MS draft in NLS's *FP*. But perhaps the punctuation here and in 41 is deliberately rhetorical, not grammatical.
  [41]  The full stop at the end of this line replaces *FP*'s comma.

*Ballad of Rebirth. New Age* XXXI (8 Jun 1922) 72 as 'Rebirth'. Muir's first published poem. *NA* has 'hoped' for 'feared' (39) and an extra stanza after 44:

> He sang, and all the sounds of heaven
> Were in his starry voice,
> He laughed, and the wide deep out-broke
> In a wild, wandering noise.

Based on a dream recorded in *A* 163–4. 'It was not 'I' who dreamt it, but something else which the psychologists call the racial unconscious, and for which there are other names.'
  cf. 'The Fall' (*JP*).

*Ballad of the Soul. New Age* XXXI (6 Jul 1922) 121–2 as 'Ballad of Eternal Life'. 'The dream was wonderful but the poem is all wrong'.

Based on a waking trance recorded in *A* 159–63, discussed in *A* 165–7, and described as 'the most strange and the most beautiful experience I have ever had' (*SL* 102).

Muir took more trouble over this poem than over any other. He radically rewrote the *NA* version for *FP*, wrote copious amendments in the NLS copy of *FP*, and revised it again near the end of his life. On 8 September 1958 he wrote to T.S. Eliot that he would like to add some poems from *FP* to the new *CP*, but that he could not find his copy. He must have found it, and done the rewriting, using and going beyond the amendments in it, in the next few days. On 19 September he sent Eliot TSS of the three extra poems, saying he was still not satisfied with 'Ballad of the Soul' (*SL* 209). So this is one of his first and probably, in its final form, one of his last poems. Indeed work on it may have inspired his very last one, 'I have been taught by dreams and fantasies' (*LP*).

cf. 'Logos' and 'Ballad of Rebirth'; and many later poems which use images from the dream, e.g. *VTT* III, 'The Fall' (*JP*), 'The Human Fold' (*NP*), 'The Journey Back' (*L*). The Prague notebook shows Muir planning a long poem, 'A Vision', based largely on the dream. See headnote to *L*.

For the *FP* text see Appendix II.

*Section I* Condensed from I and II in *NA* and *FP*. The extent of the revision and the improvement is exemplified by quoting *NA*'s I:

> All things are mortal arrows drawn
>   Up from the wide abyss,
> Through the swift sheath of life and death
>   In unreturning bliss.
> I fled adown Death's gates wide thrown
>   On slumber's noiseless feet
> To where Chaos flings in fettered rings
>   Its maddened waters fleet,
> A flood that shakes like swift black snakes
>   Escaping from a snare.
> A woman stood as carved in wood,
>   A firm-set pillar there,
> Her deep eyes shone like meteors wan
>   Through the dark hurtling air.

The image in lines 1–4 of this was used again in *VTT* III 8–11 and 'The Prize' 2–3.

[9–12]  *A* 166: 'The woman . . . seemed . . . to be a prophecy of a remote future age; as if, long before the existence of mankind, the animal soul was dreaming of it, and yearning towards it'.

cf. 'Then' (*NP*).

[36]  After this in *NA* and *FP* came the dragons weeping tears of gold, who are to appear in similar contexts in 'The Fall' (*JP*), '*The Human Fold*' (*NP*) and 'The Journey Back' (*L*).

*Section II* Corresponds to *NA* and *FP*'s III. Only one line survives unchanged from *NA*. The early versions' attempts to explain ('I battle up to man') are eliminated.

*Section III* Corresponds to *NA* and *FP*'s IV. 'End here' is written at the end of this section in the NLS *FP*.

[109–16] *A* 165. 'The battle with the wheeling sun, which, after running through all its revolutions, becomes the sphinx, is the last battle with time, after which time releases the spirit into eternity.' The sphinx appears in similar contexts in 'The Fall' (*JP*) and 'The Human Fold' (*NP*). A figure-head on a ship appears also in 'The Town Betrayed' 3–6 (*JP*); and the image is discussed in a late essay 'Toys and Abstractions': 'One can think of the figurehead of a woman laced to the bow of a sailing ship as passing through horizon after horizon . . . She, a creation of art, looks out at our world. We, looking at a statue, look the opposite way.' The forehead as prow journeys to a more optimistic end in a Diary entry given in 'The Face' (*NP*) n.

*Section IV* Corresponds to *NA*'s V and *FP*'s V and VI. The first three stanzas are adapted from separated stanzas in *FP* V, the fourth from 'Ballad of Rebirth' 29–32; the fifth avoids *FP*'s assertive ending by returning to the beginning of the poem.

[125] *Two linked*, for *FP*'s 'We linked', makes the speaker a spectator. *FP*'s identification of the one with whom hands are linked with the Woman in Section I is eliminated.

*Ballad of the Nightingale.* Based on the millennial dream recorded in *A* 54–6, tacked on to the Heine story. See also *A* 114, 116 and *PT* 102–6.
 cf. 'The Transfiguration' (*L*).

*Ballad of the Monk. Scottish Chapbook* I No. 12 (Jul 1923) 346–7.
[3/19] *dowie*: dismal; delicate.
[7] *soomed*: swam.

*Ballad of the Flood. Scottish Chapbook* I No. 12 (Jul 1923) 339–43.
 Lines 45–8 were added in *FP*. For *CP* 60 Muir eliminated some Scotti-cisms – gashly (ghastly), oot, aboot, hoose, doonward, noo, focht, droon.
 At Dresden, where they lived from April to June 1922, Mrs Muir began a play in modern terms on Noah and his family; but was discouraged by Muir who turned the story into a ballad 'which he thought a more proper way of handling an ancient theme' (*Belonging* 72). She would have brought the story into the modern world; he pushed it further into the realm of fable by adding the 'twining worm' (3) as, rather than God who plays no part, the causer of the flood, and the dragons (115–24). The 'worm' probably derives from a story Muir remembered reading in a newspaper about a dragon which in its death-agony 'wrapped its body round the earth like a great belt' (*A* 78–9). This is the Stoor Worm of Orkney legend (Marshall, *In a Distant Isle* 65–6), but apparently Muir didn't know that. For Willa's play see her deposit in St Andrews, Box 9/6.
 John Holms wrote to Hugh Kingsmill that 'this poem was written at an astonishing speed, in two or three days I think'.
 Suggesting poems for an anthology of Scottish verse Muir wrote to Doug-las Young in 1950 that 'the most Scottish poem I ever wrote is the 'Ballad of

the Flood' . . . I'm fond of it myself' (*SL* 156–7); and to T.S. Eliot in 1958: 'I hope you will like 'Ballad of the Flood' in ballad Scots, which is so different from that of Burns' (*SL* 208–9).

[2]  *dirl*: stroke.
[5]  *ganted*: yawned.
[43]  *soomed*: swam.

## CHORUS OF THE NEWLY DEAD

London: Leonard and Virginia Woolf at the Hogarth Press, Jul 1926.

Parts had appeared earlier:
—*New Age* XXXII (19 Apr 1923) 401. 'The Larva', an early version of 'The Saint'.
—*Scottish Chapbook* II No. 1 (Aug 1923) 2–8. 'Chorus of the Newly Dead', including opening and final choruses and monologues by Idiot, Beggar, Coward, Harlot (early version), Saint and Hero. The monologues had been translated into German by Gerda Krapp before May 1923. (Muir's dating in *A* 223–4 is wrong.)
—*Calendar of Modern Letters* II (Dec 1925) 244–7. 'Poems from 'Chorus of the Newly Dead'.' Monologues by Coward, Harlot (new version) and Mystic (new).

The Hogarth Press *CND* has one new monologue, by the Poet, who takes the place of the Saint, and new choruses after each of the first six monologues, and a new final chorus. *Scottish Chapbook*'s versions of Harlot, Saint and final chorus are given in Appendix II.

Muir wanted to reprint *CND*, revised, early in the thirties and in 1936. The revisions in two printed copies were presumably made at this time. In the NLS copy these are fairly numerous, but less radical than in the BL copy, in which 'Newly' is deleted from the title, the Harlot's monologue and all the choruses except the opening and closing ones are deleted, and the Poet's and Hero's monologues and the final chorus much revised.

That was not the end of Muir's interest in the poem. The Author's Note to *CP* 52 shows that he thought of including parts of it in that collection; for he says that *CND* 'has been omitted entirely, as I feel it cannot be quoted piecemeal'. Then in August 1955 he wrote to Kathleen Raine that he had 'got the idea for a long poem, after re-reading a miscarried attempt long since . . . and realising that I could do it better now and in quite a different way' (*SL* 173). On sheets in NLS he wrote notes on the intended poem – the beginning of a dialogue between 'Philosopher' and 'Chorus', lists of lines and ideas from earlier poems, plans. 'State of this place: pure silence never heard [?] before, pure sound, absence of time but true memory of time, quite beyond desire (with some) or still mingled with desire: light in itself, deep darkness . . . New heaven and new earth – still to come. The discomfort, the bewilderment, being out of time.' The dialogues 'Returning from the antipodes' (*LP*) and 'I have heard you cry' (*LP*) may be offshoots from this project. In summer 1957 he was still talking about writing a long poem.

See letters to Schiff in *SL* 37, 43, 45–6. In an unpublished letter to him 12

Jul 1926 Muir says the Chorus 'is to me the best thing I have ever written; there is most of myself in it'. See *A* 223–4; and Willa Muir's *Belonging* 103: 'The material . . . he was now shaping . . . was made up of painful emotions which had been working like yeast inside him ever since those first five years in Glasgow when his father, his two brothers, his mother had died . . . He was making his first poetic attempt to come to terms with Death by looking for a transcendental meaning in Life.'

**[86–9]**   cf. 'The Ring' (*NP*).

**[90–101]**   Instead of these three stanzas *Scottish Chapbook* has two:

> I stood where lustrous houses reared
> White pillars changelessly,
> I could not stir although I feared
> They would fall down on me.
>
> I saw the shadows on their walls
> Move in a wheeling line.
> (There still each moving shadow falls
> Like an inhuman sign.)

Willa Muir tells of their early days in London, when 'Sometimes he felt that buildings were going to crash on his head' (*Belonging* 36).

**[100–1]**   cf. 'Hölderlin's Journey' 45–6 (*JP*).

**[149]**   cf. 'Hölderlin's Journey' 7–9 (*JP*), et al.

**[After 153]**   *Scottish Chapbook* has extra stanza:

> I turned back to the town again,
> And hid myself in crowds of men,
> But like lost packs through every street
> They drove; fear trampled in their feet.

**[232–55]**   Letter to Schiff 1 February 1925: 'The poet begins the new movement, away from suffering to its transmutation; and the Hero emphasizes that movement; but I have another figure, I don't know what to call him, perhaps the Mystic, in which all life will be affirmed' (*SL* 45). Earlier the affirmation was expressed through The Saint (App. II).

**[318–22]**   cf. 'The Road' 3–10 (*JP*).

**[354–61]**   Muir comments on these lines in *A* 223–4. The last four call to mind Hölderlin, on whom Muir published an essay in 1923, in which he translates the opening lines of 'Patmos': 'Near is and hard to grasp the god. But where danger is there arises the saviour also. In distance dwell the eagles, and fearless the sons of the mountains go over the abyss on light-built bridges' (*TI* 170). In a later essay on 'Patmos' (*1ELS* 101–2) he translates lines from near the end of the poem:

> the will of the Eternal Father
> Pointed to thee. Quiet is His sign
> In the thundering sky. And One stands beneath
> His life long. For still lives Christ.

and comments, 'Christ was the one symbol which united for him the two truths he perceived in existence: a truth transcending time, and a truth immanent in time: permanence and alternation'.

## VARIATIONS ON A TIME THEME

London: J.M. Dent, April 1934. All but IV, V, and VII had appeared in periodicals with separate titles. II, VI, IX and X were included in *CP 52*; the rest restored in *CP 60*.

Written at a time when the Muirs were translating Kafka and Broch, and when he was using Scottish history and his own early life as bases for his novels *The Three Brothers* (1931) and *Poor Tom* (1932). Willa Muir wrote: 'Broch's ambience of bleak despair affected us deeply enough during 1931, and set the tone for Edwin's next book of poems' (*Belonging* 152). The ambience (e.g. I 1–7) and theme (quest-unattained, confusion of times, generalised 'I') recall also T.S. Eliot's *The Waste Land*.

*Epigraph.* Daniel 7: 24–5. This passage was used by John Knox as the text for his first sermon, and is described by Muir as 'inexplicably obscure' (*JK* 22). But Daniel the dreamer would appeal to Muir. The dream in Daniel 7 is of four beasts, the slaying of the last of whom leads to the appearance of 'one like the Son of man', whose 'dominion is an everlasting dominion'. This is, like the dreamer's battle with the Sphinx in Muir's own long dream, 'the last battle with time' (*A* 165). The possibility of such a consummation is hinted, with perhaps deliberate obscurity, by the choice of epigraph.

*VTT I. Spectator* CXLIX (9 Dec 1932) 827 as 'Interregnum'.

[4–7] *SJ* 123–4. 'To the south-east between Polmadie and Rutherglen [Glasgow] ended when I came to it first in country which could only be called slum country.' After 'several rows of squalid miners' houses' and 'a piggery of surpassing stench . . . came a country road called the Hundred Acre Dyke, dotted with a few ringwormed trees, and affording a bleak prospect of smoking pits and blackened trees'. See also *SJ* 169–70 and *A* 92.

[26–34] cf. Adam's Dream (*OFE*) 53–4, 'time was strange/To one lately in Eden'.

[35–42] cf. 'The Difficult Land' (*OFE*).

*VTT II. Listener* X (16 Aug 1933) 255 as 'The Riders'.

*L* has at the end.

> As if it were all.
> So we dream on.
> This is our kingdom.

See *The Modern Poet* (1938), edited by Gwendolen Murphy, an anthology which included this poem and two letters from Muir to the editor, parts of which are reprinted in *SL* 213–14. 'The Horses, as I see them, are an image of human time, the invisible body of humanity on which we ride for a little while . . . Yet the steed – mankind in its course through time – is mortal, and the rider is immortal. . . . The painful emotion in the poem comes from a simultaneous feeling of immortality and mortality, and particularly from the feeling that we, as immortal spirits, are imprisoned in a very small and from all appearances fortuitously selected length of time: held captive on the "worn saddle", which in spite of our belief in our immortality has power "to charm us to obliviousness" by "the scent of the ancient leather".'

' "The autumn light" (40) . . . is an attempt to suggest those isolated moments of pure vision which have a feeling of timelessness . . . They may cast a momentary reflection on the glossy hides, but it fades almost at once. This instant fading makes them "autumnal". At the moment we are aware of them we are released from the presence of Time: our limbs are "weightless". Our silvery breaths going on before us . . . is an extravagant way of describing this state of freedom.' This last image was based on an actual scene, when in autumn in Sussex he saw a boy ploughing and a moving column of breath going on before him in the light, clear air.

[46]   *Troy*. cf. 'No more of this trapped gazing' 1–4 (App. I).

*VTT III. Spectator* CL (26 May 1933) 764 as 'Autobiography'. *S* has two extra lines at the beginning: 'Ages with ages, states with states hold strife/In this my brief immeasurable life'; and has 'immortal' for 'mortal' (34).

*A* 48–9: 'It is clear that no autobiography can begin with a man's birth, that we extend far beyond any boundary line which we can set ourselves in the past or in the future, and that the life of every man is an endlessly-repeated performance of the life of man.' cf. 'Ballad of the Soul' (*FP*), 'The Fall' (*JP*), 'The Journey Back' (*L*).

[1–3]   *A* 25: 'Our first childhood is the only time in our lives when we exist within immortality'.

[9]   *arrow*: the incarnate soul shot into time. cf. early version of 'Ballad of the Soul' 1–4, quoted in note.

[11–16]   cf. 'The Private Place' 11–17 (*JP*), 'The Journey Back' section 3 (*L*).

[42]   Exodus 16:2–3. Set free from Egyptian bondage, the Israelites nevertheless hanker after the flesh-pots.

*VTT IV*
[1–4]   cf. 'The Road' 1–4 (*JP*).
[5]   cf. 'The Threefold Place' (*JP*).
[6–8]   Calls to mind 'The Return of the Greeks' (*V*) and the Sonntagberg (*A* 222), but is perhaps deliberately unspecific. The references (e.g. Exodus 4:3, 13:21, 40:34–5; Deuteronomy 3:27) to the Israelites' journey are mixed with glances at other journeys and quests.

*VTT V*
*VTT* has at the beginning:

> The infidel congregation of mankind
> Flap sullenly upon the grinding storm,
> Slow-motion flight over a bottomless road,
> Or clinical fantasy begotten by
> The knife of demon Time the vivisector
> Incising nightmares.

In the BL copy Muir wrote a large delete sign against this paragraph, an instruction which, understandably, the editors of *CP* 60 did not obey.

*VTT VI. Modern Scot* IV (Jul 1933) 138–40 as 'In the Wilderness'. *MS* has for 65: 'Of our deliverance. Though the way/Is hidden from us, and the day/We know that we shall leave this sand . . .'

[**7–10**]  Numbers 20:10–11.
[**14–28**]  Exodus 24:15–16; 32:4,19,25.
[**21**]  cf. 'The Transfiguration' 47–8 (*L*).

*VTT VIII. New Verse* 6 (Dec 1933) 3–4 as 'Threefold Time'. *VTT*'s 'slick' (12) and 'close-hidden' (38) were amended in BL's copy to 'wise' and 'un-hidden'. cf. 'The Threefold Place' (*JP*) and 'Three Tales' (*LP*).
[**5**]  *Sebastian*: Christian martyr. Often portrayed looking up to heaven while, tied to a tree, being shot with arrows by soldiers.
[**10–13**]  Alcibiades (*Symposium* 220–22) says that Socrates was a brave soldier, able to bear all hardships, though subject to fits of abstraction, once standing a whole day and night fixed in thought. Born in 469 BC he was not at the battle of Marathon (c.490 BC).
[**44**]  *banneret*: knight entitled to bring vassals into the field under his own banner. Title became obsolete when Baronets were created.

*VTT IX. Spectator* CLI (22 Dec 1933) 932 as 'The Dilemma'.

*S* has 'lubber' for 'demon' (22), 'typist's' for 'beggar's' (33), for 34–43:

> For every shame, every delight,
> The fear of children in the night,
> The conqueror before his fallen foe
> (Fingering his useless sword he cannot go,
> But stands in doltish silence), the despair
> Of thought that finds no ending anywhere,
> And size and shape, and time and space,
> And every poor and smiling place,
> And simple flowers that cannot hide,
> By boys or winds left desolate,
> And the tree patient to its fate,
> With black rain trickling down its side,
> And all that have to die and that have died.

and after 58: 'And endless partings last a parting's space,/And grief is but a shadow on the face'.

cf. 'The Private Place' (*JP*), 'The Intercepter' (*L*), extract from a diary in *SF* 250: 'Looking at [ordinary people in Edinburgh], I felt neither grief nor satisfaction – merely that official indifference in which we pass ninety-nine hundreds of our lives. I sat and looked at them almost contentedly through the scales that covered my eyes . . . while something far within me . . . cried that I wanted to see.' This was a few days after he had looked at similar scenes 'in astonishment and horror, feeling . . . the enormity of human life'.
[**33**]  *beggar's*: The echo of *The Waste Land* III in the original 'typist's' is eliminated.

*VTT X. Spectator* CLII (9 Mar 1934) 375 as 'Heraldry'. On the meaning of heraldry see *A* 46–8. cf. 'The Covenant' (*V*).
[**1–3**]  In Daniel 7:4 'The first [beast] was like a lion, and had eagle's wings: I beheld till the wings thereof were plucked, and it was lifted up from the earth'. And in 7:12 the beasts 'had their dominion taken away: yet

their lives were prolonged for a season and time'. Possibly the lions on the royal arms of Scotland may be glanced at.

[22–4] 'crucified' prompts a Christian reading; but Muir's dragons are not usually associated with evil – *A* 160, 167; 'Ballad of Eternal Life' 49–52 (App. II), 'The Fall' 21–6 (*JP*), 'The Journey Back' 90–2 (*L*), 'Dialogue: Returning from the antipodes' 3, 45 (*LP*.). Even in *CND* the treatment of the dragon is equivocal.

## JOURNEYS AND PLACES

London. Dent. September 1937. Sixteen poems were included in *CP 52*, and Muir added eight for *CP 60*, leaving out only 'Judas'.

*Dedication.* To two friends who had from their Samson Press, Warlingham published in April 1932 in a fine limited edition *Six Poems* – 'The Stationary Journey', 'The Field of the Potter' ['Judas'], 'The Trance' ['The Enchanted Knight'], 'Tristram Crazed' ['Tristram's Journey'], 'Transmutation' ['The Threefold Place'], and 'The Fall'.

Stephen Spender reviewed *JP* in *London Mercury* XXXVI (May-Oct 1937) 579–80, describing Muir as a metaphysical poet. 'His style is epigrammatic, his symbols, beautiful and living as they are, are not sufficient in themselves, they carry always the weight of their reference to an argument, which although it is contained within the poem, exists outside the poem'. Muir wrote to him on 6 October 1937, accepting the point about the argument existing outside the poem. 'The remedy . . . is for me to get more outside myself, and I think I have been able to do this a little more recently' (*SL* 97–8).

*The Stationary Journey. Bookman* LXIX (Jun 1929) 355–6; *Six Poems. B* has after 32:

> Here this long *now*; all else the void.
>   Yet through the void forever go
> Great energies past death or thought;
>   I know them yet I only know
>
> Vast hieroglyphics where power in
>   Solidity more pure . . .

and then, after the rest of 38–40, stanza 33–6; and has after 56:

> And Ilium's tumbling towers
>   Hang stationary in the air,
> And Hector holds the unshaken walls:
>   All are there, or nothing's there.

In the final revision Muir restored *B*'s and *SP*'s 'Plato's' after *JP*'s and *CP 52*'s 'Caesar's' (36). This vacillation points to uncertainty whether to include a hint of a more optimistic view of time and eternity.

In *TB* 330–2 Muir puts much of the content of this poem into the mind of David Blackadder. David thinks that to God the full round of Time is eternally present – 'Eden and Adam and Eve unfallen . . . and Christ in the ox's stall, and Christ on the Cross, eternally suffering and eternally dying'. He calls up images in his own mind – of 'ships keeled over for ever at the same slant by an invisible and eternal storm', of 'Caesar with the knife in his breast . . . eternally stationed between life and death', of Judas 'innocent for ever and guilty for ever'. His mind 'flew at last for comfort to thoughts of the end. Reviving as from a great defeat, I saw that all mankind, yes that the very world and the stars and the sun, hasten irrevocably towards their end, where all labour and suffering and joy are consummated'. He then has his vision of the Last Judgement, which is used in 'The Day Before the Last Day' (*LP*). This poem, however, returns the speaker to imprisonment in the astronomic world.

*The Mountains. Spectator* CLV (19 Jul 1935) 93 as 'The Journey'. *S* has 'distant' for 'single' (3), 'which way lies home' for 'where lies my way' (13) and 'heavenhigh' for 'single' (27).

In *SJ* 211–25 Muir describes a journey through the North-West Highlands of Scotland and arrival at a village from which he sees the Orkney hills in front. 'All the impressions of the day . . . seemed to have built up an impregnable barrier' between him and the place he started from in the morning. 'Yet at the same time I could see myself starting the car from that very place . . . This double sensation of time was confusing and yet pleasant', evoking a 'vivid sense of the simultaneity of many lives and towns and landscapes'. He can envisage the world as an entity, but fails to do so in relation to Scotland.

[22]  cf. 'A Trojan Slave' 10–12; Hölderlin's 'Patmos' 9–10, 'round are piled (gehauft)/The peaks of Time'.

*The Hill. Spectator* CLIV (7 Jun 1935) 980. *S* has instead of 9 'Green islands drinking the blue waves'; after 11 an extra line 'To climb like fountains back again'; 'rest' for 'gladness' (13); 'higher up' for 'somewhere else' (18).

[1–7]  In *SJ* 83–4 Muir describes driving by car through hilly country in south-west Scotland, mounting a rise and seeing Girvan, the sands, the sea and 'the blank red cone of Ailsa Craig . . ./I could not make out at first what the crowd of tiny louse-like forms could be that were crawling over the broad, soiled, mud-coloured sands, until I realised that they must be bathers'.

[8–18]  In *A* 115 he describes a dream of bathers in a great river, whose waters could easily wash away any impurity entering 'higher up'.

[17]  *far inland*: cf. 'The Town Betrayed' 13, 38; 'The Unfamiliar Place' 18.

*The Road*
[3–10]  cf. *CND* 318–22; 'To J.F.H.' 22–3 (*NP*); *A* 224.
[18–20]  cf. 'Time Song' 38–9 (App. I).
[26–8]  cf. 'The Enchanted Prince' (*FP*); 'The Enchanted Knight'.

*The Mythical Journey. Spectator* CLVI (15 May 1936) 886 as 'The Journey'. *S* has 'dead' for 'twice-dead' (6), 'cant' for 'edge' (10), no stop after 'valleys' (16) and for 17–18 'Of the green world. That whose form and features,/Race and speech he knew not, faceless, tongueless,'; 'vision' for 'meaning' (25) followed by extra line 'The meaning, the consummation. And not a meeting.'; 'consummation' for 'fulfilment' (34 and 44); for 35–6

'The plain like glass beneath him/And in the crystal grave that which had sought him,'; 'heavy' for 'mountainous' (39).

Muir wrote to Aitken 28 May 1940: 'I have been pursued by these little hills often without quite knowing where they came from: I realised as I wrote the autobiography' (*SL* 121). He wrote in *A* 14, 15, 40, and 57 of a roofless chapel, a damp green meadow and the remains of an old castle on a small green hill near his childhood home on Wyre; and in *A* 55 of a dream of 'little conical hills a little higher than a man's head'. In a diary entry for 17 May 1938 he mentions among other dreams 'sailing up from the north, the brief year night, Greenland on my right as a dark fleecelike shape, and the golden streaks of light broadening and running along the oily waters'; and a dream of 'the gods on the two islands'. cf. 'Hölderlin's Journey' 6–8.

[15–16]   cf. 'Hölderlin's Journey' 21, 'The Question' (*NP*).

[35–6]   cf. 'Merlin' 1–2 and n.

[37–9]   Probably includes reference to Yggdrasill, the world tree in Norse mythology, as well as to the Trees of Life and of the Knowledge of Good and Evil in Eden.

[39–41]   cf. 'The Labyrinth' 48–60 (*L*). Willa Muir (*Belonging* 75) says 'To Edwin Hölderlin's gods sitting on their mountains became very dear.' But Muir's main source was his own dream.

*Tristram's Journey. Atlantic Monthly* CXLI (May 1928) 627–8 as 'Tristram Crazed'. *AM* has an extra stanza after 24:

> And now he saw a tower, and now
> Slow-moving past a spectral brake,
> Amid black hills a gleaming swan
> Upon an ebon lake.

See Malory *Morte D'Arthur* VIII xxxi for Tristram's fight with Palamides; IX xvii-xxi for his estrangement from Iseult.

[1–3]   Tristram wrongly thinks Iseult has betrayed him because she has sent a letter to another knight.

[69–72]   In Malory the knights 'brought [Tristram] well to his remembrance' by bathing him and giving him 'hot suppings'. Later the dog causes him to be recognised.

*Hölderlin's Journey. Criterion* XVI (Jan 1937) 26/–8. In autumn 1936 Muir sent this poem to Stephen Spender, with whom the year before he had planned a volume of translations from Hölderlin. 'It is a purely imaginary and I am afraid personal description of Hölderlin's real journey, which has haunted me ever since I first read about it, why, I don't know enough about myself to say.' And later 'I am glad you liked the Hölderlin, which was not, of course, in the least like Hölderlin' (*SL* 92/93). In 'Author's Note' to *JP* he says that Hölderlin in summer 1805 [actually 1802] suddenly set out on foot from Bordeaux, where he had been a tutor; passed through Arles, and arrived in Germany 'ragged, emaciated, and out of his mind'. Susette Gontard, the woman he loved and who was the Diotima of his poems, 'was dead when he arrived. He partly recovered, and during that short period wrote some of his finest poetry; but he presently relapsed again, and for the last forty years of his life suffered from a form of insanity'. Muir probably knew the story,

mentioned by Hellingrath in his edition, of Hölderlin appearing at a chateau near Blois, staring long at statues on the terrace, and impressing the residents by his yearning look, intelligence and derangement.
  cf. 'The Mythical Journey'; and see P.H. Gaskill 'Hölderlin and the Poetry of Edwin Muir' for the relationship to Hölderlin's poems, especially 'Patmos', 'Mnemosyne' (3rd version), 'Menons Klagen um Diotima' and 'Hyperions Schicksalslied', and for the inaccuracies in Muir's account.
  [22]  *sought and seeker*: cf. 'The Mythical Journey' 36, 'The Question' (*V*).
  [34]  *Diotima*: In *Symposium* 202–3 Socrates' teacher about love. She says love is the mediator who spans the chasm between gods and men, 'and through him all is bound together'. For Hölderlin the death of Susette/Diotima means that he can no longer bring together appearance and reality. 'Menons Klagen um Diotima' st. 4: 'But my home is desolate now, and they have taken away my eyes, and together with her I have lost my own self.'
  [57–60]  After his breakdown in 1806 Hölderlin lived in a carpenter's house in Tübingen, writing simple pastoral and moral poems. Huberman (*The Poetry of Edwin Muir* 95), unusually, says the poem ends with 'a kind of victory', the hills of lies being erased by the green hills of peace and holiness, where it is fitting to give thanks; but Gaskill points to 'No more of this trapped gazing' 20–22 (App. I):

> Mad Hölderlin
> Praised God and Man, cut off from God and Man
> In a bright twisted world.

*The Fall. Modern Scot* I No. 4 (Jan 1931) 10–11; *Criterion* X (Apr 1931) 421–3 as 'After the Fall'. Mrs Muir says that Muir sent this poem to T.S. Eliot 'about the end of 1927' (*Belonging* 146–7). So *C*'s version is the earliest. *C* has 'Celestial happenings' for 'Forgotten histories' (4), 'From some wide-opening mountain place' (6), 'The changing and the unchanging land' (12); extra stanza after 20:

> The countless worlds of sport and play
> Where my armorial comrades were
> The low-browed voiceless animals:
> What sights and shapes did I see there?

'may' for 'must' (25), 'gate' for 'wall' (27), 'foundered in' for 'swam upon' (40), 'And smite the marble smiling brow' (43).
  cf. 'Ballad of Rebirth' (*FP*), 'Ballad of the Flood' (*FP*) and 'Ballad of Eternal Life' (App. I), 'The Human Fold' 15–22 (*NP*), 'The Journey Back' section 2 (*L*); and the dreams in *A* 56 and 159–67.
  [15]  *Lear*: 'The extreme age of the King brings to our minds the image of a civilization of legendary antiquity; yet that civilisation is destroyed by a new generation . . . a gang of Renaissance adventurers' ('The Politics of King Lear' in *ELS* 35).
  cf. 'The Ring' 1–3 (*NP*) and n.
  [27–32]  cf. 'Ballad of the Soul' 109–16 (*FP*) and n.
  [35]  *Venusberg*: mountain in which Venus held court and into which knights were enticed in Wagner's *Tannhäuser*.

*Troy. Listener* XVII (2 Jun 1937) 103.

Muir may have adapted the story in Sophocles' *Ajax* of Ajax in madness attacking the army's flocks and herds, imagining the rams and bulls to be Argive chiefs.

cf. 'No more of this trapped gazing' 4 (App. I) and the 'treasures' in 'The Ring' (*NP*).

*A Trojan Slave. London Mercury* XXXV (Mar 1937) 450 as 'Troy'.
[10–12]   cf. Hölderlin's 'Patmos' 9–10, 'The Mountains' 21–2, 'Merlin' 13.
[51]   cf. 'Ballad of the Soul' 99–112 (*FP*).

*Judas. Six Poems* (1932) as 'The Field of the Potter'.
cf. 'The Transfiguration' 62–5 (*L*), 'Effigies' No. 2 (*OFE*).
[13–15]   cf. 'The Ring' 7–8 (*NP*).
[20]   cf. 'Merlin' 1 and n.
[25]   *TB* 332: 'I saw Judas innocent and Judas guilty; and he was innocent for ever and guilty for ever.'

*Merlin. Spectator* CLV (27 Sep 1935) 461. *S* has 'Burst through the gates of history' (9) and 'sorcery' for 'magic' (11).

In a broadcast selection of his poems on 3 September 1952 Muir said, ''Merlin' I can scarcely say how I came to write; it more or less wrote itself'.
[1]   *crystal cave*: In *Morte D'Arthur* IV i Merlin is imprisoned under a stone by Nimue. In *Welsh Triads* there is a story of his setting out to sea in a house of glass. But probably the stone becoming a crystal cave and references to 'the crystal grave' ('Mythical Journey' 35), a 'fence of glass' ('Judas' 20), 'crystal walls' ('Three Tales' 22 (*LP*)), a 'crystal chasm' ('The Refugees' 7 (App. I)) and 'a cage of glass' (*TB* 63) derive from Muir's memories and a dream rather than from any literary source. At the time of his childhood 'fall' he went about in a world of fear 'divided by an endless unbreakable sheet of glass from the actual world' (*A* 34), and later, in Glasgow, moved 'in a crystalline globe or bubble, insulated from the world around me' (*A* 149). In a dream used in 'Ballad of Rebirth' (*FP*) his soul saw his body fall to death on ice and be resurrected (*A* 164). Can Merlin escape from imprisonment, and be reborn like the dreamer?
[11–14]   cf. 'Time Song' 11 15 (*App. I*).

*The Enchanted Knight. Saturday Review* (London) CXLIV (23 Jul 1927) 130 as 'The Trance'.
cf. 'The Enchanted Prince' (*FP*), 'The Interceptor' (*L*) and n.

In *A* 144–5 Muir mentions a poem by Heine in which a dead man hears a knocking at his grave and his sweetheart calling him to rise, but he cannot. 'I identified myself with the dead man who knew so well that he was dead. Something in myself was buried.'

*Mary Stuart. Spectator* CLVIII (12 Mar 1937) 469.

James Stuart, Earl of Moray (1531–70), illegitimate half-brother of Mary, was her chief adviser until falling from favour and going to England; returned, became Regent, and after her flight used the Casket letters to prevent her return; was assassinated by someone he had treated cruelly.

*Ibsen. Listener* XVII (13 Jan 1937) 62. *L*'s 'Solness' has been restored for later 'Sollness'.

In *The Master Builder* Solness ('a man somewhat akin to me', said Ibsen), whose hubris has damaged his wife and family, falls to death from his newly-built tower. The other Ibsen characters mentioned all exhibit illusions, false values. The poem connects with others in *JP* on illusion and discovery.

[15–20] The (false?) 'Pillars of Society', satirised in the play of that name, are seen as falling with Solness. Thus revealing the true values? But see *A* 229, where Muir says that Ibsen's destruction of supposed illusions has left people like the free-lovers of St Tropez in a freedom which is not real, 'an open landscape, without roads, or a stopping place, or any point of the compass'.

*The Town Betrayed. London Mercury* XXXIV (Oct 1936) 486–7. *LM* has 'venturous' for 'painted' (5), 'waste' for 'field' (11), 'bloody' for 'dubious' (15), 'answering' for 'word, no' (17).

Possibly memories of 'Fairport' (*A* 139) may have contributed to this landscape.

[3–6] The daughters have some resemblance to the Sphinx in 'The Fall' 27–32. See 'Ballad of the Soul' 109–16 n; 'Industrial Scene' (App. I) 15–17 and n.

[9–12, 29–32] cf. 'The Escape' 9–16 (*V*), and *A* 262, where the Gestapo men, on whom 'the usurpers' are based, cannot enjoy the beauty around them.

[33–40] cf. 'The Usurpers' (*L*), where also the speakers are troubled by 'ghosts' from the past; 'No more of this trapped gazing' 2–4 (App. I) and 'The Place of Light and Darkness' n.

*The Unfamiliar Place. London Mercury* XXXI (Dec 1934) 114–5 as 'Double Vision'. *LM* has 'Or sleeping' for 'Sleeping' (16), 'lemur and' for 'many a' (17), 'only' for 'dark and winding' (20); and extra lines at the end:

> The secret is in this place,
> Visible under the sun,
> Here where I still run
> Unchanged my changing race.

*The Place of Light and Darkness. Modern Scot* V (Jan 1935) 266–7 as 'The Harvest'. *MS* has for 7 'In darkness', and then extra lines:

> (So might Agamemnon
> Have viewed the Grecian tents one fatal night,
> Had They been life and Troy eternity.);

and for 11–14:

> Homeless and whole.
>      What day shall break for them?
> He sees the rolling hills of grain,
> A day all yellow and red, flowers, fruit and corn,
> In darkness. The brown hair harvest-white
> In darkness. Children playing;

and 'where Christ the Sun' for 'wherein a sun' (32).

Sending this poem, 'Merlin', 'The Unfamiliar Place' and 'The Original Place' to D. Kilham Roberts for *The Year's Poetry* Muir wrote, 'I myself think 'The Harvest' easily the best'.

[**22–26**] In *A* 225 he records a dream in which he found himself in a high field dotted with little heaps of dead leaves; 'as I drew near the leaves turned to stooks of corn, but when I went closer I saw that they were the dead, lying two by two, a numberless host who were harvested here'. cf. *CND* 315, 'The Threefold Place'.

[**26–32**] In *A* 64 he records a dream of bringing a clay image to life by the power of a sun blazing in his breast. In another dream (*A* 108–9) the dreamer brings a young girl to life, says 'Look! I have brought her to life!', and hastily adds 'Look! God has brought her to life!'. Contrast the change here from 'Christ the Sun' to 'a sun'.

*The Solitary Place. London Mercury* XXXII (Sep 1935) 421–2. *LM* is divided into sections I and, after 30, II; has full stop at end of 6 and for 7 'These false fields will change/Beyond interrogation or reply,'; has 'Babel's demon Towers' (25), an extra line after 34 'And only to me', 'lonely' for 'lost' (43), 'father and brother' for 'brother and sister' (45); and after 47 and a space:

> But if there is another light
> That is not cut and grooved into my sight,
> That is not I and not I,
> And a breath within the light
> That breathes on me and questions me,
> A light shaken
> Across the light that shows myself to me
> And masks myself in me,
> A grace taken
> From something far from me and strange to me –
> If when I stretch out my hand a hand comes towards me
> To lead me out of me,
> And when I question a mind answers me.
> And enters into me that was not before in me,
> O then I am not sole, secure, forsaken.

A letter to Spender on 9 April 1935 speaks of an idea for 'a sort of "dialogue of one", one voice stating pretty much the same attitude as the *Variations*, and the other answering it in a more positive way', the argument being 'largely from an "I" to a "we".' This plan is obscured by the deletion of the last section. Another letter to Spender on 4 September 1935 says that the theme of the poem is 'the modern historical view of the world, in which there is no reality except the development of humanity – humanity being in that case merely an I and not I, a sort of long and interminable monologue of many' (*SL* 85–6). The poem reaches beyond the contemporary to glance at German idealist philosophy, the phrase 'I and not I' recalling Fichte (1762–1814), whose *The Vocation of Man*, partly in dialogue, moves from apparent solipsism ('all knowledge is merely a knowledge of thyself . . .

what thou assumest to be a consciousness of the object is nothing but a consciousness of thine own supposition of an object') to a denial of mere subjectivism.

[14–16] Rivers uniting places, times, states of being are found in several poems (e.g. 'The Days' 35–6 (*OFE*)), but a 'double-threaded' river only here. Fichte, with his 'double series' – of events *in* consciousness and of consciousness *of* those events – may be in the background.

[43] cf. 'The Unattained Place' 42.

*The Private Place. London Mercury* XXXIII (Mar 1935) 477 as I of 'Four Poems'. *LM* has 'conqueror' for 'stranger' (1).

[11–17] cf. 'Ballad of the Soul' 99–136 (*FP*); 'The Fall' 41–52.

*The Unattained Place. Outlook* I No. 4 (Jul 1936) 98–9 as 'Poem'. *O* has 'I' for 'we', 'my' for 'our' throughout; for 5 'And have not crossed there from the ungathered dead'; extra lines after 62 'Forgotten and unforgotten,/Begotten and unbegotten'. *O*'s and *JP*'s comma at end of 59 has been restored in place of *CP* 60's full stop.

Possibly this is the poem referred to in Muir's letter to Spender 4 May 1935: 'The first poem is elaborated from a nightmare I had one night in Orkney. I showed it to a friend and he objected that the rhythms were all broken, but I think they should be, and I wish they were more so. But I'm doubtful of this poem.' Lines 15–17 might be the nightmare.

*The Threefold Place. Bookman* (NY) LXX (Nov 1929) 233 as 'Transmutation'; *SP*. *B* has 'squadrons blest' for 'armies drest' (17); *B* and *SP* have extra stanza at the end:

> So my deep dread is lightly taken away,
>> Now that the old blind mass dissolves, gives way (*B*)
>> Now that to three the old blind mass gives way (*SP*)
> In this won space Beauty and Hope and Faith
> May walk and draw terrestrial breath.

Hermann Broch's translation, from *SP*, as 'Verwandlung' appeared in *Die Literarische Welt* VIII (2 Sep 1932) 5. See Gaskill 'Hermann Broch as Translator of Edwin Muir'.

See 'The Place of Light and Darkness' and n.

*The Original Place. Modern Scot* V (Autumn 1934) 159 as 'The Stronghold'. *MS* does not differentiate the stanzas typographically, and has 'our' for 'your', 'we' and 'us' for 'you' in first and third stanzas; has 'endless mines' for 'turning maze' (7), 'sublime' for 'of time' (8), 'fate is' for 'arms are' (30).

cf. 'The Debtor' 8–10 (*L*).

*The Sufficient Place. London Mercury* XXXIII (Mar 1936) 478–9 as III of 'Four Poems'. *LM* has for 9–10 'With living treasure, leaf and bird and leaf/Inwoven in silence. In the doorway stand'; 'Prototypes' for 'Archetypes' (19), 'vast' for 'wild' (23), 'blessed' for 'changed' (25).

See *A* 24–5, 64–5, 212, 241–2.

*The Dreamt-of Place*

[1–3] See *A* 278; 'The Annunciation' (*OFE*) and n; Dante, *Inferno* V 136.

[14] cf. 'It might be the day after the last day' (App. I).

## THE NARROW PLACE

London: Faber and Faber. February 1943; 2nd impression September 1943.
The division – thematic, roughly chronological – into 'The Narrow Place'
and 'Postscript' was not preserved in the collected editions, perhaps because
of the rejection of 'Isaiah', appropriate introducer of the second part. All
the poems were written during the Muirs' stay at St Andrews (Aug 1935-
Mar 1942). Those in 'Postscript' reflect his rediscovery of Christianity (Mar
1939), and the serenity and heightened awareness of love for his wife
attained during his enforced rest after illness (Spring 1941). 'The Refugees',
'Scotland 1941', 'The Narrow Place', 'The Wheel', 'The Shades', 'Isaiah'
and 'The Question' were omitted from *CP 52*. All these except 'Isaiah' were
restored in *CP 60*.

*To J.F.H. (1897–1934)*. *Listener* XXVI (24 Jul 1941) 116.
  For Muir on John Holms, the chief friend of his youth, see *A* 177–81, and
for Holms on Muir *A* 167–9. Holms died from heart failure during an opera-
tion for a small injury from a fall from a horse. Muir wrote after his crema-
tion, 'a dreadful violation of death, too horrible for tears . . . I cried at the
thought that he had died so easily . . . as if Death had told him to come, and
like a good child he had obeyed' (*SF* 256). In a letter to Raymond Tschumi
on 10 June 1949 he tells of walking, after an illness, in St Andrews and
seeing a young soldier, very like his dead friend, dashing by on a motor
cycle. 'I was in one of the curious moods which sometimes come with
convalescence: at any rate I did not know for a moment where I was; the
worlds of life and death seemed to fuse for an instant' (*SL* 152–3).
[1–2]  cf. 'The Journey Back' 184 (*L*).
[16–17]  Huberman (*The Poetry of Edwin Muir* 109) compares with lines
from Rilke's 'Todeserfahrung', which she translates, 'But when you went,
there broke on this scene/A streak of reality through that crack/Through
which you went.'
[23]  cf. 'The Road' 1–5 (*JP*).

*The Wayside Station*. *Listener* XXV (20 Mar 1941) 411 as 'Poem'. During
winter 1940–41 Muir travelled from St Andrews to work in the Food Office
in Dundee, changing trains at Leuchars. 'In mid winter the dawn had still
hardly come as I stamped up and down to keep warm; and over everything
hung the thought of war' (BBC 3 Sep 1952).

*The River*
  Letter to Raymond Tschumi 10 June 1949: 'This poem was written . . .
soon after the invasion of France [May 1940], which brought images of
universal disaster to so many of us. Frontier walls seemed to be beyond
saving just then, and I had an image of a Europe quite featureless, with all
the old marks gone' (*SL* 153).

*Then*. *New Alliance* I No. 1 (New Series) (Mar 1940) 8. *NA* has 'But bone
grinding on bone' (2).
  Muir told a Newbattle student that the words of the first line came to him
as he was wandering along the beach at St Andrews. 'It was some time

before he could link them with any unified idea or theme, but he felt they *must* be the beginning of a poem he was to write' (letter to editor from Ian MacArthur).

**[6–7]** cf. description of the Stations of the Cross at Salzburg in *Marionette* 38–9, and *A* 216.

**[17–20]]** cf. 'Ballad of the Soul' 9–12 (*FP*) and n.

*The Refugees. New Alliance* I No. 1 (Autumn 1939) 61–5.

This is the final chorus, omitting the first thirteen lines, of the work in *NA*, the rest of which is printed in App. I. *NA* has colon at end of 1 and extra line 'We did not see it', full stop at end of 3 and extra line 'We did not flee it/But. . .'; 'And all the voices from their sea-castle calling?' (30); semi-colon at end of 35 and extra line 'For all are guilty: all'.

The original version probably owes something to conversations with Hermann Broch, a refugee from Austria, who stayed with the Muirs in St Andrews in summer 1938. See *SF* 252–3.

Diary 4 June 1939, 'I have started on a poem 'The Refugees' from which I hope a great deal'.

Letter to Aitken 4 January 1940, 'It was inspired by quite sincere feeling but never rose to the right height, the pity and indignation never transmitting themselves, except in one or two lines in the last part.'

**[1–3]** Marshall (*In a Distant Isle* 42) connects with the flagged floors of Orkney houses, with insects coming up through the cracks. See *A* 21.

*Scotland 1941. New Alliance* II No. 3 (Apr-May 1941) 9.

*NA* has 'And huddled all the harvest gold away' (9) and, instead of 39–41:

> If we could raise these bones so brave and wrong,
> Revive our ancient body, part by part,
> We'd touch to pity the annalist's iron tongue
> And gather a nation in our sorrowful heart.

cf. 'The Book of Scotland', a series of broadcasts by Muir on Scottish history. The first, on 21 October 1941, was 'a story of disunity growing into unity' – through the spread of Columban Christianity, colouring Scots' attitude to the natural world, 'which became impregnated with Christian poetry and legend'; through the achievement of nationhood in the thirteenth century and the sense of being a people during the popular uprisings under Wallace and Bruce.

cf. 'The Fathers' (*V*).

**[1]** cf. 'The Ring' 1–2.

**[8–11]** cf. 'The Incarnation' (*OFE*). Knox robbed 'Scotland of all the benefits of the Renaissance' (*JK* 309); Andrew Melville (1545–1622), leading Presbyterian, was expert in invective; Sandy Peden (1626–86), Covenanter, is mentioned in *JK* (306) as an exponent of the tradition of denunciation stemming from Knox, which is still a destructive feature of Scottish life.

**[18]** *oak*: associated with the Stewarts.

**[30]** See *SS* 11–12 (Scott), 28–9 (Burns).

**[35]** Montrose (1612–50) late in the day went over to the losing Royalist cause; Mackail (1640–66), Covenanter, was tortured and executed for his faith; both the 1st (1598–1661) and 2nd (1629–85) Marquesses of Argyll tended to take the losing side and were executed. All exemplify the 'thrift-less honour', characteristic of the seventeenth century, which helped to destroy the kingdom but which is preferred to the 'pride of pelf' of a later time.

*The Letter. London Mercury* XXXVII (Nov 1937) 7 as II of 'Letters'. For I see App. I.

Probably connected with fierce attacks on Muir, especially by Christopher Grieve, following publication of *SS* in 1936.

*The Human Fold. Listener* XXI (4 May 1939) 938 as 'The Burden'. *L* has 'ever striving' for 'ever-moving' (3) and 'free' for 'dark' (39).

Muir's comment in a broadcast selection of his poems 3 September 1952: The poem 'is an attempt to describe the human situation in its greatness and littleness and confusion; you will detect in it . . . the shadow of the war. The refrain . . . came to me in a dream, and the whole poem grew from it'.

'Extracts from a Diary': 'A dream, or rather a voice, which came to me in half-sleep this morning, after being knocked up. The voice spoke from behind and a little above me, and said, 'I lean my cheek from Eternity for Time to slap'. At the same time I had a faint image of someone in white – a dim impression of a shroud – pushing his or her cheek against some transparent thin substance, slightly crinkling it; a feeling of an insubstantial displacement. I am certain I could never have framed that sentence except in sleep, though it seems so wonderful to me now, awake'. (*SF* 240–1).

cf. 'The Usurpers' 37–40 (*L*).

[15–20]   cf. 'The Fall' 21–40 (*JP*).

[49–52]   Diary 22 February 1939: 'Another dream consisting of a sentence which impressed me very deeply, but has only a feeling of impressiveness and mystery now, for the words, as far as I can remember, were: 'They loved each other, and they would have loved each other forever; if it had not been for public trouble and private care: these were the only two things that could prevent them'. Obviously a reflection of these troubled times, but something more in it. I thought the two were princes.'

*The Narrow Place. London Mercury* XXXIX (Apr 1939) 533–4 as 'The Narrow Country'. *LM* has 'our' for 'this' (8), 'thought' for 'blood' (12), 'mound' for 'hill' (40), and an extra line after 41, 'It is your eyes; it is your mind'.

[31–5]   cf. 'The Sufficient Place' 5–9 (*JP*), and *A* 64–5.

*The Recurrence. Listener* XXIII (13 Jun 1940) 1130 as 'The Eternal Recurrence'.

[34–9]   cf. 'The Window' (*V*).

[40–6]   cf. 'Robert the Bruce' 21–8. See *A* 128, a dream of Nietzsche on the Cross.

*The Good Man in Hell. New Verse* No. 28 (Jan 1938) 3 as 'Poem'. *NV*'s 'could wander' became 'could enter' in *NP* and 'would enter' in *CP* 60 (18).

*The Wheel. New Alliance* III No. 5 (Aug-Sep 1942) 3. *NA* has for 8 'That lie within the never-sleeping hill –/Conspiracies and disputes of the stinging dust'; lacks 14; and has for 28–9:

> Unless a Grace
> Come of itself to recreate
> Our souls in peace . . .

*The Face. Listener* XXVII (30 Jul 1942) 149.

*A* 144–5: 'I think it must have been out of my obsession with animal traits flitting across human features that a poem called 'The Face' emerged like a frightening monster.' Probably written early 1938, at the time of the diary entries with which *A* connects it. Contrast the more positive vision in Diary 13 August 1938: 'Sat in my bed looking at myself in a mirror hanging on the wall opposite. My face, especially the bony expanse, *came out*, and I saw the skin and flesh shrivelling from it, and the bone beneath: a terrifying, absolute vision, like the stripping off of time. And simultaneously a feeling of journeying on, with the forehead as a prow, beyond time, and the assurance that the naked bone, there, would flower into angel's flesh, and sprout angel's hair, fragrant and beautiful beyond conception.'

*The Law. London Mercury* XXXIII (Mar 1936) 477–8 as II of 'Four Poems'. Excluded from *JP*.

**[19–23]**   cf. 'No more of this trapped gazing' 16–19 (App. I).

*The City. Spectator* CLX (25 Mar 1938) 511 as 'Poem'. *S* has comma at end of 16; 'Even to the beasts' for 'We looked away' (17); comma at end of 24, and instead of 25–8:

> Who would not let us pass. Their arms were old,
>     Their swords rusted, their generals deaf and blind.
> If we had bribed these men, would they have sold
>     The sacred place? If we had fought them, signed
>
> A hurried peace? We do not know. We saw
>     In thought the holy streets running with blood,
> And centuries of fear and power and awe,
>     And all our children lost in the deadly wood.
>
> So we went home. Before we went our eyes
>     Saw wingéd men walking along the wall.
> We have made an order natural and wise
>     Here, like a dream, until the destiny fall.

cf. 'Outside Eden' (*OFE*). The 'wingéd men' appear again in a fragmentary draft mentioned in 'The Day before the Last Day' (*LP*) n.

*The Grove. New Alliance* II No. 2 (Feb-Mar 1941) 11.

cf. *CND* 268–79.

**[15]**   cf. 'Dialogue: I have heard you cry' (*LP*), 25–8.

*The Gate*

See *A* 14–15, where memories of playing with his sister near the remains of the Castle on Wyre are immediately followed by memories of the little general; *A* 33–5, 64–5; *PT* 110–13.

*The Little General. Listener* XIX (9 Jun 1938) 1232 as 'Poem'. *L* has 'emblems' for 'ritual' (4) and for 13–14: 'Tale of a rustic war half human and half feathered/Legend and truth embattled on one shield.'

See *A* 15, 47–8; W.P.L. Thomson *The Little General and the Rousay Crofters*.

*The Prize. Listener* XXVI (30 Oct 1941) 586.

Letter to Aitken 12 June 1941. He has been living in a state of enforced tranquillity after straining his heart. One result 'has been a little freshet of poetry. I'm enclosing some of it, not knowing how you will like it, for it seems to me different from most of my poetry: there's no effort in it, for at present I'm unable to make such things as efforts; and I'm afraid it lacks intensity, but it may have some other quality that makes up for that' (*SL* 129–31). The poems sent were 'The Question', 'The Guess', 'The Prize' and 'The Old Gods'.

**[2–3]** cf. first version of 'Ballad of the Soul' 1–4 (*FP*); *VTT* III 8–11.

*The Ring. Spectator* CLXVII (26 Dec 1941) 596. *S* has 'As in a dream the half-remembered word' (22).

**[1–3]** Letter to Spender 2 August 1940: 'My mind is being teased by fragmentary intimations of poems more than it has been for some time, . . . lines like:

> We were a tribe, a family, a people,
> King Lear was our father.'

In 'The Politics of King Lear', two conceptions of 'nature' are contrasted. 'Lear is very old, almost Saturnian in his legendary age; the kingdom in him exists as a memory and no longer as a fact, the old order lies in ruin, and the new is not an order. The communal tradition, filled with memory, has been smashed by an individualism that exists in its perpetual shallow present' (*ELS* 49).

**[10–11]** *A* 53: 'Goneril, Regan and Cornwall are merely animals furnished with human faculties.' cf. Archie Blackadder in *TB* 204, people in Glasgow in *A* 52–3, himself in 'The Face'.

*Isaiah. Glasgow Herald* (7 Mar 1942) 3. *GH* has 'Playing their parts eternally' (3), 'triune' for 'triple' (12).

See Isaiah 6:1–8, the prophet's vision in the temple of God and angels; 11:6–9, his vision of unity between animals, men and God. cf. 'The Covenant' (*V*).

**[1]** See 1 Kings 7:23–37, where ledges are mentioned as features of the Temple's architecture. The temple was next to the palace. But 'ledge' may also suggest a viewpoint in mountains as in *CND* 259 and 292, 'Adam's Dream' 13 (*OFE*).

*The Return of Odysseus. New York Times* (31 Aug 1942). Printings before *CP* 60 entitle 'The Return' and have 'Ulysses' for 'Odysseus' in 1, 21, 27.

Letter to Spender 2 August 1940 quotes 'The doors yawned open in Ulysses' house' among fragmentary intimations of poems, and says it has turned into a poem (*SL* 124).

cf. 'Telemachos Remembers' (*OFE*) and n.

*Robert the Bruce. New Alliance* I No. 4 (Jun-Jul 1940) 9 as 'Robert the Bruce Stricken with Leprosy: To Douglas'.

cf. 'Ballad of the Black Douglas' (App. I).

Bruce, dying of leprosy in 1329, having failed to fulfil a vow to make a pilgrimage to Jerusalem, entrusted his heart to Douglas to take to the Holy Sepulchre. In 1306 he had slain John Comyn, a possible rival for the throne, in a Dumfries church. Wallace had been hung, drawn and quartered in London in 1305.
[5–8]   Nearly a repetition of 'The Town Betrayed' 13–16 (*JP*).

*The Trophy. Listener* XXVI (18 Dec 1941) 811.
cf. 'The Fathers' and n (*V*); 'The Three Mirrors' 36–53 (*V*).

*The Annunciation. NP* has 'spirits' (32).

*The Confirmation.* Willa Muir says (*Belonging* 210–11) that it was during Muir's enforced rest in bed in spring 1941 that he wrote some love poems to her. One was this poem, which 'sent me into a passion of tears, because I knew too well that I was only a botched version of what I was meant to be'; the others presumably 'The Annunciation' and 'The Commemoration'.

*The Old Gods. New Alliance* II No. 5 (Aug-Sep 1941) 7 as 'To the Old Gods'. For early version sent to Aitken 12 June 1941 see *SL* 129; and see 'The Prize' n.

*The Guess. Spectator* CLXVII (18 Jul 1941) 57.
See 'The Prize' n.

*The Swimmer's Death. Listener* XXVII (11 Jun 1942) 742.
Letter from Neil Gunn to the editor: 'Edwin told me that the poem exactly described a dream which he had had. I know we talked of the wonderful clarity and radiance of the light – of the sea – which remained in our minds from early boyhood years in that northern world. But I cannot remember if I mentioned a word in the poem which had affected me, that word "homing". I may have been diffident about mentioning it because I felt that such a word gave a warmth to radiance, appeared to add human experience to austere vision, and that some of his poems might gain by having it here or there, if only in the sense of gaining more readers' (*SL* 151).

*The Question. Spectator* CLXVII (11 Jul 1941) 33; *Poetry* (Chicago) LVIII (Sep 1941) 323 – in both as 'The Finder Found'. *P*, presumably the earlier version, has 'in the buyer's hand' (7), for 8 'And there, the prize, in freedom rest and roam', and other variants. cf. 'The Mythical Journey' 15–16 (*JP*).
Letter to Spender 2 August 1940 quotes among fragmentary intimations of poems: 'He who has not been yet will be some day,/The gatherer gathered, the finder found' (*SL* 124).
See 'The Prize' n, and letter to Peat 28 February 1940: 'I have had something like a sense of the presence of God, a sense which I have never consciously been aware of before' (*SL* 118).


## THE VOYAGE

London: Faber and Faber. Apr 1946; 2nd impression 1947. All the poems except 'Sappho', 'Dialogue', 'The House', 'On Seeing Two Lovers in the Street', 'Song of Patience' and 'Song: "Here in this Corner"' were included in *CP 52*; all except 'Dialogue' and 'Song: "Here in this Corner"' in *CP 60*.

# Notes

All were written during the Muirs' time in Edinburgh (Mar 1942-Autumn 1945), where he worked for the British Council.

Dedication: Lumir Soukop and his Scottish wife were friends of the Muirs in Edinburgh, and later in Prague, where he worked in the Czech Foreign Office.

*The Return of the Greeks. New English Weekly* II (May 1945) 35–6 as 'The Return'.

*The Escape. Listener* XXXIII (4 Jan 1945) 12.

In a letter to Oscar Williams 19 November 1944 Muir said this poem was suggested by a novel by David Scott, *Corporal Jack*, (which he had reviewed in *Listener* (29 Jul 1943) 134) about an English soldier's escape from prison camp, wanderings through France and arrival at Gibraltar. It reminded him of other such wanderings through Europe, for instance after the failure of the Crusades. 'The escape I try to describe in the poem is partly realistic and partly symbolical' (*SL* 140).

[9–20]  Jack walks south through rural France, and is kindly treated by a family in a village, where he is known; but also sees the effects of war and suffers nightmares: cf. 'The Town Betrayed' 9–12 (*JP*).

[25–40]  He thinks that if he can get out of Occupied France he will be safe, but finds the German influence still strong in the Unoccupied zone and even in Spain, where he is arrested, escapes by jumping out of a train in a tunnel, comes out to see Barcelona in golden light, is re-arrested, beaten and for a time thinks he is going blind.

[48–52]  cf. 'The Bridge of Dread' 21–5 (*L*).

*The Castle. Listener* XXXIV (8 Nov 1945) 520.

Muir's first St Andrews home was just opposite the Castle, where Cardinal Beaton was murdered in 1546 by a group of Protestants, who got in probably with collusion from inside. He wrote of this in *JK* 19, and in *TB* 6–16, where the sensitive boy David's father explains how assassins might get into a strong castle by a 'wicked-looking, wee gate'. In *TB* 61–4 the father tells of a visit to a deserted chateau near Paris and of seeing the great silver pointer of a clock lying broken on the cobbles. 'The chateau seemed terrible all at once, as if the murder of Time had coincided with some incomprehensible event.' David was entranced by this story, which 'seemed more wonderful than those in which things happened', and saw 'an invisible ruin sweeping through the chateau as if from a secret chamber in the centre, and breaking off the dial hand like a leaf'.

cf. 'The Town Betrayed' (*JP*).

*Moses. Listener* XXXIV (22 Nov 1945) 586.

[1]  Deuteronomy 34:1–4. Moses sees into the promised land, but dies without entering it. The next book, Joshua, tells of the Israelites crossing the Jordan and possessing the land, but also of their continuing troubles and rebelliousness.

*Sappho*. Makes use of Ovid's apocryphal story of Sappho throwing herself from a cliff for love of Phaon.

[13–24]  Reverses the naming enacted in 'The Days' (*OFE*).

335

*The Covenant* See *A* 46–8 on 'the timeless, crowded age of organic her-aldry'.

*The Voyage. Orion* II (Autumn 1945) 7–9. *O* lacks 25–8 and 77–80; has 'For freedom alone was then our joy' (81), 'Compass and chart would never yet/Fail him;' (90–1). All printings before *CP* 60 have extra stanza at end:

> The crowds drew near, the toppling towers;
> In hope and dread we drove to birth;
> The dream and a truth we clutched as ours,
> And gladly, blindly stepped on earth.

Eric Linklater to editor 6 August 1963: 'It was during the war, and I had been spending a few days with soldiers and sailors training for combined operations . . . On the way back I was talking to an elderly man who had gone to sea in stick-and-string days, and rejoined (Merchant Service) for war-time duty. He told me of a voyage to Australia in which, because of persistent bad weather (fog and storm) they had, for week after week, got no sight of the sun nor spoken another vessel. And presently a fo'c'sle rumour began to spread: Perhaps the world had come to an end, and they alone were left alive? . . . There was no panic . . . but an ever-growing fear and foreboding. And when at last, after a voyage that seemed interminable, they saw land, there was no rejoicing, but a sort of dismay of another sort.' When Linklater told him this story Muir at once asked if he could have it. 'His poem is his . . . own creation – but my story was the yard from which he launched it.'

*The Fathers. Orion* I (Spring 1945) 42.

The second and third stanzas were read in 'The Inheritors', a BBC pro-gramme by Muir on Scottish history, on 27 March 1955, the narrator com-menting, 'We are the descendants of the victors, but also of the defeated . . . You have victory and defeat within you, and the rage of the quarrel'. A voice asks whether the curse can be lifted, and the narrator answers, 'Yes, if you accept the curse and change it into a blessing; if you give thanks for the victory and show pity for the defeated'. Then the second stanza of 'The Trophy' (*JP*) was read; and at the end 'The Debtor' (*L*).

cf. 'The Wheel' (*NP*).

*The Three Mirrors*

From 'Yesterday's Mirror: Afterthoughts to an Autobiography': 'Art is the sum of the moments in which men have glanced into that yesterday which can never change . . . that mirror in which all the forms of life lie outspread'. There are 'three ways in which men may look into that mirror – . . . the glance of experience which discerns a world where wrong triumphs and right suffers; . . . the glance of the man who in maturity has kept a memory of his childhood', and who 'sees in the mirror an indefeasible right-ness beneath the wrongness of things'; and the vision of the mystic, who sees 'a world in which both good and evil have their place legitimately: in which the king on his throne and the rebel raising his flag in the market place, the tyrant and the slave, the assassin and the victim, each plays a part in a supertemporal drama which at every moment, in its totality, issues in glory and meaning and fulfilment'.

**[39–43]** cf. 'The Trophy' (*JP*).

*The Rider Victory. Horizon* X (Dec 1944) 376. Included in *The War Poets: An Anthology of the War Poetry of the Twentieth Century* (1945).

In summer 1944 Muir wrote to Spender that a reading of C.M. Bowra's *The Heritage of Symbolism* had made him realise that he 'had been writing symbolist poetry very frequently for years without knowing it. He inspired me to write one deliberately, which I enclose . . . I shouldn't have written it quite like that but for his book'.

The Rider has some resemblance to 'The Conqueror' (*LP*) and to the figure on a bridge in 'Extracts from a Diary': 'Another image of Time, which came to me this morning between asleep and awake. A legendary female figure on a bridge, with the blind or all-seeing eyes of a tragic Greek statue. This figure faces the future. The past lies behind her, clear and definite, a world of forms. The future lies in front, shapeless and increate, an ocean of irridescent colours. This is all she can see; she can never turn her head and look at the creation. This figure seems to be in perpetual motion, but is stationary, and stands on a narrow bridge' (*SF* 237–8). Recording the poem at the Library of Congress in 1955 Muir said that in it he 'tried to express the limitations of victory'.

*The Window. Poetry-Scotland*, Third Collection (Jul 1946) 47–8. *P-S* has 'revivals' for 'marvels' (10), 'mound' for 'mount' (12).

*The Myth. Orion* I (Spring 1945) 41–2.

*On Seeing Two Lovers in the Street. Listener* XXXIII (28 Jun 1945) 706.

Morley Jamieson, writer and bookseller, and his wife Flora lived with the Muirs in 8 Blantyre Terrace, Edinburgh from 1943 to 1945. When Muir met them walking hand in hand in the street, 'he seemed', Jamieson remembers, 'to wake up as we approached and an engaging smile would spread over his face'.

**[10–14]** cf. Donne 'The Extasie' 15–16, 41–5.

*Reading in Wartime. Listener* XXX (8 Jul 1944) 40 as 'Reading'.
**[18]** *The Death of Ivan Ilych* (1886), a novella by Tolstoy.
**[35]** cf. 'The Brothers' 27 (*LP*).

*The Lullaby*. Sent to Oscar Williams on 19 November 1944 for an anthology of war poetry, but not included in it (*SL* 139–40). 'The Rider Victory' was substituted.

*Song of Patience. Poetry-Scotland*. Second Collection (1945) 12.

*Sorrow. Poetry-Scotland*. Third Collection (Jul 1946) 47 as 'Song of Sorrow'. *P-S* has 'must' for 'cannot' (9), and for 17–24:

> I can't want it so!
> For joy was all my trade
> Till sorrow on sorrow
> Unmade what joy made.
> O joy must still renew
> Both joy and sorrow too,

Else I'd have nothing, so, or so,
And all must go.

*Epitaph*. *Scottish Art and Letters* No. 2 (Spring 1946) 23.
[5–6]  cf. 'To Franz Kafka' 9–10 (*OFE*), more characteristic of Muir.

*Comfort in Self-Despite*. *Scottish Art and Letters* No. 2 (Spring 1946) 23.

*The Transmutation*. *Listener* XXXIV (26 Jul 1945) 96.

To Douglas Young 15 Jul 1950, suggesting poems for an anthology:
'Among the Sonnets I like best "Transmutation"' (*SL* 157).

*For Ann Scott-Moncrieff (1914–1943)*. *New Alliance* IV No. 3 (Apr–May 1943) 7 as 'To Ann . . .', which remained the title until the final revision.
*NA* has extra stanza after 16:

> Here I can say at last
> What I could never say
> Until your mould was cast,
> Perfected and laid away.
> I could have learned from you
> In the common course of time
> What I learned from a few
> When I hurried past my prime
> To Plato and Dante to school
> And conned immortality,
> And tried to put off the fool,
> And, a being, strove to be.

and has 'on' for 'in' (39).

Ann Scott-Moncrieff, née Shearer, an Orcadian, wife of George Scott-Moncrieff, was author of *Auntie Robbo* (1941), etc.

*A Birthday*. *Poetry-Scotland* No. 1 (1943) 12–13. *P-S* has 'memories' for 'travellers' (29).
See 'In Love for Long' n.

*In Love for Long*
To Douglas Young 15 Jul 1950, suggesting poems for an anthology, 'I'm fond of "I've been in love for long"' (*SL* 157). In 'The Poems of Edwin Muir', BBC broadcast 23 September 1952: 'The genesis of . . . "In Love for Long", I can remember vividly. I was up at Swanston in the Pentlands one Saturday during the War. It was in late summer; a dull, cloudy, windless day, quite warm. I was sitting on the grass, looking at the thatched cottages and the hills, when I realised that I was fond of them, suddenly and without reason, and for themselves, not because the cottages were quaint or the hills romantic. I had an unmistakable warm feeling for the ground I was sitting on, as if I were in love with the earth itself, and the clouds, and the soft subdued light. I had felt these things before, but that afternoon they seemed to crystallise, and the poem came out of them'. Mrs Muir (*Belonging* 210) says that 'A Birthday' also was composed at Swanston.

Richard Wilbur, American poet, to editor 8 August 1964: 'I recall his asking his audience [at Harvard] to imagine or remember the sort of experience men sometimes have – the experience of sitting, perhaps, on a hillside in the country and feeling oneself swept by a deep and sudden love for no particular thing. This was by way of preface to his poem 'In Love for Long', and during that preface I saw heads everywhere begin to nod, Ivor Richards' among them; it was as if he were telling a happy secret about us all which had never been told before.'

[34–6]   cf. 'Ballad of the Nightingale' 53–6 (*FP*).


## THE LABYRINTH

London. Faber and Faber. June 1949. 2nd impression 1950.

All the poems were included in *CP 52* and *CP 60*. Probably all were written during Muir's time as Director of the British Council Institute in Prague between September 1945 and July 1948. A letter to Joseph Chiari (*SL* 141) shows that only 'The Child Dying' had been completed by July 1946. In September 1947 he told him that on holiday at Mariánské Lázne he had been able to get out a number of poems that had been dammed up in him, and that he had almost enough for a volume. 'I intend to call the poems *Symbols* or something of that kind, for they all deal with symbolical human situations and types' (*SL* 146). By September 1946 Faber had accepted the volume, which he thought 'the best I have done yet' (*SL* 150).

In a notebook in NLS, used between 1946 and 1948, are plans, jottings, and more or less complete drafts of 'The Interrogation', 'The Way', 'The Labyrinth', 'Soliloquy', 'Too Much', 'The Return', 'The Helmet', 'The Transfiguration', 'The Usurpers' and 'The Good Town', interspersed with workings towards parts of 'The Journey Back'. At the beginning, in a list of 'Ideas for poems', is 'The Dream of the mythological vision'. Soon afterwards is a sketch for this, headed 'The Vision': 'The first breathings. Water. The sun and stars: the lights. God was there though we knew not God. The low-browed animals. The dragon. The sphinx: fear. Knowledge. Birth. The fluttering spirit. The creation of the universe in the mind [?]. God in the sky, man in the centre, the animal world. The Transfiguration. The angels and immortality.' Muir was hoping to use the material from his London dream (*A* 159–163) more adequately than in 'Ballad of the Soul' (*FP*). Other unfulfilled ideas are for poems on The Last Supper and The Return of the Crusaders.

*Too Much*. Listener XXXVII (24 Apr 1947) 623 as 'Sonnet'.
   cf. 'The Bargain'.
[12–14]   cf. 'Oedipus' 53–5; 'Milton' (*OFE*).

*The Labyrinth*. Listener XXXVII (20 Mar 1947) 432.
   In the notebook draft, headed 'Theseus', the first sentence (1–35) is directly answered by 'This is illusion' and a draft of 47 to end. Then 'And then I'd stumble' (35) to 46 is drafted.
   In a BBC broadcast on 3 September 1952 Muir said that the poem 'started itself' in Dobřiš Castle near Prague, given by the Czech government as a retreat for writers. 'Thinking of the old story of the Labyrinth of Cnossos and the journey of Theseus through it and out of it, I felt that this was an image of human life with its errors and ignorance and endless intricacy. In

the poem I made the labyrinth stand for all this. But I wanted also to give an image of the life of the gods to whom all that is confusion here is clear and harmonious as seen eternally. The poem begins with a very long sentence, deliberately labyrinthine, to give the mood.' The formal garden at Dobřiš, full of statues of classical gods and heroes, may have contributed to suggest the theme, but the maze ('The Lost Land' revised 26 (App. III), 'The Original Place' 7 (*JP*), 'The Prize' 17 (*NP*)) and the gods on islands ('The Mythical Journey' 39–41 (*JP*)) had already appeared in poems.

[20–3]   Theseus gets out by help of a ball of thread, given by Ariadne.

*The Way. Listener* XXXVII (6 Mar 1947) 334.

*The Return. Listener* XXXVIII (18 Sep 1947) 479. *L* lacks 17.
See *A* 64–5, his dream of the Bu, 'strangely transfigured and transposed'. cf. 'The Sufficient Place' (*JP*).

*The West.* Jottings early in the notebook look forward to the concluding lines of this poem and to 'The Journey Back' section 7, both of which work to reconcile opposed points of view in the jottings. See 'The Journey Back' n.

*The Journey Back.* Section 1 in *Listener* XL (19 Aug 1948) 279; sections 3, 4, 7 in *Poetry - London* No. 15 (May 1949) 2–4. *L* has extra line after 22 'With slow and patient pace treading the ground'; 'In trust and candour' for 'In patient trust' (23); extra line afteer 31 'Sleep in the rain, beg, rob, lie in rich beds'; 'helpless' for 'hapless' (60).

The notebook shows the poem growing from widely-dispersed jottings and drafts, probably not at first seen as parts of a whole. The first start from the present, 'Yet blessing in spite of all on this time and place', and became the second half of section 5. An argument follows between a speaker who says 'We live but here and now' and one who asks 'How could we live if all were not in all?' The 'here and now' was developed into the conclusion of 'The West'; the idea of all being in all was eventually used in section 7 of 'The Journey Back', but now leads into an early version of section 2:

> Then come the god, and come the beast, and aid
> My soul to fight against this time mismade
> Before the land rose from the sea I was
> In a dream, in a sleep, in a trance. I kept the laws
> Of the great universe.

Material from the old dream is coming in and is seen as relevant to 'this time'; but there is no clear plan. Fragments ('And there was consternation among the dead'; 'And the yellow harvester in the sunset') which were later to find their places are followed by workings towards sections 3 and 4. Later is a draft of the first half of section 5, not yet connected to the 'blessing' passage. Only towards the end of the notebook do we come to the first draft of section 1. Perhaps it was now that the poem took shape in Muir's mind. The journey back through the ancestors could be used to connect the calamities and blessings of the present with the 'Vision' material on man's origin and end. This stage was probably reached in Spring 1948, when, on 7 April, Willa wrote in her diary,

'Edwin has written some magnificent poetry. Beginning of a series called "I" and two short ones . . . "I" is going to be a great work'. Next in the notebook are workings towards section 2, now in stanzas and short lines; then, at the very end, a bringing together of the two halves of section 5. Apart from odd lines there has been no sign of section 7, which was probably added deliberately as a conclusion.

**Section 2**

**[84]** *consternations*: punning on German stern — star.

**[90–2]** In the draft, 'Sometimes I feel again/The mortal anguish when/The dragon died'. The dragon does not have the usual evil associations. It belongs in the world before the Fall. Its appearance is several times followed by that of the Sphinx ('Ballad of Eternal Life (App. II)', 'The Fall' 21–6 (*JP*), 'The Human Fold' 16–20 (*NP*)), associated with time and with fear. In the notebook, during the first attempt at section 2, there is a marginal note 'The Sphinx to be brought in here', and in the second attempt there are lines on 'The . . . Sphinx/With dead and moveless wings'.

**[96–8]** In *A* 166 he writes of an 'intuition that long before man appeared on the earth he existed as a dream or a prophecy in the animal soul'.

**Section 3**

**[115]** *third*: cf. 'Ballad of Rebirth' (*FP*), where the soul watches his body fall to death and be reborn; *VTT* III 15–16.

**Section 6**

In the middle of the draft of section 1 is a draft of a poem on music:

> And once I saw one with a radiant face,
> Illuminated and blind, whose name was Music,
> And he spoke to the emptiness as none were there.
> And so he said 'Behold, all things speak through me,
> Living and dead, Austria and France and Egypt,
> America, Hellas, India and Judaea,
> And tongues forgotten that shall never be known again,
> Silences and voices of beasts who have no language,
> And trees and rocks and waters and buried places.
> For I am music, and through me speak all things,
> Yet I can never know that which I say.

This may have been intended for 'The Journey Back' and been replaced by a poem which is music, inspired by the vision of angels in *A* 162. But 'The angels and immortality' was part of the original plan for 'The Vision'; so the draft on music may be quite separate.

cf. Hölderlin's 'Schicksalslied', part of which Muir translated: 'You wander up there in the light, on soft lawns, spiritual beings. Fateless, like the sleeping child, breathe the heavenly ones. Chastely nourished in separate buds, the spirit blooms in them forever, and the spiritual eyes gaze in still, eternal clarity. But to us is given in no state to rest . . .' Hölderlin, Muir comments, was haunted by the thought of the dual existence of the gods and of men. Why should they both exist, and why should there be an unbridgeable gulf between them? ('A Note on Friedrich Hölderlin', *TI* 18).

**Section 7**

cf. 'To J.F.H.' (*NP*).

**[209]** '*golden harvester*': harvest moon made golden by the light of the sun which has set.

cf. 'Double Absence' (*OFE*).

*The Bridge of Dread. Listener* XXXIX (1 Jan 1948) 16.

cf. Ballad 'A Lyke-wake Dirge':

> From Brig' o' Dread when thou may'st pass
> Every nighte and alle
> To Purgatory fire thou com'st at last;
> And Christe receive thy saule.

cf. 'The Grove' 41–9 (*NP*), 'The Escape' 45–52 (*V*).

*The Helmet. Listener* XXXVIII (9 Oct 1947) 625. *L* has 'comfort' for 'sweetness' (15).

The notebook draft is more optimistic:

> A helmet on a beloved head
> Glazes and blinds the remembered face,
> And brings another in its stead . . .
> Take off your helmet and let me see
> You and me as we were before
> Put from your heart all enmity . . .

In *A* 254–5 Muir tells of being stopped, at the frontier to Russian-occupied Czechoslovakia, by a soldier whose eyes were 'quite expressionless and giving out the interior light of glowing, highly polished stones'. His party was kept waiting a long time, looking at the soldier and at horses grazing in a field nearby. cf. 'The Interrogation' and 'The Usurpers'.

*The Child Dying. Listener* XXXVII (26 Jan 1947) 994.

To Chiari 27 July 1946: 'I have written only one poem since I came, a very curious one about the thoughts of a child dying – where it came from goodness only knows! . . . I've been trying for some years to write poetry that was both simple and unexpected; and if this poem is good – I can hardly tell whether it is or not – I think I have succeeded' (*SL* 141–2). The version sent to Chiari has 'A passing grace, a single face' (16), and *L* 'A fleeting grace'.

cf. Rilke *Duino Elegies* I, and see Ritchie Robertson in *Edwin Muir: Centenary Assessments*, 113–14.

**[25–30]** Later this year Willa wrote a poem:

> If my hand should die in yours
> or yours die in mine,
> how long could the clay-cold corse
> with living flesh entwine?
>
> That deadly chill would numb the wrist,
> shoulder, bosom, heart,
> yet what could make our hands untwist
> or rive us two apart?
>
> Since the quick blood could not warm two,
> however close the hold,

better to let it ebb than flow
till both alike were cold.

*The Combat. Listener* XXXVIII (4 Sep 1947) 386.

See *A* 65 for the dream from which this poem was developed; *A* 106–8 for in some ways similar incidents and another dream; *Belonging* 238 for the circumstances in which it was written.

To Douglas Young 15 July 1950; 'I think "The Combat" is one of my best poems' (*SL* 157).

From comment after recording the poem: 'Helpless little animal – might stand for something in humanity that can be killed, that cannot be killed actually – it is very valuable that, after being beaten, it does return – it's an expression of hope, at the end – it might be taken as humanity and all the enormous forces, particularly nowadays, ranged against humanity in every way' (Tape 2 H).

*The Intercepter. Scottish Periodical* I No. 2 (Summer 1948) 111.

cf. *VTT* IX, 'The Private Place' (*JP*). Indifference, the Intercepter and the trickster (*SF* 258–9) are internal obstacles to the true self. Willa Muir identifies the Intercepter with Indifference. He 'represented, I thought, the influence that had led him in earlier years to shut doors so often on his feelings . . . Now in Prague, he had reacted to the Putsch [Feb 1948] and his difficulties in the Council by again showing signs of withdrawal . . . The conclusion I came to eventually was that the demon Indifference, The Interceptor cutting Edwin off from natural feeling, was his own defence against the doctrine of Original Sin . . . It was the Fall of Man and the consequent inherited guilt of the whole human race that kept haunting his imagination, and, I suspected, at times had paralysed him like his own Enchanted Knight' (*Belonging* 248–9).

[11–12] cf. *VTT* IX 12–13, 42.

*Head and Heart. Scottish Periodical* I No. 2 (Summer 1948) 112.

Letter to Richard Church 15 December 1941: 'You have a combination of emotion and thought which gives your poetry an exciting living quality which I envy very much . . . These poems [*Fifty Poems*] . . . moved and delighted me with a sense of significant living experience fully expressed, while it is most living, not merely in memory, as too much of my own poetry tends to be'.

*The Interrogation. Listener* XL (2 Sep 1948) 347.

See 'The Helmet' and n, 'The Border' and n.

*The Border.* Probably the poem referred to by Willa Muir in her diary entry 7 April 1948 about Edwin having written two short poems 'about crossing frontier, the first, very neat, very simple'. Probably the other is 'The Interrogation', which, drafted earlier, may have been put into final form at this time.

*The Good Town. Listener* XL (25 Nov 1948) 807.

Comment in BBC broadcast 3 September 1952: 'A little after writing "The Labyrinth" . . . I had an idea for two poems about towns, one to be called "The Good Town" and the other "The Bad Town"; and I intended the towns to stand as symbols of two ways of life. But as things were then shaping in Prague, I saw that the only way to treat the theme was to describe a good town turning into a bad one. Yet the poem is not really about Prague or any other place, but about something that was happening in Europe. Stories of what was occurring in other countries to whole families, whole communities, became absorbed into the poem, which I tried to make into a symbolical picture of a vast change'. The position of the draft near the end of the notebook suggests that it was written after the Communist takeover.

*The Usurpers. Listener* XL (1 Jul 1948) 27; *Virginia Quarterly* XXXV (Jul 1949) 386–7. The *VQ* text, having 'do not like' for 'never seek' (26), 'cheek' for 'face' (38) and other slight variations, is presumably the earlier.
    See *A* 260–2, story of Gestapo atrocity and description of young Gestapo men who stare out of a photograph 'with the confidence of the worthless', but no satisfaction and no hope.
[38–9]   cf. 'The Human Fold' 35–6, 66–7 and n (*NP*).

*The Bargain. Listener* XXXVII (22 May 1947) 791 as 'Sonnet'.
*L* has 'eye' for 'mind' (8), 'unmoving' for 'unfading' (12).

*Oedipus. Listener* XXXVIII (16 Oct 1947) 681.
    Written at about the same time as an essay on Kafka, published in 1947, in which Muir speaks of Kafka's 'theory of the irreconcilability of divine and human law' (*ELS* 123), and implies that he rejects it.
[31–4]   cf. 'Too Much' 12–14.
[76]   cf. 'The Church' 37 (*LP*); Dante *Paradiso* XXXIII 145.

*Circle and Square. Scottish Periodical* I No. 2 (Summer 1948) 110.

*Soliloquy. Listener* XXXVIII (30 Oct 1947) 779.
[67–73]   Drafted immediately after the first jottings towards 'Too Much'; probably written at about the same time as another related poem, 'The Bargain'.

*The Absent. Scottish Periodical* I No. 2 (Summer 1948) 109.
    *SP* has a break after 14, 'For They are not here' (15), 'Those' for 'These' (16). cf. 'The Refugees' 33 (App. I).
[22]   *usurpers*: Though the attitude of the speakers is different, this poem is linked with 'The Usurpers', probably written about the same time.

*The Transfiguration. Listener* XXXIX (19 Feb 1948) 59.
    *L* has 'delusion' for 'a vision' (13).
    Comment in BBC broadcast 3 September 1952:
    'I had always been deeply struck by the story of the Transfiguration in the Gospels, and I had felt that perhaps at the moment of Christ's transfiguration everything was transfigured – mankind and the animals, and the simplest natural objects. After the poem appeared in *The Listener*, I had a letter from a lady [Miss Maisie Spens, author of *Receive the Joyfulness of your Glory*] who had made a long study of the subject, and to my surprise I found that the idea which I had imagined myself possessed a whole literature, and that in some Russian churches it was often represented pictorially. Perhaps in the imagination of mankind the transfiguration has become a

powerful symbol, standing for many things, and among them those trans-formations of reality which the imagination itself creates.' See letter to Miss Spens (*SL* 148).

See *A* 54–6 for the millennial dream on which the poem is based, *A* 114 for a real-life experience of the feeling 'that all substance had been trans-muted' (described also in *PT* 102–6). cf. 'The Nightingale' (*FP*) which at the beginning keeps closer to the dream.

[62–4] 'The idea of Judas going back into innocence has often been with me' (*SL* 148).

*The Debtor*. cf. 'The Trophy' (*NP*), 'The Fathers' (*V*).
[8] *strong hold*: cf. 'The Original Place' 24–31 (*JP*).

*The Toy Horse*. Listener XXXIX (8 Jan 1948) 59.
 *L* has 'still' for 'calm' (18).
 cf. a late essay, 'Toys and Abstractions': 'By virtue of one front leg raised as if for pacing, the toy horse creates a road to lie before it, and the road may in turn evoke little rivers and hills to be crossed, a small landscape, a small world ruled, like the actual world, by the law of departure and return . . . Regard this toy horse and you will see that it has at the same time the qualities of motionless and motion, and that while unchanged it suggests countless images of change. The explanation is that every true imitation of an object becomes a pattern and has the power to gather round it the world of patterns'.
 In the Library of Congress recording Muir spoke of 'a toy horse which I remembered as a boy', and read 'wandering' for 'wondering' (3).
 cf. 'The Emblem' (*OFE*).

## ONE FOOT IN EDEN

London: Faber and Faber. March 1956. New York: Grove Press 1956. Written during Muir's time as director of the British Institute in Rome (Jan 1949-Jul 1950) and as Warden of Newbattle Abbey College near Edin-burgh (Jul 1950-Aug 1955).

To Joseph Chiari 20 December 1949: 'I'm much struck with Rome, and all its wealth of associations; you feel the gods (including the last and great-est of them) have all been here, and are still present in a sense in the places where they once were. It has brought very palpably to my mind the theme of Incarnation and I feel that probably I shall write a few poems about that high and difficult theme sometime: I hope so. Edinburgh I love, but in Edinburgh you never come upon anything that brings the thought of In-carnation to your mind, and here you do so often, and quite unexpectedly. I'm rather afraid of writing on such a theme and though it occupies my mind whenever my mind is free from daily affairs, I feel nothing is ready yet to be written down. I haven't written much at all, a poem about the first seven days, and one about day and night, and one, with which I'm not very pleased, about the gods hanging round a ruined temple' (*SL* 154–5).

*OFE* was a Poetry Book Society choice, and Muir wrote in the Society's *Bulletin* No. 9 (Mar 1956): 'From all I can learn, it is a common experience among poets to have some line occur to them spontaneously, almost capriciously, and this line, being a question, somehow or other builds a poem round itself. About half the poems in this collection began in that way; the rest started from a general conception or subject which could be dealt with in a more systematic fashion. I imagine there is not much difference between the poems which began in these two separate ways, for the working on a poem seems to be what gives it character'.

In correspondence with Eliot at Faber Muir suggested changing the title to *The Succession*, but was dissuaded (*SL* 172). He left five poems – 'The Christmas', 'The Son', 'Lost and Found', 'The Lord' and 'The Choice' – out of *CP 60*, the religious ones (the first four) seeming to him to be 'quite inadequate' (*SL* 206).

A few pages of a notebook used at Newbattle (NLS 19657) have drafts, ideas for poems, a dream. This will be referred to as the Newbattle notebook.

*Milton. London Magazine* I No. 5 (Jun 1954) 15.
[9–11]   cf. *Paradise Lost* VII 25–38.
[13–14]   The last line and a half are carved on Muir's tombstone at Swaffham Prior.

*The Animals. Botteghe Oscure* IV (1949) 388. *BO* has 'by words' for 'with names' (7), 'words was shaped' for 'names was built' (9) and 'Mud' for 'Dust' (11).

Ritchie Robertson (*Muir's Contact with German Literature* 194) compares this poem with the eighth of Rilke's *Duino Elegies*, in which 'Raum' (the domain of the animals) is contrasted with 'Welt' (of man). Raum 'is a state of completeness, in which subject and object are not separated by uncertainty or desire . . . Animals are directly conscious of their environment and of God . . . They are not conscious of themselves, or of death, or of time . . . Human beings suffer from a consciousness which is divided between subject and object. We can apprehend Raum only occasionally' (as children, lovers). Muir's vision is his own, but his language ('world') may owe something to Rilke.
[20]   Deviates from Genesis 1:24–8, which places the creation of animals and man on the sixth day.

*The Days. Botteghe Oscure* IV (1949) 386–7. *BO* does not have 5–11; has extra line after 12, 'Opening, opening into time and space'; 'through the seven great doors' for 'from the doors' (13); extra line after 26 'Shadow on shadow'; 'On the sixth day fell' for 27; for 32–5:

> Here looking across the lake and the wooded plain
> From this the sixth day where my work is done,
> I see the mountains stand in the third day
> (Where they shall always stay)
> And think or feign
> That thence I watch an endless river run
> Through the separate days away,

And other slight variations.

*Adam's Dream. Listener* XLIV (14 Sep 1950) 352. *L* has 'seemed' for 'were' (20), 'They ran a while, till by some accident/They . . . (41–2), no 'it seemed' (61).

In the Library of Congress recording: 'I imagine [Adam] having a picture of time having been cast out of Eden, and not understanding what it could be.'

cf. *Paradise Lost* VIII 292–311, XI 556 – XII 623.

**67–72]** Cf. 'Dialogue: I have heard you cry' (*LP*).

*Outside Eden.* The Newbattle notebook has a draft towards a poem which split into 'The Incarnate One' and this poem: 'Thoughts that fly to the other side of time' . . . to 'The archaic peoples' . . . who saw 'The far side of the Cross' . . .

> Fly farther yet
> To the untutored toilers [?] who till their fields
> Not far outside the crumbling walls of Eden
> Held there by memories of innocence,
> And guilt dissolved [?], they who were the most guilty,
> And first and least [?] offending' . . .

cf. 'The City' (*NP*).

*Prometheus.* One of Faber's series of Ariel poems for Christmas, published in October 1954 with illustrations by John Piper. Having been asked by Eliot to contribute Muir wrote to him 1 August 1952, 'I have no poem ready at the moment, but one is in course of formation' (*SL* 162); and on 27 August sent an early version without lines 37–50, 'I am not pleased with it . . . Dante said more in a single line [*Paradiso* VIII 6] which has been running in my mind, 'Le genti antiche nell' antico errore'' (*SL* 163). On 10 October he agreed to alter 'Jove' and 'Cupid' to 'Zeus' and 'Eros' (33–4) and to add a paragraph (37–50) to meet Eliot's comment, 'it is a little unexpected to find Prometheus surviving into our own epoch, since one started with the usual assumption that one is being taken back to the era of early Greece' (*SL* 163); and sent the enlarged version on 20 November.

**[33]** See *A* 45–7.

**[47–9]** A recurring image in Muir – *The Marionette* pp. 64 and 157, *VTT* VI 46–9, 'Dialogue: Returning from the Antipodes' (*LP*) 13–14.

*The Grave of Prometheus. Listener* LIII (13 Jun 1955) 67.

*Orpheus Dream. Listener* XLV (31 May 1951) 863 as 'Eurydice'. The Newbattle notebook has jottings towards this poem:

> Eurydice – Orpheus' dream.
> A boat – taking them both.
> E. young and innocent – as if time had carried her
> Swiftly towards
> Free.
> Even their remembered love not as          as this
> As if they were souls
> So secure they could look back and see
> Without

> Eurydice and Pluto side by side
> Wordless and motionless in their ? chair
> Eurydice
> Sleep waking in her mouldering chair
> in Hades empty hall.

In NLS there are also four pages of MS workings.

[14–18] Reverses, though with precedent in the earliest version of the myth, the best-known version in which Orpheus loses Eurydice by looking back; and Plato's in *Symposium* 179, where Phaedrus says 'The gods sent Orpheus away from Hades empty-handed, and showed him the mere shadow of the woman he had come to seek'. Muir habitually reshaped legend to his purpose; so a variation, used by Euripides, of the story of Helen is probably a parallel rather than a source – only Helen's ghost went to Troy with Paris, the real Helen waiting in Egypt until Menelaus reclaimed her and took her home by boat.

cf. 'Time Song' 22–7.

*The Other Oedipus. New Statesman and Nation* XLIII (14 Jun 1952) 706. Published not long after 'The Charm' and perhaps deriving from it. If the guilt-ridden Oedipus could take Helen's drug he would have happiness – of a kind.

*The Charm. Listener* XLVI (30 Aug 1951) 336.

In *Odyssey* IV, visiting the court of Menelaus and Helen, Peisistratus weeps for the death of his brother Antilochus and Telemachos for the feared loss of his father Odysseus. To relieve them Helen slips into their wine a drug 'that had the power of robbing grief and anger of their sting and banishing all painful memories. No one that swallowed this dissolved in wine could shed a single tear that day, even for the death of his mother and father, or if they put his brother or his own son to the sword and he were there to see it done' (Trans. Rieu p. 70).

cf. 'The Other Oedipus'.

*Telemachos Remembers. Listener* XLIX (18 Jun 1953) 1011.

Closely related to 'Song for a Hypothetical Age', qv and n.

[1] *twenty*: As often Muir alters the source for his purpose. In *Odyssey* XIX Penelope tells how her nightly unpicking was betrayed and she was forced to complete the shroud in the fourth year.

[18–20] To Douglas Young 24 June 1953: 'I was not trying to give a correct account of what Odysseus was doing, but conveying the anxiety and bewilderment of Telemachos and his mother, and I think the picture of someone wandering about in a circle gives a better impression of persistence and frustration over a long stretch of years than any nautical image could possibly give . . . I think I have read the Odyssey about twenty times' (*SL* 167).

[26–30] Kathleen Raine in *Defending Ancient Springs* (1967) 11. The weaving and unweaving is 'an emblem of that daily life which is always an imperfect realization of the Fable. The loom cannot, indeed must not, be finished, yet life must never be relinquished . . . Woman as the weaver of lives is an old theme . . . a Scottish theme; . . . but Muir could take such symbols, and in his hands they seem neither old nor new'.

*The Heroes. The Sun* (Newbattle Abbey College, Spring 1952) 30 as 'The Shakespearean Heroes'.

Diary 7 May 1938: 'My dream that I was to be publicly executed, which makes me understand the "last words" of the great Elizabethans. You are raised up in a sort of ecstasy.' Reflected on in *SF* 241–2.

*Abraham. Listener* LIII (27 Jan 1955) 158.

*The Succession. Listener* XLIV (2 Nov 1950) 457.

*The Road. Listener* XLVII (3 Jan 1952) 8 as 'Sonnet'.

*L* has 'us', 'we', 'our' for 'them', 'they', 'their' throughout; 'We thought we' for 'Yet they' (3).

[5–8] See *SF* 258–9 on the trickster, an aspect of himself, who keeps diverting him from his proper road. 'And when we have struggled back to the right road – the return journey is always much harder than the first one; great boulders, even dangerous chasms, appear in it, though it had seemed perfectly smooth before.'

cf. 'My Own'.

[14] cf. 'Journey Back' 169 (*L*).

*The Annunciation. Botteghe Oscure* VI (1950) 330–1 as 'From a Roman Bas-Relief'. *BO* has 'Have passed beyond the door of space' (4), comma at end of 21 and extra line 'That was ordained in eternity'.

In *A* 278 Muir tells of a plaque on the wall of a house in the Via degli Artisti in Rome representing the Annunciation: 'An angel and a young girl, their bodies inclined towards each other, their knees bent as if they were overcome by love, 'tutto tremante', gazed upon each other like Dante's pair, and this representation of a human love so intense that it could not reach farther seemed the perfect earthly symbol of the love that passes understanding'. In Dante Paolo and Francesca's kiss (*Inferno* v 136) leads them to hell; but for Muir there is no incongruity in bringing together Dante's pair and the Annunciation. Fra Angelico's 'Annunciation' was one of his favourite pictures.

*The Christmas. Observer* No. 8429 (21 Dec 1952) 7 as 'The Year's Christmas'.

*The Son. Botteghe Oscure* V (1950) 308–9.

cf. 'Thought and Image' (*V*).

*The Killing. Botteghe Oscure* IX (1952) 156–7.

The Newbattle notebook has under heading 'Ideas' jottings for a poem called 'A Walk':

> A walk up to the Hill, at the Crucifixion
> Idle people, staring idly at the three figures.
> Or in hatred – both parties equally enraged,
> the Pharisees and the Publicans.
> The hearts beating.

cf. Soliloquy 2–9 (*L*).

*Lost and Found. Partisan Review* XX (Nov-Dec 1953) 634, one of 'Two Sonnets', the second being 'The Lord'. *PR* has 'You through whom' for

'That by which' (1), 'You' for 'It' (3,9), 'it's said' for 'by grace' (14). A TS sent to Janet Adam Smith has 'They through whom' (1), 'They' for 'It' (3,9), 'Inextricable' (11), 'they say' (14).

*Antichrist. Listener* XLVIII (17 Jul 1952) 99.
   *L* and *OFE* have extra line after 4, 'In him all is reversed; evil is good'; *L* has extra line after 9, 'The perfect image of his opposite'.
[1]   cf. 'glass' images mentioned in 'Merlin', n (*JP*).
[10–11/24–7:   cf. *A* 128, dream of Nietzsche.

*The Lord. Partisan Review* XX (Nov-Dec 1953) 634, second of 'Two Sonnets'. *PR* has 'summons' for 'whisper' (14).

*One Foot in Eden. Listener* XLIII (25 May 1950) 924 as 'Loss and Gain'.
[20]   cf. descriptions of desecrated country near Glasgow in *A* 92, *SJ* 124, *VTT* I.

*The Incarnate One. Saltire Review* I (Apr 1954) 7.
   Near the beginning (before ideas for 'Orpheus' Dream') of the Newbattle notebook are jottings for a poem 'The Legend' on:

> The story of the time-beloved God
> Preserved        on Padua's walls
> Where the Italian splendour [?] falls
> On Giotto the Tuscan shepherd's dream,
> Until it faded in this our northern land
> Huddled into a        word . . .

Several pages later are jottings towards an untitled poem which split into part of 'Outside Eden' (qv and n) and part of this poem:

> Thoughts that fly to the other side of time,
> The back of the worlds, the lovely [?] tumbling waters,
> Fly free, fly free . . .
> Cross safe the invisible barrier, be among
> The archaic peoples in their ancient error
> (These too your kindred) who can only see
> The far side of the Cross, the visible ashwood
> The smooth and shaven wood, an empty sign
> Set on a hill like any other hill
> Unscarified by the heavenly agony,
> Stain [?] of celestial blood. Fly farther yet . . .

[18]   Adapted from Dante's line 'le genti antiche nell' antico errore' (*Paradiso* VIII 6) about the worship of Venus, Cupid, etc.
   See 'Prometheus' n.

*Scotland's Winter. Listener* XIII (6 Feb 1935) 226.
   Printed at the end of the chapter on Edinburgh in *SJ* 38. 'My impressions of Edinburgh, or rather of historical Scotland, and feeling of the contrast between the legendary past and its tawdry present, crystallised several months later in a poem.' It was brought to Muir's attention by Douglas Young, who included it in his anthology *Scottish Verse 1851–1951* (1952).
   12–15]   cf. 'Robert the Bruce' and n.

[18] In a BBC reading in 1955 'songs' was substituted for 'singers'. When Young pointed this out Muir wrote, 'I cannot remember what I wrote first, but I think 'songs' is better than 'singers'.

*The Great House. Listener* LII (15 Jul 1954) 87 as 'Sonnet'. *L* has 'clouded' for 'hidden' (6), 'wisdom' for 'bravery' (8).

*The Emblem. Listener* XLVI (6 Dec 1951) 964; *Hudson Review* VII (Spring 1954) 49, in both as 'sonnet'. *HR* has 'withered' for 'shrivelled' (3), 'rank' for 'place' (13).
    cf. 'The Toy Horse' (*L*).

*To Franz Kafka. Listener* XLVI (1 Nov 1951) 759. *L* has 'twisted' for 'secret' (13).

*Effigies.* No. 2 in *Botteghe Oscure* IX (1952) 157–8 as 'The Betrayer'; Nos. 1, 3, 5 in *New Statesman and Nation* XLVIII (27 Nov 1954) 712. Sending Nos. 1, 3, 5 to Janet Adam Smith Muir wrote that he wouldn't mind if she omitted the second one, 'for I don't like it as well as the others' (*SL* 169); and he wrote to Kathleen Raine that the three poems have 'a little infusion of poison in them except for the third, which comes from an old memory' (*SL* 170–1).
[No. 1] In NLS there is a later draft of a rather similar poem about an old man who will live to be a hundred and be 'carried to his grave/Become a part of England and at last of life'.
[No. 2:11] *let*: restored from *BO* and *OFE* after *CP* 60's 'led'.
[No. 5] cf. 'An Island Tale'.

*The Difficult Land. Botteghe Oscure* XV (1955) 91–2. *BO* has extra lines – after 3 'The grub and the patient caterpillar batten', after 7 'No substance or coherence, life or meaning', after 10 'Clowns raising a dust to entertain some audience/Not in this world or any other world'; after 18 'We are afraid when the very earth grows strange', after 28 'Hopes, fears, despairs, knowledge of their recurrence;', after 32 'Our customs stale, our speech soured on our tongues;', after 33 '(which yet are knit to us as flesh to bone)'; and has for 40–2 'By faces of goodness, courage, fidelity/And love . . .'
[9–12] cf. 'The Cloud' and n.
[17–18] The Newbattle notebook has jottings for a poem 'The Creation', including:

> turned in the silver daybreak
> The flight of stars to a flock of blackbirds flying.

[19–21] From 'The Inheritors', BBC programme by Muir on Scottish history 27 March 1955: 'And for long other men from over the sea came among us in spring, trampling our young corn and killing our cattle and carrying away our women. And they at last mingled with us: Celt and Norsemen and Saxon and Dane. And we, who were a hantle of tribes, became a people.'

*Nothing There But Faith. New Statesman and Nation* XLIII (3 May 1952) 529 as 'Sonnet'.

*Double Absence. New Statesman and Nation* XLV (23 May 1953) 618 as 'Newbattle Abbey'. *NSN* has comma after 'Atlantic' (5) and extra line 'This brooch, this cloak, hung in the darkening sky'.

To George Mackay Brown 31 March 1953, sending him two poems, this and 'The Northern Islands'. 'You will recognize the islands; the other, vaguely about Newbattle, really began with a moon and a cloud I saw one evening. They're not very like my other poems, at least as far as I can judge.'

*Day and Night. Listener* XLII (29 Dec 1949) 1142 as 'Night and Day'. *L* has 'space' for 'light' (8), 'gave' for 'showed' (13), 'word' for 'speech' and 'speech' for 'tongues' (16–17), 'lighted' for 'visible' (31).

From a diary (1941): 'Lying in bed late at night, something in the quality of the darkness outside and the soughing of the wind must have brought back my childhood, for I found myself saying: "I wrap the old night around me." When we are children all our perceptions are fresh, and the night seems very old compared with the day, which is always new and displays nothing but a glittering arrangement and collection of new things. Last night was very dark, not a star even, a seamless blanket of darkness; the soughing of the wind, coming out of the boundless reaches of space, sounded like the unending mournful voice of age itself.'

From the Prague notebook: 'Now I lie down and wrap the night around me' – a detached entry in midst of working out of 'Soliloquy'.

See E. Huberman 'The Growth of a Poem: Edwin Muir's "Day and Night"'.

*The Other Story. Listener* XLIV (6 Jul 1950) 26.

*Dream and Thing. Listener* L (30 Jul 1953) 178.

*Song for a Hypothetical Age. Glasgow Herald* (4 Jul 1953) 2. *GH* has 'very thought' for 'other side' (25).

In a broadcast reading on 23 May 1954 Muir said that 'Telemachos Remembers' (qv and n) and this poem 'were in a sense born out of each other'. The Song 'was suggested by a fancy . . . that if Penelope had finished the web, she would have achieved the supreme work of art, but in doing so would have renounced her humanity. The poem is a fanciful statement of the claims of life and art, and describes the desolation which would follow if they were quite divorced from each other, as fortunately for us they cannot be'.

cf. 'Impersonal Calamity' (*LP*).

[9–16]  cf. 'The Brothers' 29–34 (*LP*).

*The Young Princes. Listener* XLIX (19 Feb 1953) 296.

In BBC broadcast 23 May 1954: ' "The Young Princes" is about childhood and the fact that we all come into the world unspoiled, as if we were stepping into an Eden, but that sooner or later doubt falls across our lives so that we pass out of innocence into experience. The young princes in the poem are children; and the last two lines suggest that we only know what we are by remembering our first state.'

*The Cloud. Botteghe Oscure* XV (1955) 90–1.

[2] *Writers' House*: Dobřiš Castle near Prague, maintained by the State for the use of writers.

[9–19] cf. 'The Difficult Land' 9–12.

[22] *preacher from Urania*: Communist lecturer on materialism, from Russia, supposedly an ideal, 'heavenly' state.

[29] *the change*: Communist take-over in February 1948.

*The Horses. Listener* LIII (10 Mar 1955) 429.

Letter to Derek Hawes 7 Jul 1958. The horses are not wild, but 'good plough-horses and still have a memory of the world before the war. I try to suggest that they are looking for their old human companionship. As for "tapping": have you ever listened, on a still evening, to horses trotting in the distance? The sound is really a pretty tapping. The drumming sound indicated that they were drawing nearer: the hollow thunder when they turned the corner meant that they saw the village or farmstead and found their home. I think I am right in the choice of verbs here' (*SL* 205).

*Song: 'This will not pass'. Listener* (4 Dec 1952) 932. *L* has 'rejoice' for 'cry' (9).

In BBC broadcast 23 May 1954: 'The last two poems are more in the nature of songs, with only a floating residue of meaning, and a faint echo of thought. The first has to do with the eternal return of things; the second ["The Late Swallow"] with the bourne towards which all things move.'

*The Island. Botteghe Oscure* VI (1950) 331–2 as 'The Mediterranean Island'. *BO* and *OFE* have extra line after 9, 'And dynasties stretched beneath the grass'; 'winding' for 'garrulous' (19).

From a notebook (NLS 19658) used for drafting new chapter of *A*: 'After Italy Sicily [where the Muirs went on a lecture tour in May 1950] seemed to belong to an earlier world . . . The hills were covered, mile after mile, with yellow grain, ready for harvesting. By the road we watched oxen trampling out the corn on a threshing floor in the middle of a field, while a group of peasants stood about, winnowing the chaff from the grain with huge, unwieldy flails. On the road we met occasional carts glittering with painted scenes of medieval battles or religious scenes and drawn by horses with scarlet plumes and embossed trappings; the driver sometimes asleep in his seat.' They were taken up Mount Etna, seeing vines growing luxuriantly out of sooty earth, and deep sulphurous yellow flowers. These experiences were used also for 'The Desolations' (*LP*).

*Into Thirty Centuries Born. Botteghe Oscure* XV (1955) 88–90. *BO* has for 16 'The clown, the counsellor and the King', after 36 extra line 'But time drives on: To be! To be!', for 39 'What does half-blind tomorrow bring?', for 63 'The bird song and the burning briar'.

In *EP* 80–89 Muir wrote of the imagination that makes 'us feel the grief of Priam and Hecuba over the death of Hector, dead thirty centuries ago', and which liberates us from the cage of the present. 'We are bound to the past generations by the same bond as to our neighbours, and if only for the sake of preserving the identity of mankind we must cherish memory'. In *EP* 60 he quoted Yeats writing to Dorothy Wellesley of the difficult poetry of the present, which 'is not your road or mine, and ours is the main road . . . and we have thirty centuries on our side'.

[12]    *Ilium*: The inner citadel of Troy, burnt by the Greeks.

*My Own. Listener* XLVI (27 Sep 1951) 515 as 'Sonnet'.
  cf. 'The Road' and n (*OFE*).

*The Choice. The Sun* (Newbattle Abbey College, Summer 1952) 33 as 'The Refuge'; *Botteghe Oscure* IX (1952) 158. *Sun* and *BO* lack 8; for 'the riddling sages' (9) *Sun* has 'the laconic sages' and *BO* 'the brave and the wise'.

*If I Could Know. Glasgow Herald* (17 Apr 1954) 3 as 'To Know'. *GH* has 'This Life' (2), 'These countless shapes, and each itself and free' (8).
  cf. 'The Solitary Place' (*JP*).

*The Late Wasp. Botteghe Oscure* V (1950) 310.

*The Late Swallow. Listener* XLVI (13 Dec 1951) 1025.

George Mackay Brown (a Newbattle student 1951–2) in *Edwin Muir: Selected Prose* 210: 'I . . . was deeply impressed by the imagery, the movement – made memorable by the rhymed interweaving of short and long lines – the perfect workmanship. I told Willa how much I admired it. "It is Edwin's epitaph", she said.'
  See 'Song: This will not pass' n.

*Song: 'This that I give'. Listener* XLIX (26 Mar 1953) 506.


## LAST POEMS

This section includes all poems written after *OFE* was sent to Faber in January 1955. At least one, 'The Song', was written before Muir went to USA in August. By the following February, he told Kathleen Raine, he had written eight or nine poems there, 'mostly from lines that came when I was waking' (*SL* 179); and on 10 April he wrote to her that he had 'been writing some very queer poetry since I came, with a good deal of new horror in it . . . Horrible thought: I don't know whether Eden was ever here' (*SL* 185). This may refer to 'The Tower' and 'After a Hypothetical War', certainly written by then, and to any of 'After 1984', 'The Strange Return', 'The Desolations', 'The Voices', 'Nightmare of Peace' and 'Ballad of Everyman', drafts towards which are found on the backs of drafts of parts of his second set of Harvard lectures, delivered in March. He returned to Britain in May, and settled at Swaffham Prior near Cambridge. In April 1958 he told Norman MacCaig that he had almost enough poems for a new volume. 'Half of them I intend to put under the heading of "Ballads", though only one or two will be in strict ballad form: they will be mostly on half-narrative, half-legendary themes. I think there is still a great deal to be learned from the ballads, especially a tight attention to the theme' (*SL* 203). In correspondence with T. S. Eliot that summer it was agreed that 'a little over twenty' new poems should be kept for a new volume, not included in the projected *CP*. A MS list of twenty-two poems (each of 'Images' mentioned separately) was presumably made at this time. It includes all the poems in *LP* I except 'Complaint of the Dying Peasantry' (probably rejected), 'The Voices' and 'Impersonal Calamity' (perhaps not in final form by then); and includes 'The Good Man' ['A Righteous Man'?] and 'The Breaking'. After Muir's death Willa Muir and John Hall edited 'Poems Not Previously Collected' for *CP 60*, dividing the poems into three sections – poems published by Muir, unpublished poems found in TS, and poems found in MS. Three poems have been added in later editions of *CP*, and some amendments have been made to the texts. In this edition the same general arrangement has been followed. But 'A Righteous Man', 'The Breaking' and 'Sunset' have been put in section II, since they are in TS; the sonnets 'You will not leave us' and 'Do not mourn still' have been transferred to Appendix I, since they could have been, and were not, included in *OFE*; four unfinished poems have been put in a new section IV; and the poems have been arranged in a conjectural order of writing in each section. Some amendments have been introduced after fresh study of the MSS.

Muir habitually, sometimes extensively, revised for volume publication poems that had appeared in periodicals, writing amendments on printed or TS copies and then making a new TS, not always incorporating all the MS amendments; he had already begun this process for several poems in *LP* I. When the amendments are written on a printed copy and are confirmed in a later TS, they may confidently be introduced into the text, as has been done in 'The Last War'. But when they are written on an undated TS or are not confirmed in a later TS it has been thought safer to leave the text undisturbed, though the amended TSS of 'The Brothers' and of a version of 'The Voices' contain characteristic revisions. See notes to those poems.

## I

*The Song. London Magazine* II No. 8 (Aug 1955) 13–15.
In BL a copy of the printed version cut from *LM* has extensive MS revisions. The revised version is printed in App. III.

*The Tower. Adam International Review* No. 250 (1955) 6; Tape 1 H (Nov 1955) and Tape 2 H. Tape 1 was spoken from memory, and has several small variants.

*Images. Encounter* V No. 6 (Dec 1955) 52.
[I] Kathleen Raine *Defending Ancient Springs* 2. Muir 'once described to me a dream that at the time seemed to convey to him the deepest truth about writing. The dream was a very simple one: it consisted of a semicolon. The meaning of this semicolon, as it revealed itself to the dreamer, was that the poet never knows all that he writes; he writes only, as it were, as far as the semicolon; beyond the statement is something more, that completes his meaning. We can never define it, yet it is part of the poem, and part of what the poem communicates to the reader'. cf. 'The Poet'.
[II 10–12] In *A* 227 Muir tells of seeing, during a time of dejection, a robin. 'As I stared at it out of my worry, which was a world of its own, the small glittering object had an unearthly radiance, and seemed to be pouring its light into the darkness without and the darkness within myself. It astonished and reassured me.'

[13–14]   cf. 'The Animals' 1–2 (*OFE*).
[15–18]   See *EP* 28–30 on the importance of story for poetry.

*The Church. Encounter* VII No. 1 (Jul 1956) 55; *New Poems 1956: a PEN Anthology* (1956). *PEN* and two TSS in NLS have 'Father and Son' for 'God and Man' (15); *Encounter* and *CP 60–84*, surely by inadvertence, omit 'in dust' after 'heaven' (16).

   Willa Muir in *Belonging* 298–9: 'From the first days in our sitting-room [in the Hotel Continental, Cambridge, Massachusetts] we saw a new church being built outside; day by day it grew, until one day the skeleton of its spire was set up, delicately pencilled against the autumn sky with a small gilt cross on top . . . That it was, as he knew, a Mormon church was a matter of no moment to him.'
[37]   Dante *Paradiso* XXXIII 145.

*After a Hypothetical War. Listener* LV (5 Jan 1956) 15 as 'The Bad Lands'. *L* has for 19: 'The bad lands: did they breed this tribe, or has/The tribe infected them with enmity'.

*Complaint of the Dying Peasantry. Saltire Review* III (Spring 1956) 11. Sending this to Alexander Scott for *SR* Muir wrote, 'It came from another reading of the ballads, which I've always loved above any other Scottish poetry. And they were still alive in Orkney when I was young'. See the first of his Harvard lectures (*EP* 1–22).

*Salem, Massachusetts. Botteghe Oscure* XIX (1957) 77.
   Willa Muir in *Belonging* 299: 'One day in spring [1956] we went to Salem with the Wilburs, following the "Witches Trail" . . . The wooden houses with their handsome pillared porticoes looked what they were, dwellings of rich burgesses.' Muir sacrifices history to his pattern of fire images. Trials in 1691–2 led to the *hanging* of nineteen 'witches', not all women, on Gallows Hill.
   cf. Robert Lowell's 'Salem' and 'Children of Light.'
[18]   The House of the Seven Gables was made famous by Hawthorne's novel of that name, concerned with the consequences of a curse by a male victim of the trials. It was not burnt.

*After 1984. New Statesman and Nation* LI (22 Dec 1956) 821 with 'The Strange Return' under heading 'Reports on Time'; Tape 2 H. The tape has 'world' for 'life' (38).
   These two poems grew from a single root, a draft headed 'A possible sonnet "1984"' on the back of a sheet in NLS used for *EP*. The draft is not in sonnet form, and grew mainly into 'The Strange Return'; but lines near the end approach 'After 1984' 27–8:

> I made that prison once
> I alone, and most stubbornly
> Locked myself within.

   Later 'I' became 'We', and two poems were developed – one on the communal escape from Orwellian nightmare, the other on escape from personal neurosis.

*The Strange Return.* See 'After 1984' n.

The draft mentioned above is of the first paragraph – first on the escape, then in a marginal addition on the 'they' who may be plotting. A line 'How had he come into the day' may have prompted the thought of Lazarus, not in the draft; and then of other re-entries, or entries, maybe reluctant, into life. Jottings for another poem on a sheet of Newbattle paper in NLS were brought in to form the basis of the second paragraph:

> Echoes of earth 'Let me be!' 'Do not go' . . .
> The vertical cleft above the young girl's eyes
> That have seen too much.

[29–32]cf. 'Dialogue: I have heard you cry' 52–7.

*The Desolations. Botteghe Oscure* XIX (1957) 76–7; Tape 2 H. The tape has 'Where only what is harvest is gathered in' (14); omits 28, 'if you listen' (29) and 'Love is at home' (30).

Drafts towards this poem and part of 'The Voices' are written on the versos of three pages of drafts for *EP* in NLS. In the first draft the desolations are exemplified at length ('Bellowing of beasts . . . the cry of leaves shrivelling in autumn frost', etc) and their voice is likened to 'a cashiered and spavined army of horse', etc ('The Voices' 8–11). At the end the counter-voice 'Love is at home' is introduced without any mention of Sicily. In the second draft the spavined army has gone; and Sicily (see 'The Island' and n) is introduced to give a local habitation to the positive voice.

*The Voices. London Magazine* V No. 8 (Aug 1958) 11.

See 'The Desolations' and n. On another sheet of *EP* paper in NLS are two drafts for an untitled poem, which were ultimately to develop into this one. It resembles 'The Desolations' in moving from 'desolations' to a more positive voice, and the first draft of it in having lines on the 'spavined army'. Since these are here less developed these drafts must be earlier than 'The Desolations' drafts. Perhaps 'The lid flew off' poem was put aside when 'The Desolations' was written on a similar theme. Then the idea, first appearing in the margin of the second draft, of having the desolate voice be poured out at a 'ceremony' may have suggested a way to make 'The lid flew off' sufficiently different. 'The spavined army' lines, rejected from 'The Desolations' were taken back.

In NLS there is also a TS, with MS amendments, of this poem headed 'The Ceremony', varying considerably from *LM*. Since the *LM* version is the only one certainly endorsed by Muir it has been printed as the main text, but it is possible that the TS as amended represents his final intentions, and it is given in Appendix III.

[11]  cf. 'Into Thirty Centuries' 25 (*OFE*).
[20–6]  The first draft is more declamatory:

> Push back that agony under the ground
> Before the earth is torn asunder.
> How can we bear that sound
> Although it is ours, is ours, that world-wide thunder?
> Or listen to this small still voice
> That through the clamour says, 'Rejoice

You are redeemed today,
So go your way'.

Some phrases in the drafts suggest the atomic bomb in the background. The MS amendment from 'calmly said' to 'seemed to say' in the final line in 'The Ceremony' TS is a farther move away from the confidence of the first draft.

*An Island Tale. New Statesman and Nation* LII (6 Oct 1956) 428 as 'A Country Tale'. *NSN* has 'And so she made herself our own' (10). cf. 'Effigies' No. 5 (*OFE*).

*The Two Sisters. Nation* CLXXXIII (10 Nov 1956) 409. First collected in *CP 63*. A draft in NLS has extra line after 13, 'On those she loved too well'.

*Three Tales. Botteghe Oscure* XIX (1957) 75–6.
[22]  *crystal walls*: cf. 'Merlin' 1–2 and n (*JP*).

*The Brothers. Botteghe Oscure* XIX (1957) 77–8; Tape 2 H.

*BO* has 'The reckless and the gentle one' (2), 'either head' for 'head to head' (12), extra lines after 24, 'At deadly cost our joy was bought', and after 25, 'We were not ours; we loved and fought', 'imprisoned' for 'buried' (28). The tape follows *BO* except for 'As if they were two gamboling suns' (11), 'hung on' for 'covered' (25) and other small variations. Two TSS in NLS, the second incorporating MS revisions in the first, follow *BO* in 2 and 28, omit 6 and 12 as well as *BO*'s extra lines and have 'bright' for 'strong' in 13; there is a full stop after 'care' (5) and then a space, and no stop after 'suns' (11). This slimmed version was sent by Willa Muir to the BBC early in 1959. Later some authority, not extant, must have been found for the *CP 60* version, whose variations in 2, 12 and 28 from the three other versions cannot be merely editorial.

On two sheets of MS workings in NLS, after the heading 'My brothers: Willie and Johnnie', the first jotting is 'the strict dry mid-days of the law'.

Letter to Kathleen Raine 24 January 1957: 'I'm trying to write [a poem] now about a dream I had recently about my two brothers, Willie and Johnny, dead fifty years ago. I watched them playing in a field, racing about in some game, and it was not a game which either of them was trying to win (there was no winning in it), and because of that they were infinitely happy in making each other happy, and all that was left in their hearts and their bodies was grace. It is very difficult to convey this in a poem. I had not thought of them for a long time. And when I did know them (I was little more than a boy then) there was affection, but also little grouses and jealousies, assertions of the will, a cloud of petty disagreements and passions which hid their true shape from me and from themselves. In the dream it seemed to me the cloud was dispelled and I saw them as they were. I'm sure Blake could have told me everything about it' (*SL* 191). Willa Muir says that one afternoon when Kathleen Raine and Muriel Bradbrook were in their sitting-room at Swaffham Prior 'Edwin came downstairs with his finished version . . . and read it aloud there and then, his face illumined' (*Belonging* 309).

*The Conqueror. Listener* LVIII (18 Jul 1957) 99. A TS sent to BBC by Willa Muir in 1959 has for 4 'So perfect he need hardly go'.

# Notes

In Daniel 7, a chapter already used in *VTT* epigraph, and in II Esdras 13 there are apocalyptic visions of a man coming in clouds; in Esdras he annihilates those who oppose him with fire from his mouth. 'Encrimsoned cloud' suggests the thought of a modern atomic apocalypse.
cf. 'The Rider Victory' (*V*).

*Dialogue: 'Returning from the antipodes'. New Statesman* LIV (2 Nov 1957) 572.
[1–11]   cf. 'Ballad of Eternal Life' 49–52 (App. II); 'The Fall' 21–6 (*JP*); 'The Journey Back' section 2 (*L*).
[13–14]   cf. *VTT* VI 48–9.
[51–61]   cf. 'Double Absence' (*OFE*).
[59–61]   cf. 'Three Tales' 12–16.
[72–6]   cf. 'The Journey Back' section 6:12 (*L*); 'The Road' (*OFE*).

*Penelope in Doubt. Listener* LIX (23 Jan 1958) 152.
Swaffham Prior notebook 9 November 1957: 'Towards evening went for my usual walk in the Station Road. Cold. While wandering along, I remembered the meeting between Penelope and Odysseus, and thought the only thing which identified him for her (after 20 years), was a brooch he described from memory, a brooch of beaten gold showing a dog and a fawn, the dog fastened to the fawn's throat, the fawn striking at him with his slender hoofs, the brooch lost now and the combat still going on, unchanged. She remembers it when he spoke of it. Then he spoke of the time he was hunting on Parnassus and a wild-boar gashed him on the thigh high up. The scar was still there. The brooch and the scar, these were all that brought him back to her. For his hair was grey, his shoulders had shrunken, though his back was still straight, and his eyes were cold and pale, as if they had looked at things she would never know, or had been bleached in the snows of time. Were these enough to make her know in her heart he was Odysseus? A poem somewhere out of this.'
In *Odyssey* XIX Penelope does not recognize Odysseus when, pretending to be a Cretan, he describes the brooch so as to convince her he has known Odysseus; it is Eurycleia who recognizes him by the scar. In book XXIII Penelope is still in doubt even after being told by Eurycleia of the scar.
Sending some poems written since his return to Britain to Jack Sweeney on 12 December 1957 Muir wrote 'I like the "Penelope" best myself'.
There are MS workings out in the BL notebook. A little later in the notebook there is an idea for another poem, 'Odysseus' meeting in Hades with his mother' (*Odyssey* XI).

*Sick Caliban. Listener* LIX (6 Feb 1958) 244.
Two TSS with MS revisions in NLS, headed 'Every Man', are early states. The earlier omits 4 and has after 5:

> Or Adam, first and hapless king,
> Who has not learned to die, or that poor man
> Stretched by the highway that runs everywhere,
> And waiting for a good Samaritan
> Who does not pass that way?

Has nothing corresponding to 7–11, has for 28 'By his last breath', and for 32–6:

> Saying little. But love still stood at that first turning.
> Even now if he could fix his eyes
> On that one place, walk backwards to the grave
> Seeing that image only, would it save
> Something perhaps? Would he find breath to call
> The others, and all be changed, that thing, and all?

There are also in NLS a cutting from *L* with MS amendments; and a TS identical with *CP 60*. This TS may be assumed to be Muir's since it incorporates some, but not all, the MS amendments to the cutting. The most significant variants are in 35–6, where *L* has 'Would all find breath to call/To each other . . .' amended in MS to 'Would each find breath to call/To the others . . .'. *CP 60* returns, substantially, to the 'Every Man' version.

*Impersonal Calamity. London Magazine* V No. 8 (Aug 1958) 12.

A draft, untitled, on a sheet of Newbattle paper in *BL* is written in the first person singular; it begins 'I a respectable man saw terrible things/For five whole years . . .', and ends:

> Oh now I would be changed
> Now I would be estranged
> From my own self, be sent abroad
> From this ? self and semblance and take my road.

cf. 'The Last War' 48–52; 'The heart could never speak'.

*The Last War. New Statesman* LV (14 Jun 1958) 770.

NLS has a cutting from *NS* with MS amendments, and a TS incorporating these amendments, which have now been introduced into the text: 'boundless' before 'air' deleted (5), 'to attempt', after 'way' deleted (6), 'order' for 'pathos' (10), 'there' added after 'be' (27), 'Pilfering' deleted at beginning of 56, 'senseless' for 'idle' (57. This appears only in the TS; in the cutting 'idle'is deleted without any replacement); 'By' for 'In' (66).

The Swaffham Prior notebook in NLS records on 6 November 1957 two dreams – one of 'the watchers in a dark place', their 'faces strongly radiant, serene, almost indifferent' but with 'a hidden tenderness'; the other 'of a woman, or muse or sibyl, speaking . . . of human life . . . in a dark and very spacious place'. 'On wakening I could not remember what she said, but thought it told of our life from birth to death, a great story, with nothing small or mean.' He associated both dreams with the Well of Life. These dreams led to the planning, on two sheets in NLS, of a poem in terza rima on Lazarus. 'Lazarus, on his return to life, as it were has second birth, remembers being with the guardians [?] of the Well of Life'. He 'sees first what seems the starry head of a serene divinity quite near the ground . . . Then, farther away, other divinely serene heads all illuminated by a light that flows along the ground . . . Next the hand of his Friend. Sees Jesus and his two sisters . . . Ordinary sounds'. Near the beginning of the BL poetry notebook are a few lines on a sibyl speaking in darkness in a great hall; but no more progress was made with the Lazarus poem. Farther on, after drafts of other poems, is a draft beginning 'A tree wounds the heart', which was to become 'The Last War' IV; then, after other matter, a draft on a future war, which was to become sections I and II, and then, headed 2, further thoughts on death in a future war, part of which was to go into section III and part into 'The Day before the Last Day'. Probably at this stage the three themes – The Well of Life/Lazarus, the 'sick tree', and the future war – were not yet seen as parts of a whole. On 23 April 1958 he wrote to Norman Mac-Caig: 'I've been rather daunted in the last year or two by the fear that I am keeping on writing the same poem . . . I have written very few poems lately, but many parts of poems which ceased when they seemed to be taking the same old course. Some of the parts are quite good, I think, and perhaps the best thing . . . would be to integrate . . . them in a longish poem' (*SL* 202–3). Probably this refers to 'The Last War', then thought of as including part or all of what later went into 'The Day before the Last Day'. Jottings in NLS headed V ('Yet should it come . . . And we accomplish our own nonentity') suggest that it would have ended with a vision of the last day. But instead the Well of Life dreams were brought in. Thoughts of future war were linked back to the present attitudes that might cause it and farther back to the origin of life, leaving the looking forward to Judgement for a separate poem, which was completed later.

[31–35]   cf. 'The refugees born for a land unknown'.

[48–61]   As often the draft is more explicit and prosaic:

> A crooked smile twists inward through the mind
> Until it finds its place
> And settles in comfort there
> They say that is an ancient art.
> Look long: you shall not find
> The only archetypal head
> For here face mirrors face
>               our eyes are led
> A thousand times by the impure reflection
> In other eyes.          the blind
> Are saved from seeing . . .

cf. Muir's thoughts in the Swaffham Prior notebook on his dream of the Sibyl. He has fancied that the Well of Life dream showed 'how she would have begun her story, and that the rest of it would have been told in the same spirit, exalted and mysterious, to the end . . . I've reflected since that, seen in this way, humour and irony are mere devices to hide the real nature of our life, which is infinitely serious and real, and a great event'.

[51]   cf. 'Impersonal Calamity' 22.

## II

*Nightmare of Peace/Ballad of Everyman.*
The Newbattle notebook records a dream: 'We were at some place in Europe, Willa and I, and a friend of ours was there too; in a hotel at some conference. Our friend, something like Alec Reid [student, later lecturer, at Newbattle], had left the room; hotel detectives came to ask about him; he did not come back; we began to fear he had been seized and taken away by

the Police, perhaps taken to Prague. Then we were in the air, I think in a helicopter, and looking at the country below. Came to a little village and a tangled knot of people engaged in something we could not make out, packed very close, and with something that looked like a tail coming from it, as if a beast were somewhere in the ? , some strange wild beast and an enormous tail. Could Alec be in there? The dream tried to explain the tail by saying that it was a bull's tail, cut off, which someone was carrying. Did not convince the dreamer. After that all faded out.'

In NLS are two pages of MS drafts, on back of drafts of *EP*, towards 'Nightmare of Peace' 10–59. 'Nightmare', which is closer to the dream, was presumably written first. The more concise 'Ballad' was probably intended to replace it.

Muir's old vision of men as animals ('The Ring' (*NP*), etc) reappears in a new context in 'Nightmare' 33–54 and 'Everyman' 29–38.

*The Poet. New Statesman* LVIII (3 Oct 1959) 434.

To Janet Adam Smith 22 September 1956: 'It started from something a Harvard student said. She had attended a lecture of Ivor Richards, and he had set off on one of those wonderful inspired passages of his, so that the poor girl was left, as she told me, and as she told him, 'in bewilderment'. And his reply struck me as very fine, and seems to have struck her too: 'That's splendid. That's where one should start.' But the poem is not at all equal to that.' On the 26th he sent her the poem, 'but not for publication. It is only a note that might turn into a poem, as I see it now. I think if I found an "objective correlative", it would come to life; and I think I have found one, the poet Hölderlin in his half-mad prophetic phase' (*SL* 186/187). After Muir's death Janet Adam Smith published the poem as sent to her in 1956.

In NLS there is a MS draft on the back of a sheet used for Harvard lectures:

### A Mad Poet

His eyes had looked so long on change
That to him they had grown more strange
Than all he saw. He scarcely knew
If the common light was true,
Tell the far presence from near.
And there lingered in his ear
Melodies he had never heard,
Reverberations of the Word?
So now his tongue must make known
Wondrous tidings not his own
And in his bewilderment
Utter thoughts mind never meant,
From lands where traveller never went.

In line 3 'all he saw' is deleted, and replaced by, I think, 'miracle'.

cf. draft poem on music in 'The Journey Back' section 6 n (*L*); and Muir's discussion of Plato's *Ion* and poetic madness in *EP* 24–7.

*Petrol Shortage.*
A TS with MS amendments in NLS has extra stanza after 8, deleted:

> The very trees look different
> Though clad in no Wordsworthian glory,
> They rise from nothing but the ground,
> The brightening buds relate no story.

Petrol rationing was imposed, as a result of the Suez crisis, from December 1956 to May 1957.

*The Breaking.* First published with 'A Righteous Man' in *Times Literary Supplement* (21 Dec 1979) from TSS with MS corrections in NLS. Added to *CP* in 1984. Position of a note – 'The Breaking: Came on a walk to the railway station' – in BL notebook shows this probably written before November 1957, in similar circumstances to 'Petrol Shortage'.

*A Righteous Man.*
See 'The Breaking' n. The TS in NLS has three extra lines at the end, deleted in MS but included in *TLS* and *CP 84*:

> Lord, fling into his face
> The gift, it seems, that never can be
> His choice, Your grace.

*Sunset.* There are MS workings in BL notebook, and a TS with MS amendments in NLS. Line 10 was originally 'Saying, a bush, a tree'.

Swaffham Prior notebook 8 November 1957: 'My thoughts and feelings a little while ago, walking along the quiet road to the railway station. The evening extraordinarily still, bright clouds in the west, soft and suffused with all the colours of light flowing through them almost horizontally, yet lingering, reluctant to go. The trees along the road seemed conscious of this image of peace, and three horses in a field were subdued by it. Nothing which appeared to be unaware of it. Strange perfection of a common mood, sky and light and cloud and tree and the horses: I felt it too.'

## III

*'The heart could never speak'.* MS workings on the same page as a TS of 'Petrol Shortage' in NLS show that this was originally written in the first person singular. Connected with 'Impersonal Calamity', also originally an 'I' poem. cf. 'The Last War' 48–52.

*'Our apprehensions give'.* Drafted on a sheet in BL used also for 'The refugees born for a land unknown'.
Muir wrote in *EP* 86 of 'the forlorn Utopias of Aldous Huxley and George Orwell . . . Our imaginations when they have nothing better to do, project these vast distorted nightmares into the future. I think we all make these projections, for in states of apprehension or foreboding we live more in the future than in the present, and are troubled by both'.

*The Day before the Last Day.*
On 26 October 1957 Muir wrote to Professor Joseph Summers, who had sent him a copy of an essay in which he had quoted from David Blackadder's

vision of a worm in his hand and meditation on the cruelty of the universe in *TB* 269–74: 'I had forgotten that passage from *The Three Brothers*, and I was surprised that I wrote anything so good so long ago, in that very unequal story, and do not even have a copy of it now' (*SL* 195–6). He must have found a copy; for he was soon using not the passage quoted by Summers but David's vision of the last Judgement in pp. 333–7. About this time he was beginning to write the fragments which were to coalesce into 'The Last War', including a draft towards section III containing lines on the aloneness of those awaiting Judgement based on *TB*. Then he must have decided that the *TB* vision could be used as a major part of a poem. A long TS in NLS follows it very closely. It is numbered '2', which suggests that it may have been seen as the conclusion to the long integrated poem mentioned to Norman MacCaig (see 'The Last War' n). Then the Well of Life was brought in to conclude 'The Last War', and the *TB* vision, much modified, was formed into a separate poem, drafted near the end of the BL notebook. There is a much-corrected first draft and a carefully-written fair copy. It is probably Muir's last completed poem.

[15–16] An early state of these lines shows Muir still battling with an old enemy:

> Technological parody of the Judgement Day
> Where none is judged and all are dammed, the thought
> Even of Calvin spurned [?], that incomprehensible
> Yet irreprehensible judgment.

Calvin wrote in the *Institutio* of the 'just and irreprehensible but incomprehensible judgment.'

[17/18] The space in *CP* 60, not in the drafts nor the fair copy, has been eliminated.

[52–7] In the TS in NLS the speaker is 'I', and a voice *is* heard saying 'There shall be no more time', etc:

> And the voice was heard by all that congregation,
> The aged and young, the dying and newly born,
> And many, when they heard, fell to the ground
> And called on the earth to cover them, and the sea
> To swallow them up, because they could not bear
> The radiance and stillness of eternal day.
> But others took the splendour on their flesh
> And were from head to foot transfixed and still.
> I thought, These are the inconquerable ones
> Who have endured to the end. I am not of them.
> And a voice cried: 'Choose! Choose! you who are chosen'.
> But I was filled with joy for the eternal day,
> And with despair at the stationary sun
> That would not set again, and I could not choose.

In *TB* this was a vision of the Last Judgement which brought David 'great comfort'; for finally he saw himself turning 'to the ranks of the blessed'. In the TS the speaker is left suspended between joy and despair, eternity and time, and cannot choose. In the completed poem 'all' have chosen 'this' – the destruction of the world by war. The bringing of the dream into association with the last war has quite altered its meaning. It is no longer a vision of the Last Judgement, but a 'mechanical parody of the Judgment Day' – not God's judgment, but what man might do to himself. That the original vision with its optimistic end was still running in Muir's mind is shown in a fragmentary draft on a sheet in NLS used also for 'The Two Sisters'. There were to be three stanzas beginning 'What do you believe?', 'What do you know?', and 'Where do you go?'. In the third the speaker is:

> a foot length from eternity
> And cannot lift my foot.
> So I must choose,
> While here I stand and dream
> That ringed by an angelic multitude
> That without moving [?] from eternity have stood
> I scale the ramparts of eternity.

Earlier are lines derived from a related vision used in the first version of 'The City' (*NP*):

> But once I saw waking or in dream
> Great wingéd men striding on the walls of Heaven.

[58]  'stationary' is written over 'real' in the fair copy.


## IV

*'There's nothing here'.*
    Note in *CP* 60: 'This poem is probably a soliloquy by Edwin Muir's cousin Sutherland, awaking after death to find himself in heaven . . . *Orra* means without regular employment, working here and there as required; *old-farrant* means old-fashioned; and *dander* means to dawdle or stroll.' For Sutherland see *A* 16–17.

*The refugees born for a land unknown.* An unfinished draft on a sheet in BL used also for 'Our apprehensions give'; probably abandoned when lines were used in 'The Last War' 32–4. Punctuated differently from in *CP* 60.
[2]  *dismissed*: may be 'discussed'. Originally:

> We have met them in our own or others' houses
> Not knowing what to say, have wisely [?] discussed [?] their griefs
> Their little judgment days lost in the dark
> While we sat by the fire or in the window seat.

Cf. 'The Refugees' 15–16 (*NP*).
[3/4]  There are deleted transitional lines, including 'And once I heard one say'.
[14/15]  There are deleted transitional lines, including 'And I have heard in thought another voice'.
[15–18]  A version of these lines is written on a sheet in NLS used for 'And once I knew':

> Sound of four feet on the stair, two light, two heavy
> And then the door opened. 'What are your names?'
> 'Where do you come from?' And that was all.

[16]  *knew*: deleted and replaced, but not by *CP 60*'s 'remember'. First written was 'and since then I know no more/Than this cell . . .'. This speaker has not escaped.

[19–20]  Not in *CP 60*. Taken from the other side of the sheet in BL. Originally 'they' in line 19 was 'the refugees'.

*Dialogue: 'I have heard you cry'.*

A difficult MS draft in BL is the only authority. The text was slightly amended in *CP 63*, and the following further amendments have been introduced in this edition: 'Could' for 'Would' (3), 'woke' for 'awoke' (14), 'and bud' deleted (21), 'come and' inserted (22), lines 25 and 26 put in reverse order, 'strong resolve' for 'the commandment' (26), 'away' inserted (47). Some amendments have been made to punctuation and capitalisation.

This is probably an offshoot of the plan to write a new *CND*. There are variants of lines 2–3 and 53–6 in the workings towards a new 'Chorus' mentioned in *CND* n. 53–6 are similar also to 'The Strange Return' 26–33. 41–2 are almost the same as lines in the fragmentary poem mentioned in 'The Day before the Last Day' n.

[14, 19–24]  Cf. 'Adam's Dream' (*OFE*).

[20–1]  Originally after 'this my only road' was 'Or take a different road/From this' – deleted, but might have been replaced. The meaning intended, I think, is that Adam chose 'this' road where his kindred come and go rather than some 'other' road where other flowers gem. Cf. 'The Journey Back' sections 6 and 7 (*L*).

[25–6]  Reversed from *CP 60*. I think the line inserted at the side 'On which I read . . .' belongs with 'the face'.

[26]  'strong resolve': deleted, but printed because the last clearly legible words. What is substituted may be 'the commandment'.

[57]  *drab Penury*: *CP 60*'s reading, conjectural. The first word may be 'dumb'.

*'I have been taught'.*

A difficult MS draft at the end of the BL notebook is the only authority. Earlier in the notebook are notes for a poem on old age:

> Now the only true
> Poetry is Plato's dream
> Time has gone on so long
> Time sings this song,

and for one 'About my father and mother. Realising long after their deaths their virtue and goodness. How could they have been what they were but for Incarnation. The incarnation of a soul in a body. Simplicity, grace, infinite patience and kindness'. There is a moving entry about his parents in the Swaffham Prior notebook (quoted in my *Edwin Muir: Man and Poet* 286–7).

[18]  It is clear in the draft that 'The' at the beginning, having been deleted, was re-instated. This, with the addition of a comma after 'forever', is the

only amendment made to *CP 63*, though the readings of lines 2, 3, 7, 8 and 15 are conjectural.

## APPENDIX I: UNCOLLECTED POEMS

*To a Dream. New Age* XXXIII (24 May 1923) 63.

*Ballad of the Black Douglas. Scottish Chapbook* I (Jul 1923) 344–5. cf. 'Robert the Bruce' (*NP*). Douglas died fighting the Moors in Spain.
[30]   *den*: narrow valley.

*Pastoral. New English Weekly* V (26 Jul 1934) 349; *Scottish Journey* (1935) 100–1. Text as in *SJ*.

*Industrial Scene. Time and Tide* XVI (9 Mar 1935) 344; *Scottish Journey* (1935) 152–3. Text as in *SJ*, the most important variant being that *T and T* has 'The Communist contemplates the promised land' as the last line.
*SJ* 152: 'As I can speak with no exact knowledge of the rich in Glasgow, I shall give instead a short poem which took shape during my journey [in summer 1934] through the industrial regions, and arose from my sense of the violent contrasts that I saw on every side. The only excuse I give for it is that contrast can be more briefly expressed in verse than in prose, and can form a synopsis of a complex scene.'
[15–16]   Is there some connection between these daughters and the 'harlot daughters' in 'The Town Betrayed' 3 (*JP*), and of both with Muir's employer's daughters 'lying under the hawthorn bushes with their lovers' at their 'ostentatious villa' (*A* 139)?

*Time Song. Listener* XIV (28 Aug 1935) 339.
[11–15]   cf. 'Merlin' (*JP*).
[22–7]   cf. 'Orpheus Dream' (*OFE*).
[38–9]   cf. 'The Road' 18–20 (*JP*).

*'No more of this trapped gazing.' London Mercury* XXXIII (Mar 1936) 479, IV of 'Four Poems'.
    If, as seems probable, this is the fourth of four poems sent to Spender on 4 May 1935 Muir's comment applies, 'The fourth I like only for one or two lines, and may give up altogether' (*SL* 84); and his statement on 13 June 1935: 'I have not been able to write any poetry except for one poem following from the last of the four I sent you, which . . . has fallen into a sequence in my mind – I mean that there are several other poems that will arise out of it in time.' Poems published not long after which may have arisen from 'No more' include – from lines 2–4 'The Town Betrayed' (*JP*); from 16–19 'The Unattained Place' (*JP*), 'The Law' (*NP*); from 20–22 'Hölderlin's Journey' (*JP*).
[9–15]   *Odyssey* VI–VII.
[16–19]   cf. 'The Incarnate One' 15–21 (*OFE*).
[23–4]   Letter to Spender 4 September 1935. The feeling that there is a reality outside humanity in its historical development 'you get in all the greatest poetry and music, in Beethoven for instance' (*SL* 85).

*'It might be the day after the last day'. Spectator* CLVIII (19 Mar 1937) 514.

To George Barker 14 February 1936: 'We look straight out to sea [from their house on the Scores, St Andrews] over a medieval castle, and there are the loveliest grassy cliffs a little distance along the shore . . . I have got a very good first line, I think, which I have been boasting about:

I think the day after the Last Day
Will be like this.

But the ones that follow do not come up to the sample, I'm afraid' (*SL* 87/88).

cf. 'The Dreamt-of Place' (*JP*).

*Letters I. London Mercury* XXXVII No. 217 (Nov 1937) 6–7. No. II is 'The Letter' (*NP*).

*The Refugees. New Alliance* I No. 1 (Autumn 1939) 61–5. The concluding lines were included in *NP* as 'The Refugees'.

*Rimbaud. New Alliance* I No. 4 (Jan-Jul 1940) 9. Rimbaud wrote his last work *Une Saison en Enfer* at the age of nineteen, renouncing his old life and ambitions in the final section 'Adieu'.

*'In a time of mortal shocks'*. Sent to Stephen Spender 2 August 1940: 'I find it hard to write anything with sense in it at present; odd lines of poetry keep coming to my mind, but no coherent argument will follow from them; perhaps that will come. I'm enclosing one poem which did get written, not for publication, for I don't know whether it is good or bad; it came simply out of distress of mind which I tried to deal with, and is probably far too monitory; and I distrust myself when I am monitory' (*SL* 124–6). Never published by Muir.

*To the Czech Language. Penguin New Writing* No. 29 (1947) 90. Jelinek: Czech poet and journalist, born 1909; was with Czech forces in Britain during the war.

*The Shrine. Botteghe Oscure* V (1950) 307. See letter to Chiari quoted in headnote to *OFE*.

*The Northern Islands. New Statesman* XLV (20 Jun 1953) 738. See 'Double Absence' and n (*OFE*).

*Sonnet: 'You will not leave us'*. Read in an anthology 'New Verse' in BBC Third Programme 14 June 1954. Like 'Do not mourn still' it could have been included in *OFE*, and so is treated as 'Uncollected' (by Muir), though it was in *CP* 60.

*Sonnet: 'Do not mourn still'. Glasgow Herald* (16 Oct 1954) 3. *GH* has 'folly this' (14). See note to preceding poem.

## APPENDIX II: EARLY VERSIONS

*Ballad of Eternal Life*. As in *FP*. Revised for *CP* 60 as 'Ballad of the Soul'.
[49–52] Omitted in 'Ballad of the Soul'. In the dream the dragon weeps its eyes, tinged blue and red and white, into a heap (*A* 160). 'The dragon and the sphinx seemed to be completely self-created; so far as I know there was no subject-matter in my mind from which I could have created them' (*A*

167). But the change to tears of gold may have been influenced by memory of Freyja, Norse fertility goddess.

[153–60]    cf. 'Ballad of the Soul' 120–24 – 'their bright wraiths', no mention of 'she who once'.

From *Chorus of the Newly Dead. (Scottish Chapbook* version). See *CND* n.

—*The Harlot*. Replaced by an entirely new version, which in turn was deleted in the BL copy of *CND*.

—*The Saint*. An amended form of 'The Larva', which in line 7 has 'brain' for 'cell'; replaced by 'The Poet'.

—*Chorus*. Replaced by an entirely new version in *CND*, which was much amended in MS in BL's copy.

[15–20]    Early appearance of an idea often returned to, for instance in 'Yesterday's Mirror: Afterthoughts to an Autobiography'.

## APPENDIX III: REVISED VERSIONS

*The Song*. Cutting from *London Magazine* in BL, amended in MS. Where words have been deleted and replaced by something illegible, the printed words have been returned to – 'For I had gone away' (9), 'identity' (10), 'fables' (11).

*The Ceremony*. TS with MS amendments in a shaky hand in NLS; an alternative version of 'The Voices' (*LP*).

[11]    What is written over the deleted 'miles or years' is faint. The suggested reading accords with an early draft:

> Against an army stretched beneath the corn
> Ten thousand years and a few feet away.

## APPENDIX IV

*Juvenilia*.

*A* 193 'I began to write poetry at thirty-five instead of twenty-five or twenty'. He continued in MS, 'for the Heinesque I sent to Orage had no resemblance to poetry'.

To Sydney Schiff 7 May 1924, referring to the epigrams from *The New Age* printed at the end of *We Moderns* – 'ill-natured couplets full of bumptious conceit, written I really cannot tell why, because I am not ill-natured, and have no ill-will, so far as I know, for anyone alive' (*SL* 35).

# SELECT BIBLIOGRAPHY
(of works used in this edition)

## 1. Muir
(i) Prose

*The Marionette*, London and New York, 1926.
*John Knox: Portrait of a Calvinist*, London and New York, 1929.
*The Three Brothers*, London and New York, 1931.
*Poor Tom*, London, 1932.
*Scottish Journey*, London, 1935.
*Scott and Scotland*, London, 1936; New York, 1938.
*The Present Age*, London, 1939; New York, 1940.
*The Story and the Fable*, London, 1940.
*Essays on Literature and Society*, London, 1949. Second ed. revised and enlarged, London and Cambridge, Massachusetts, 1965.
*An Autobiography*, London and New York, 1954.
*The Estate of Poetry*, London and Cambridge, Massachusetts, 1962.
*Selected Letters*, London, 1974.
*The Truth of Imagination: Some Uncollected Reviews and Essays*, Aberdeen, 1988.

(ii) Uncollected essays

'Yesterday's Mirror: Afterthoughts to an Autobiography', *Scots Magazine* New Series XXXIII No. 6 (Sep 1940) 404–10.
'Toys and Abstractions', *Saltire Review* IV No. 13 (Winter 1957) 36–7.
Particulars of poetry books are given in the head notes.

## 2. Books and Articles about Muir
Butter, Peter. *Edwin Muir: Man and Poet*, Edinburgh, 1966.
Gaskill, Howard. 'Hermann Broch as Translator of Edwin Muir', *New German Studies* Vol. 6 No. 2 (Summer 1978) 101–15.
— 'Hölderlin and the Poetry of Edwin Muir', *Forum for Modern Language Studies* XVI No. 1 (Jan 1980) 15–32.
— 'Edwin Muir in Hellerau', *Scottish Literary Journal* XI No. 1 (May 1984) 45–56.

Huberman, Elizabeth. *The Poetry of Edwin Muir*, New York, 1971.
— 'The Growth of a Poem: Edwin Muir's 'Day and Night'',
*Studies in Scottish Literature* XXII (1988) 106–14.
Marshall, George. *In a Distant Isle*, Edinburgh, 1987.
Muir, Willa. *Belonging*, London, 1968.
Raine, Kathleen. *Defending Ancient Springs*, London, 1967.
Robertson, Ritchie. *Muir's Contact with German Literature*, Oxford D. Phil. thesis, 1981. Available from University Microfilms.
*Edwin Muir: Centenary Assessments*, ed. C. J. M. MacLachlan and D. S. Robb, Aberdeen, 1990.

## 3. Other Works

Fichte, J. G. *The Vocation of Man*, trans Smith, Chicago, 1906.
Hölderlin, J. C. F. *Selected Verse*, with translations by Michael Hamburger, revised edition, London, 1986.
Murphy, G. (ed) *The Modern Poet*, London, 1938.
Scott, David. *Corporal Jack*, London, 1943.
Spens, Maisie. *Receive the Joyfulness of Your Glory*, London, 1952.
Thomson, W. P. L. *The Little General and the Rousay Crofters*, Edinburgh, 1981.

## 4. Bibliographies

Hollander, Robert. *A Textual and Bibliographical Study of the Poems of Edwin Muir*. University of Columbia Ph.D. thesis, 1962. Available from University Microfilms.
Hoy, Peter and Mellown, Elgin. *A Checklist of Writings about Edwin Muir*, New York, 1971.
Mellown, Elgin. *A Bibliography of the Writings of Edwin Muir*, Alabama, 1964; revised edition, Alabama and London, 1966.
— *A Supplement to Bibliography of the Writings of Edwin Muir*, Alabama, 1970.
Robertson, Ritchie. 'Some Revisions and Variations in the Poetry of Edwin Muir', *Bibliothek* X No. 1 (1980) 20–26.
Stratford, Jenny. *The Arts Council Collection of Modern Literary Manuscripts*, London, 1974. Chapter I deals with Muir's MSS, etc in BL.

# INDEX OF TITLES

# INDEX OF FIRST LINES